MEMORIES AND REFLECTIONS
1852 – 1927

Photo: Thomson

H. H. Asquith (1894)

MEMORIES
AND REFLECTIONS
1852 ～ 1927

BY

THE EARL OF OXFORD
AND ASQUITH, K. G.

VOLUME ONE

LITTLE, BROWN, AND COMPANY

BOSTON 1928

TO MARGOT

Quod spiro et placeo, si placeo,
tuum est

NOTE BY
LORD OXFORD'S EXECUTORS

L ORD OXFORD began to write this book in 1926 and his final illness overtook him before he had completed it. He had drafted for the printer at least two-thirds of the book, and had prepared all the material for the remainder, with the result that, save for a few verbal amendments, nothing now appears which has not been written or prepared by Lord Oxford himself. Nevertheless he saw none of it in print, and the responsibility for the arrangement of the part left uncompleted and for the final revision of the whole has had to be borne by the Executors. Subject to this responsibility the work has been carried out by Mr. Alexander Mackintosh, who assisted Lord Oxford throughout the preparation of this book and his two previous books. Lord Oxford had a high regard for Mr. Mackintosh's wide knowledge of political affairs and sound judgment, and the executors record with gratitude their wholehearted appreciation of his assistance.

April 24, 1928.

PREFACE

BY MARGOT OXFORD

IN July, 1926, I was dining alone with Lord Balfour. In the course of the conversation he asked me if there was any man living that I would choose to write the life of my husband. Neither he, nor I, could think of anyone that was specially marked out, and he suggested that my husband himself was the proper person to do it. To this I replied that I feared that he was too interested in other things, and too reserved to write well about himself: but I urged Lord Balfour to put the proposition before him.

My husband called for me on his return from dining at Grillion's, and after greeting my host, he listened to his suggestion. Lord Balfour spoke with conviction, and I could see that his words had made an impression. Alone with my husband I continued the conversation. I said that as he had concluded his "Fifty Years of British Parliament" I thought he should write as Arthur Balfour had suggested. He said there were events that took place in 10, Downing Street that would be of vital importance to historians, the truth of which had been obscured by misrepresentation and rumour. To contradict rumour was to make it immortal, and he did not feel that he could write freely upon matters which were of a painful and private nature. The chief events of his life were already known, and all that was of an autobiographical interest would be his private estimate of the moral and intellectual qualities of his colleagues, and their character and conduct. But to differentiate between the men he would like to write about, and the men he would prefer not to discuss, would be invidious, and he did not see his way to writing of men as different in nature and temperament as Lord Rosebery, Lord Kitchener, Lord Morley, Mr. Churchill, Mr. Bonar Law, Mr. Ramsay MacDonald and Mr. Lloyd George—not to mention the Admirals, the Generals, and the men of business who had played a prominent part in the War. A book of that length he said he would not live to finish, even if he felt tempted to write it; and the world would not thank him for platitudes.

But I could see that although to write an autobiography of an intimate kind would be impossible for him, he was not averse to the idea of publishing notes from the store of his memories, and some of the letters he had written to friends.

In the many fine and praising tributes written of my husband after his death both in the Press, and in private letters to myself, the words "lucid," "concise," "logical" and "serene" recur: and although these are apt epithets, they are obvious, and misleading. A man who becomes Prime Minister of this country must be singularly stupid if he is prolix, agitated, or obscure. But no catalogue of single words covers the ground in making a portrait of a man as elusive as my husband.

When one of the speakers in the House of Commons compared him to the Thames: "placid, calm, never boisterous or turbulent, moving with a steady and serene flow," I was not reminded of him. Few men of distinction are boisterous, and none of self-control are turbulent; nor was he fundamentally serene. It is not easy for leading men to speak in public of the dead. They think of Pitt and Burke, try to recall Grattan and Gladstone, and are impelled towards something fine and far-reaching which will express their feelings, and stir the public. They waver between the Biblical simplicity of Bright, and the moving eloquence of Lincoln, but in listening to the speakers that afternoon in the House of Commons I understood their difficulty, and knew what I would have felt had I been in their position.

My husband was patient, but not placid, and what people mistook for serenity was the perfect proportions of a mind big enough for trifles to look small in, and that was closely woven into a strong and stable character. He had a great respect for life, law, and institutions. *"La vie est une enveloppe à demi transparent qui nous enveloppe depuis la naissance de notre conscience,"* might have been written by him, and if you noticed his fine attentive face, you realized that he was a man who saw life whole.

In spite of appearances, he was, scientifically speaking, of a nervous as against a stolid temperament, and practised an iron self-control to protect himself from an acute personal sensitiveness. Understatement that amounted to taciturnity, and a certain shyness and self-discipline, made even friendly people think him inaccessible. Although he had no irritability, he was never placid, and the quickness of his understanding made him impatient of the lengthy explanations of self-centred men. But as most people are copious, and few are not self-centred, he cultivated a tolerance with his fellow-creatures which was not altogether easy for him. It was only after he had been thrown into the wide circle, which for want of a better word I will call society, that he was able to overcome his natural intellectual scorn. But that he put so many stupid men and women at their ease when conversing with them is the proof that he overcame it.

When I complained to him of his tolerance with his Cabinet colleagues, whose vagaries he appeared to me to watch more as an umpire than as a judge, he said:

"I cannot expect to find the wisdom of Crewe, the judgment of Grey, the humour of Birrell, the temper of Haldane, the intellectual refreshment of Morley, and the epigrams of John Burns in all my colleagues. The only chance a Prime Minister has of keeping his Cabinet together is to make the best use of the material he is given."

In an age of publicity and self-advertisement I sometimes regretted his self-control, for as the *Daily Mirror* of February 16 wrote this year:

"Lord Oxford always took the dangerous course of meeting misrepresentation with silence."

Before returning to this criticism I wish to put on record what an Irish newspaper wrote on the same date. Concluding its estimate of my husband, the *Irish Times* says:

"He would have been at home in the eighteenth century. In the beginning of the twentieth century he found himself the ruler of a political society which in a hundred ways was alien from his tastes as a scholar, and from his instincts as a gentleman. The soul of

honour, he became the sport of intrigue, the victim of
ingratitude and misrepresentation, but he was always
loyal, always proudly serene, most patient when provo-
cation was bitterest and least deserved. The keynote
of Lord Oxford's character was magnanimity, and with
his death a high and subtle quality has gone out of
English politics."

Although most men would agree that he was always
a knight and never a prize-fighter in the arena, it might
be said to his disadvantage that he was not a fighter.

Whether from a quiet deep disdain or from a fixed resolve to ignore his enemy, he refused to use any of his
natural weapons of self-defence. The rôle of a bruiser
bored him, and anything like a personal onslaught was
as impossible as it would have been for him to have taken
his clothes off in public. When anyone tried to warn
him of intrigue, or pointed to baseness, disloyalty, and
ingratitude, he would change the subject with a sud-
denness that was final: and neither wife, child nor
friend, could reopen it.

He enjoyed fighting purposes and not people. This
was not surprising, as it would be idle to pretend that
in the years of his Administration (from 1908 to 1916)
and later he had not ample reason to be disillusioned
by his friends even more than by his opponents.

Once he had made up his mind what he considered
was the right thing to do, no amount of argument or
persuasion could deflect him from his purpose. Fear,
indecision, even apprehension, were unknown to him,
and he left nothing to chance.

Shrinking from censure, and incapable of wounding,
he had a detached but real interest in the merits,

foibles, and vanities, of not only his colleagues, but of most men in and out of the House of Commons, and after late and weary sittings would describe them to me with sardonic humour and precision. There was a massive magnanimity and imaginative insight about him that I have never seen equalled; and he could bear with composure the heavy weight of every form of personal responsibility.

A noisy mind full of frills and fancies was abhorrent to him, and whether rightly or wrongly he neither wooed nor flattered the Press. His view was that newspapers by ignoring public men can help to obscure them, but that their prescience — and their power — is limited.

He pointed to the biggest triumph his Party had ever had when in 1905–1906 all the London newspapers of importance were against him.

There is much to be said for this point of view; but in times of war the Press can exaggerate criticism and propagate rumour to the detriment of the wisest Prime Minister, and it takes less than newspapers to frighten an ill-informed, apprehensive, and credulous public.

Having read the many signed and anonymous works upon the motives and happenings of the Government from 1914 to 1916, I am convinced that truth is never as strange as fiction. Human nature is full of vanity, and as long as this is so, there will always be back-stair busybodies who think they know everything that takes place in Downing Street. "They say . . . What say they? — Let them say," was a favourite quotation of my husband's; and nothing that I, or anyone else can write of good or of evil can affect his stainless record.

It may be said that a wife is not the proper person to describe a Prime Minister: I shall therefore refrain from writing of the personal love and loyalty that he gave, and that he inspired, to which the letters received by me since February the 15 of this year testify.

I think it both an appropriate and fitting conclusion to this Preface that I should quote what was written by Chapman in his "Revenge of Bussy d' Ambois" in 1613 of the Earl of Oxford of that day.

"He was beside of spirit passing great, valiant, and learn'd,
      and liberall as the Sunne,
Spoke and writ sweetly, or of learned subjects,
Or of the discipline of publike weales;
And t'was the Earle of Oxford."

MARGOT OXFORD,
April, 1928.

CONTENTS

CONTENTS

ILLUSTRATIONS

MEMORIES AND REFLECTIONS
1852 — 1927

CHAPTER I

EARLY YEARS

I WAS born at Croft House, Morley, on September 12, 1852.

The hamlet of Morley is of great antiquity, and gave its name to one of the West Riding Wapentakes. According to a local historian the "Old Chapel" has been "in the hands of Papists, Protestants, and Protestant Dissenters, and under some form or other a place of worship, from the era of the Saxon Heptarchy." Morley was in feudal times a Manor, and had developed into a prosperous little town, when in the reign of Edward II an invading Scottish army chose it as their winter quarters, and by their barbarous exactions and ravages reduced it to a condition of decline and almost of ruin, from which it did not recover till the time of the Commonwealth.[1] Thenceforward the woollen trade became its staple industry; "nearly every house had its loom and spinning wheel"; "the same family stock inhabited the same dwelling for generations, with scarcely the intrusion of a stranger."

Among these indigenous families were the Asquiths, one of whom, being an enthusiastic Puritan, took part in a belated and abortive effort to restore the Commonwealth—the Farnley Wood Plot of 1664. For this escapade my ancestor (if such he was) was imprisoned in York Castle.

[1] See Scatcherd, "History of Morley" (1830); W. Smith, "Rambles about Morley" (1866); W. Smith, "History and Antiquities of Morley" (1876).

The family, after machinery had begun to displace domestic handiwork, seem to have become employers on a modest scale. My paternal grandfather was able to give his only child, my father, a good education, according to the standards of those days, at a boarding school near Tadcaster, where he was allowed to keep a pony and a piano of his own. My father died prematurely, when I was less than eight years old. I gather from local and family tradition that he was a cultivated man, interested in literature and music, of a retiring and unadventurous disposition, and not cut out in the keen competitive atmosphere of the West Riding for a successful business career.

My mother also came from a Puritan Yorkshire stock. Her father, William Willans, had migrated early in life from Leeds to Huddersfield, where he developed a growingly prosperous business as a "woolstapler," and being a man of parts, with a strong personality and much public spirit, became one of the dominant figures in the life of the town. He narrowly escaped being returned to the House of Commons as its member, when he stood as the Liberal candidate in 1851. He was an ardent Nonconformist (belonging, as did my father's family in Morley, to the Congregationalists, who were in direct descent from the Independents of the Commonwealth) and an active fellow-worker with Cobden and Bright in the campaign for Free Trade. He had the reputation of being an effective public speaker, and I can remember him, though I was not more than eleven when he died, as in appearance and manner a dignified and impressive figure.

My mother inherited her father's strength of character and his range of interests. She was all her life a great reader, both of serious and of light literature — English, French, and to some extent German. She had a remarkable gift of expression both in speech and in writing, a keen sense of humour, and exceptional insight into the foibles and the excellences of her fellow-creatures. I have never known a better talker. If she had had good health, and a wider sphere of opportunity, she might have become an influential figure. But almost from her youth she was physically disabled for an active life, and though her reserve of vitality and of high spirits was unfailing, and she watched with the closest and most vivid interest the course of outside things, she had perforce to content herself with the part of observer and counsellor. She was a devoted and sagacious mother, and made herself the companion and intimate friend of her children. She died at the age of sixty at my sister's house in London in December, 1888. I used to see her constantly during her last illness, and she retained her *joie de vivre* and her interests to the end. The sittings of the Parnell Commission, in which I was counsel, had just begun, and one of the last questions which she asked me was whether I could *assure* her that the famous letters were forged. I doubt whether she was conscious that she was so near the end of her journey, but fortified, as she was, by the discipline of suffering, and by her unquenchable faith that all things work together for good, the thought of death could have had no terrors for her.

Almost my earliest recollection is of our village

celebration at Morley of the peace at the close of the Crimean War in 1856. My brother and I marched with much pride through the streets at the head of a procession of children, carrying two home-made banners, on one of which was inscribed "Peace on Earth" and on the other "Good will towards Men." We were thus unconsciously among the early pioneers of the creed of the League of Nations.

We lived in simple comfort amid semi-rural surroundings, and every Sunday went in our best clothes to Rehoboth Chapel—an Independent congregation, in which my parents were active workers and devout worshippers.

In the course of a few years we moved our home from Morley to Mirfield, then little more than a village, within a few miles of Huddersfield. It was there that my father, after an illness of only a few hours, died (June, 1860) at the age of thirty-five. He had not been able to accumulate more than a scanty provision for his family, and my grandfather Willans, a well-to-do and large-hearted man, of whom my mother had always been the favourite child, took charge of us, and established us in a house a few doors from his own in the town of Huddersfield. For a short time my brother and I attended Huddersfield College as day-scholars, but we were very soon sent as boarders to a Moravian school at Fulneck, near Leeds, where the ground floor of my education was laid. The life there was homely and indeed rough, but the Moravians were excellent teachers, and I am gratefully conscious that I owe them much.

For the first fifteen or sixteen years of my life my

Herbert Henry Asquith   William Willans Asquith
Emily Evelyn Asquith, afterwards Mrs. Wooding
A FAMILY GROUP

brother (William Willans Asquith) and I were inseparable companions. We were at school together both at Fulneck and later at the City of London. He was a little more than a year older than myself, but never enjoyed the same unbroken health. When he was about sixteen, he was, by the doctor's orders, taken away from school, and went to live by the sea with my mother. He joined me at Balliol in my second term (January, 1871), and by what was then an unusual arrangement we were allowed to share the same set of rooms on the top floor of Staircase No. IV in the Back Quad. He was a good scholar, though from bad luck he only got a Second in "Mods," and he became proficient in "Greats" Studies and got his First in the Final School in 1875. He chose the vocation of a schoolmaster, for which he had rare and special aptitudes, and spent the whole of his active life at Clifton College, first as house-tutor to Dr. Percival, and afterwards as a master with a house of his own. He never married, and usually spent his holidays in travel with an old pupil or colleague. He had a considerable knowledge of all the stages of Italian art. He died, not long after his retirement, at Hampstead in the week of the Armistice in 1918 in his sixty-eighth year. He was a born teacher of boys, as generations of old Cliftonians are ready to testify, one of his most attractive and useful qualities being a faculty of humorous expression which could at will be either mordant or playful. Though a man of small stature and seemingly frail physique, he had not the least difficulty in keeping order, and no boy ever attempted twice to take a liberty with him. Our paths in life diverged, but we had many common interests and rarely differed in opinion, and from first to last there was never any breach in our confidence and affection.

CHAPTER II

SCHOOL IN LONDON

THE death of my grandfather, William Willans, induced my mother, whose delicate health needed a more genial climate, to move to the South of England, and from the beginning of 1864 for a number of years she lived at St. Leonards-on-Sea. At the same time her eldest brother, my uncle John Willans, who had no children of his own, generously took upon himself the education of my brother and myself. His three brothers afterwards divided the burden with him, and their munificence without doubt altered the whole course of my life.

John Willans and his wife — a daughter of Edward Baines, M.P. for Leeds — lived at this time in London, and in January, 1864, my brother and I became inmates of their house, and were entered as day-scholars at the City of London School. A few years later circumstances compelled them to return to Yorkshire, and thereafter we lodged and boarded as paying guests in a family, first at Pimlico, and afterwards at Islington. From that time onwards — now over sixty years — with the exception of my terms at Oxford, I have been to all intents and purposes a Londoner.

The City of London School was founded at the beginning of Queen Victoria's reign by the Corporation of London, who utilized for the purpose an ancient and neglected endowment bequeathed by one of their mediæval town clerks, John Carpenter. They had the wisdom to select as headmaster Dr. Mortimer, a Fellow of Queen's College, Oxford, who had got a First in "Greats", in the days of Gladstone and Roundell Palmer. When I became a pupil he was just approaching the close of his headmastership and I had no actual experience of his work as a teacher. That he must have been a singularly able and efficient administrator, is abundantly clear. The number of boys at the school had risen to 650; and several scholarships tenable at Oxford and Cambridge had been endowed by City men, and the great City companies. For a school not yet thirty years old, with only a small sprinkling of pupils who were not destined to a commercial career, there was already a promising nucleus of academic distinctions, won for the most part at Cambridge. In the year 1861 two old boys—Aldis and Abbott—were respectively Senior Wrangler and Senior Classic: an achievement which I imagine to be still what is called in the language of the turf a unique "double."

I was at the City of London School from 1864 to 1870; it was from there that I won the Balliol Scholarship in 1869; and during my last year I was captain of the school. We were fortunate, for the most part, in our masters, though according to modern ideas the school was under-staffed. It will curdle the blood of the progressive educationists of to-day to be told that the class in which I started (about midway up the school) consisted of no fewer than sixty boys! We had an admirable teacher, Mr. Woodroffe, who was especially successful in developing the still much neglected faculty of articulate enunciation, and so far as my memory goes, he had never the least difficulty either in

maintaining order, or in securing not only the attention
but the interest of the boys.

But the driving power of the whole machine, no less
than the special quality of the teaching in the highest
Forms, was provided by the new headmaster, Dr.
Edwin Abbott, who succeeded Dr. Mortimer in 1865.
He had been a pupil of the school, and passed thence
to St. John's at Cambridge, where, as I have just said,
he came out as Senior in the Classical Tripos of 1861.
He was a Cambridge scholar of the most finished type
in days when that type produced some of its most brilliant specimens. Next to Abbott's name in the Tripos
of 1861 comes that of G. O. Trevelyan of Trinity, and
in the following year (1862) the Senior Classic was
Jebb, the runners-up being Graves and Henry Jackson,
either of whom (it used to be said) might have been
Senior in an ordinary year. Abbott had a natural gift
for teaching, and in the everyday tasks of translation
and composition it would be difficult to imagine a better
equipped or more stimulating master. He diversified
and enlarged the regular curriculum of a Sixth Form
by going outside the Greek and Latin Classics, and
applying the methods of exact scholarship to such
authors as Spenser, Dante, and above all Shakespeare.
His "Shakespearian Grammar" is still, I believe, a
standard authority. His lessons on the Greek Testament were the vestibule to the great edifice of research
to which he afterwards devoted the years of his retirement. He was a clergyman of the Church of England,
and well known outside as a powerful and suggestive
preacher, but there was nothing sectarian or denominational in his presentation of religion to his pupils.

Above all, he had the sovereign gift of a great personality, at once austere and sympathetic, impressive and inspiring, without which the most accomplished teacher cannot succeed in moulding and fortifying the character of the young.

A day school does not perhaps afford the same opportunities of intimate companionship as a boarding school, particularly when, as was our case, there was no playground, and cricket and all other athletics had to be practised at a distance, in Victoria Park, on half-holidays. We had one common resort, of which some of the more studious boys took advantage, almost within a stone's throw — the Guildhall Library of the City of London: an admirable browsing ground in desultory hours. I picked up there at odd times a good deal of the kind of information, especially as to our modern political history, which is not generally taught at schools, and which I often found serviceable in later life.

Two of my schoolfellows with whom I was much thrown, and who became lifelong friends, were W. G. Rushbrooke and John Cox: neither of them, alas! any longer with us. Both went to Cambridge, and achieved distinction there, Rushbrooke being sixth in the First Class of the Classical Tripos (1872), and Cox, who was a "double" man, Eighth Wrangler, and only just out of the First Class in Classics (1874). Rushbrooke, who died in 1926, became one of the greatest and most inspiring of headmasters. The school, to the service of which he gave his life, was of old origin — St. Olave's, Southwark — but hardly known to the world until his informative faculty and inspiring enthusiasm gave it a new life. He is entitled to a distinguished place in the roll of headmasters who have, mainly by their own personality, made or remade a school. Rugby under Arnold is of course a classical case. Marlborough under Bradley; Uppingham under Thring; Clifton under Percival; Manchester and St. Paul's under Walker; the City of London School under Abbott; Oundle under Sanderson — and this is by no means an exhaustive catalogue — supply other illustrations.

John Cox was a man of different type: with faculties and interests both humanist and scientific which, if he had concentrated them in a single groove, would have given him, in either, a place of exceptional distinction. He had a gentle and lovable temperament, and was wholly free from any form of selfish ambition. He was the first head of the newly-founded Cavendish Laboratory at Cambridge, and thence migrated to Canada, where, at the McGill University of Montreal, he was for years an eminent professor of physics and a potent, though always modest and unobtrusive, factor in the academic life of that illustrious home of learning and research.

As to the atmosphere and surroundings in which the boys of the City of London School received their education, I may quote a few sentences from a speech which I made at a complimentary dinner given to me by old schoolfellows, when I became Home Secretary in 1892:

We had no ancient traditions to rest upon in the academic world. We had hardly any memories of great men whom we could appropriate to ourselves. Our buildings were contracted, gloomy, and a trifle squalid: we had not that which is regarded by most people, not so much as an accident, but as the very essence of a public school, we had not so much as a playground. Instead of those spacious and attractive surroundings in which the life of most public schools is carried on, we spent our days within the sound not only of Bow Bells, but of the roar and traffic of Cheapside itself.

When I look back upon my old school-life, I think not only, and not perhaps so much, of the hours which I spent in the class-room, or in preparing the lessons at night. I think rather of the daily walk through the crowded, noisy, jostling streets; I think of the river with its barges and steamers, and its manifold active life: I think of St. Paul's, and Westminster Abbey, and the National Gallery, and the Houses of Parliament. I am certain there is not one among you who will not agree with me, that the presence and contact of this stimulating environment contributed a large and a most influential element to our education in our youth.

There are two incidents which belong in point of time to my early schooldays in London, which are perhaps worth putting on record. One morning (about February, 1864) I was walking to school up Ludgate Hill, and had come to the point where the Old Bailey debouches, when I saw, hanging in a row outside Newgate, with the white cap covering their heads, the bodies of a famous gang of criminals who were known as the " Five Pirates." In those days, before the abolition of public executions, a murderer's body was not cut down until an hour after death.

The other experience was of a less gruesome kind. I was present at the vast demonstration at the Crystal Palace (April, 1864) which was the climax of the popular welcome given to the Italian hero, Garibaldi. There was wild enthusiasm when the general in his famous red shirt appeared on the platform, while the two great operatic stars of the era (both of them vocally on the wane), Mario and Grisi, joined in a duet in the most florid Italian style.

We know from the admirable edition which Mr. Buckle has recently given us of the second series of Queen Victoria's Letters (1862–78) the feelings of growing suspicion and regret with which the Queen observed these pro-Garibaldi manifestations. She particularly lamented that "the members of the Government should have lavished honours usually reserved for Royalty, upon one who openly declares his objects to be to lead the attack upon Venice, Rome and Russia." "The Queen" (she adds) "thinks that the representatives of these countries might well remonstrate at the unusual adulation shown in official quarters to one professing objects so hostile to their royal masters."[1]

Lord Granville, to whom these complaints were addressed, replied in a letter which for courtesy, tact, and delicate irony, is, I venture to think, a masterpiece in this most difficult form of composition.[2] He wrote:

Garibaldi has all the qualifications for making him a popular idol in this country. He is of low extraction, he is physically and morally brave, he is a good guerilla soldier, he has achieved great things by "dash," he has a simple manner . . . and a pleasing smile. He has no religion, but he hates the Pope. He is a goose, but that is considered to be an absence of diplomatic guile. His mountebank dress, which betrays a desire for effect, has a certain dramatic effect. No amount of cold water would have damped the enthusiasm of the middle and lower classes. His political principles, which are nearly as dangerous to the progress and maintenance of real liberty as the most despotic systems, are thought admirably applicable to *foreign* countries.

[1] Vol. I, p. 175. [2] *Ib.*, pp. 175-6.

The joining of the aristocracy, including some Conservative leaders, in demonstrations in his favour, although making the affair more offensive and more ridiculous to foreign
nations, has been of great use in this country.   It has taken
the democratic sting . . . out of the affair.   There has been
tomfoolery and much vulgarity, but on the whole there has
also been much that is honourable to the English character.

None, however, of these apposite and nicely balanced
considerations was present to the minds of the huge
crowd at the Crystal Palace, who waved their hats and
roared themselves hoarse in honour of the Liberator
of Italy.

It is well that, in these days, Englishmen should be
reminded of the genuine and whole-hearted enthusiasm
with which their fathers and grandfathers, from school-
boys to grey-beards, of all classes and of all political
creeds, sixty years ago hailed the most romantic and
chivalrous figure of the Italian Risorgimento.

CHAPTER III

OXFORD

THE academic prizes of my old school had been, as I have said, so far, for the most part, won at Cambridge. It was, therefore, a new adventure when the headmaster advised that I should try my luck at Oxford, and compete for what was then, and has not ceased to be, regarded as the "blue ribbon" among entrance scholarships — a scholarship at Balliol.

In those days Balliol offered each year only two, and in November, 1869, when I was just over seventeen, I was lucky enough to secure the first. The candidates, drawn from all the Public Schools, were required before the examination began to have an interview with the Master. I can remember well the trepidation with which I found myself — a raw schoolboy — in the Olympian presence of Dr. Scott, whom we had all been brought up to regard with legendary reverence as one of the twin Dioscuri, Liddell and Scott. They had both graduated with distinction — Scott was an Ireland Scholar — in remote times at Christ Church; and now Liddell (a magnificent and impressive figure) was Dean of Christ Church, and Scott, who had been Jowett's tutor when he was an undergraduate, was Master of Balliol. It was the first time that the scholarship had been won by the City of London School, and I can honestly say that, after more than fifty years of later experience, this was the proudest moment of my life.

I did not go into residence until a year later (October, 1870), and in the meantime Scott had become Dean of Rochester, and had been succeeded in the Mastership by Benjamin Jowett, the greatest of Oxford tutors, who had brought the reputation of his own college, due in the first instance to the opening of the scholarships under the Mastership of Dr. Jenkyns, to a commanding and unassailable height.

I have sometimes regretted that I was too late to have been — like Bowen and Wright and Swinburne — one of Jowett's pupils. I never had the privilege, such as St. Paul enjoyed, of sitting at the feet of Gamaliel. Jowett had been in his day in the ecclesiastical world a heretic and almost an outlaw. When in 1855 he was made by Lord Palmerston Regius Professor of Greek (an office happily in the gift of the Crown) the clericals and obscurantists, who dominated the government of the University and of Christ Church, refused to raise his salary from the pittance of £40 at which it had been fixed in the days of Henry VIII.[1] There was a legend, widely circulated and believed in country parsonages, that Jowett was wont to gnash his teeth when he saw from his window the undergraduates filing across the quad to morning or evening chapel. All that mattered to the more unlettered clergy — most of whom had never even heard of, let alone read, his edition of the leading Epistles of St. Paul — was that he had been a contributor to a notorious volume (containing little which would not now be accepted as common sense, and even as commonplace, at a bishop's examination of

[1] After years of squabbling, the Dean and Chapter of Christ Church at last (in 1865) agreed to increase the salary to £500.

ordinands) which was for a time the scandal of the orthodox world — entitled "Essays and Reviews." [1]

It is hardly necessary to say that Jowett was never in temper or in doctrine an heresiarch. He had not contented himself with the old Oxford round of Plato, Aristotle, and Bishop Butler. He had studied, with an equable and eclectic judgment, the German philosophers — Kant, Fichte, Schelling, and even Hegel; but, like Erasmus, he had not the temperament of a fanatic, or even of a disciple, nor, except with many reservations, in the intellectual and theological sphere, that of a reformer. He had, what may seem to us now, the curious indifference of the Liberal Anglicans — such as his friend and contemporary Dean Stanley — to formulæ and symbols, by which they were ostensibly bound; and when a foolish and petty-minded vice-chancellor, urged on by zealots both from the High Church and the Evangelical factions, took advantage of an obsolete University statute to require him, as Regius Professor of Greek, to subscribe his assent to the Thirty-nine Articles, it was reported that his only reply was to say, "Give me a new pen." [2]

Jowett as Master was as different a figure as it is possible to conceive from the "bogy-man" who had disturbed the imagination and shaken the nerves alike of Evangelicals and High Churchmen in the middle Victorian era. It was not because, in the essentials either of his personality or his convictions, he had undergone any fundamental change. He had never been an iconoclast, or a pioneer, or propagandist of

[1] Temple, afterwards Archbishop of Canterbury, was another of the contributors.
[2] "Life of Jowett," Vol. I, pp. 238-9.

revolutionary dogmas and ideals. Even his political
Liberalism had always been of a temperate and semi-
sceptical kind, and no man was by nature and habit of
thought more repelled by what his friend Tennyson
called the "falsehood of extremes." The fervours of
Gladstone made little appeal to him, and in the political domain, though he retained his aversion for
Toryism, he found more that was congenial in Arthur
Balfour than in any other statesman of his later days.
Both as Master of the college, and as for a time Vice-
Chancellor of the University, he showed a perhaps
unsuspected faculty for the transaction of business,
and the practical aspects of administration. But largely
from the necessities of his new status, he lost the personal nexus which had bound him to generations of
undergraduate pupils, whether brilliant or mediocre;
and I cannot honestly say that in my time he was any
longer a great formative influence, though he never
ceased to be the dominating personality, in the college.

I cannot better express my own feeling, and that of
many of my contemporaries, about him than in a few
sentences from what I said at the commemoration meeting, over which Lord Salisbury presided, after his
death, in December, 1893:

We cannot hope to see again the counterpart of that refined and fastidious mind, in whose presence intellectual
lethargy was stirred into life, and intellectual pretentious-
ness sank into abashed silence. Still less can we hope to see
a character such as his: the union of worldly sagacity with
the most transparent simplicity of nature: ambition, keen
and unsleeping, but entirely detached from self, and absorbed in the fortunes of a great institution and its members. Upon his generosity no call could be too heavy: with
his delicate kindliness he was ever ready to give the best

THOMAS HILL GREEN

DR. JOWETT

TWO OXFORD PERSONALITIES

hours of either the day or the night to help and advise the humblest of those who appealed to him for aid. These are the qualities, or some of the qualities, which were the secret of his personality, and which are now buried in his grave. No man of our time, and few men of any time, can be more truly said to have lived for the sake of his work. Of that work Balliol College was from the beginning, and remained to the end, the centre and the inspiration.[1]

The old Balliol staff, which had co-operated with Jowett in building up and keeping in repair the reputation of the college, had all but dissolved by the time of his election (1870) to the Mastership. James Riddell, a pure scholar of the best type which Dr. Kennedy produced at Shrewsbury, had recently died; Edwin Palmer had become Corpus Professor of Latin in the University; W. L. Newman was unhappily a permanent invalid; and Henry Smith, the most brilliant of them all, who had in his undergraduate days achieved a unique distinction by winning both the Ireland and the Senior Mathematical Scholarships, was gradually retiring from college work. And now Jowett himself was removed from the routine duties of a tutor.

On the other side of the account was to be set the growing influence of one of the younger Fellows, Thomas Hill Green, who was reaching the maturity of his powers. It is not too much to say that by the time of his premature death, some ten years later, he had transformed both the atmosphere and the methods of philosophical thought and study in Oxford. There is a faithful, and on the whole a vivid, sketch of him in the short biography which his devoted pupil, Richard

[1] "Occasional Addresses," pp. 164-5.

Lewis Nettleship, prefixed to the third volume of his collected works. Green had been brought up in a Yorkshire parsonage, and he never "sacrificed to the Graces." He was at school at Rugby, and was an adequate, though not distinguished, scholar. As Nettleship, than whom there was no better judge, truly says: "He had not the interest either in language or in learning which makes a great scholar."[1] He was a Commoner of Balliol, got a First in Greats, and the Chancellor's prize for an English essay, and was President of the Union.

The fashionable philosophies in the University were still those of Mill and Herbert Spencer; for the neo-Kantian school (if such it can be called) of Hamilton and Mansel, though smiled upon in its day by some of the High Anglicans, had never taken deep root in Oxford.

There had been a brief efflorescence in the 'fifties of an exotic imported from France—the Positive philosophy of Auguste Comte, with its spiritual development—the Religion of Humanity. It found a seeding ground in Wadham, where it was nurtured and propagated by Richard Congreve, with a small band of brilliant pupils—Frederic Harrison, E. S. Beesley, J. H. Bridges, and others. In its full-blown form, with its Calendar, its Feast days, its hierarchy of Saints, its substitution, as the rational satisfaction of the faculty of Worship, of humanity (as someone said) with a big "H," for God with a little "g," it failed to attract either Materialists or Idealists, Theists or Agnostics. Huxley damned it in an epigram as "Catholicism

[1] "Memoir," p. xiii, "Works of T. H. Green."

minus Christianity." It was perhaps even better hit
off in a phase which Mrs. Sidney Webb, in the interesting first instalment of her Autobiography, reports as having been used to her by one of her talented
sisters—"underbred theology."[1]

Green, profoundly dissatisfied with these meagre
and arid dietaries, turned away from them, and gradually found that for which he was in quest—the basis
of a spiritual philosophy—in the speculations of Kant
and his successors, and in particular of Hegel. He
was commonly called a Hegelian, but while he was
steeped and even saturated in the dialectic of that illustrious teacher, he never lost his intellectual self-mas-
tery, and his presentation of the Hegelian doctrine
was always coloured, both in substance and in expression, by his own robust and independent personality.
He had, indeed, another side to his life and activities.
He was a man of affairs, a member for some time of the
Oxford City Council, an ardent Liberal politican, and
an energetic worker in causes, such for instance as that
of temperance, in which he thought he could discern
the germs of social progress. He was a layman, and
could have passed none of the common tests of orthodoxy, but he had a profoundly religious mind. His
lectures on St. Paul's Epistles were the best I ever
heard. The essence of his teaching on this side is to
be found, expressed with his characteristic condensa-
tion of thought and style, in his two pre-Communion
Sermons to his Balliol pupils on "The Witness of
God" (1870) and "Faith" (1877).[2]

[1] "My Apprenticeship," by Beatrice Webb, p. 148.
[2] "Works of T. H. Green," Vol. III, pp. 231–76.

Green gave a superficial impression of reserve and even austerity, but no teacher in Oxford gathered around him, as time went on, such a band of whole-hearted and enthusiastic disciples. His lectures were not easy to follow: his manner was apt to be jerky; and his style abounded in what Burke calls "nodosities." It was a familiar gibe of those who looked on from outside the fold, that by the end of the hour he had become so contorted that he had to be untied by friendly hands. It must be admitted that, while he made a deep and indelible impression, not only upon the best intellects of the place, but upon the whole course of philosophic thought in the University then and thereafter, the less well-grounded of his neophytes began to talk a jargon or "patter" which lent itself to the ridicule of the unregenerate. Jowett looked on with a certain mild and mellow scepticism at these new departures, having himself (as I have said elsewhere) in his earlier days "*déjà passé par là.*"

Between 1870 and 1880 Green was undoubtedly the greatest personal force in the real life of Oxford.

For myself, though I owe more than I can say to Green's gymnastics, both intellectual and moral, I never "worshipped at the Temple's inner shrine." My own opinions on these high matters have never been more than those of an interested amateur, and are of no importance to anyone but myself. I thought then, and still think, that the two greatest thinkers and teachers are Plato and Kant. The books which did most to clear my own mind, in the post-Kantian domain, were two, which I doubt if anyone now reads: Ferrier's

"Institutes of Metaphysics," and John Grote's "Exploratio Philosophica."

A more complete contrast to Green can hardly be imagined than Thomas Case (familiarly called "Tommy"), who in our preparation for Greats was, both in the technique of Plato and Aristotle, and in Greek and Roman history, a most efficient trainer and coach. I seem still to remember vaguely his catalogue of the thirteen good points, and the twelve or fourteen drawbacks, in the Constitution of Cleisthenes. He had equal facility in the enumeration and classification of the usual and examinable Τόποι of the "Ethics" and the "Republic." He had been (like Green) a Commoner of Balliol from Rugby, and was for four years a distinguished cricketer in the University Eleven (1864–67). He took a First in Greats, became a Fellow of Brasenose, and then migrated to the Stock Exchange. Nostalgia soon brought him back to Oxford, and Jowett, who had in these, as in other matters, a keen flair, got him to join the Balliol staff. He became, later on, Whyte's Professor and President of Corpus, and up to the time of his death, at the age of eighty or more, he contributed to *The Times* breezy and controversial letters on the decadent developments of latter-day philosophy.

In the sphere of pure scholarship, we had as good a teacher, particularly in composition, as was to be found in the University — a lovable and unconventional expert, Francis (afterwards Baron) de Paravicini.

The one serious disappointment in my academic career was my failure to win the Ireland Scholarship, for which I was in two successive years *proxime*. It was some consolation to be bracketed for the Craven in my last term with my old friend and successful rival, Henry Broadbent of Exeter, for many years a master and now librarian at Eton. In the summer term of 1874 I was (*mirabile dictu*) the only Balliol man in the Greats First Class, and in the autumn I was elected a Fellow of my old college.

During the last term of my undergraduate life (1874) I was President of the Union, one of the most important of Oxford institutions, open to members of all colleges, and with, I suppose, an outstanding fame among the debating societies of the world. Its popularity ebbs and flows from generation to generation; it sometimes suffers from the particularism of colleges which have clubs of their own; in my time it was fortunate in enlisting almost all the best of the younger men in the University. It was, in those days, overwhelmingly Conservative in politics, with the result that active Liberals, like Milner and myself, were almost always in a small minority. He and I were generally in agreement, but once at any rate we spoke on different sides. A young Canadian, G. R. Parkin, afterwards secretary to the Rhodes Trustees, introduced a motion in favour of Imperial Federation, which was supported by Milner and opposed by myself. I remember that on the celebration of our Jubilee in 1873 the Cambridge Union sent over a deputation of three undergraduates to take part in our debate. It was then that I first formed what proved to be a lasting friendship with two of the most ingenious thinkers and distinguished teachers, in different fields, who have illustrated the annals of Cambridge in our time —

A. W. Verrall and F. W. Maitland. My interest in the fortunes of the Union has never ceased, and it was a great satisfaction to me that in course of time two of my sons (both Balliol men) succeeded me in the Chair.

A full and detailed picture of the Oxford Union in those days (1870–75) has been drawn by Sir Herbert Warren, the President of Magdalen, who was one of my most intimate friends.[1] His account of my own performances is coloured by friendly partiality, but I may cite a passage which indicates on my part a certain bent towards administrative activity of a controversial kind:

He signalized his tenure of office (as Treasurer) by one permanent and most beneficial reform: the introduction of smoking and of afternoon tea, then a somewhat novel institution in Oxford and indeed the country, into the Union. Obvious boons as these were, they were not conferred without much criticism and opposition. The Treasurer himself was one of the foremost in demonstrating their utility. A steady smoker and a great reader himself, he used to advise his friends to spend one hour every afternoon in general reading at the Union.

A typical specimen of what was commended as " general reading" was Trollope's novels. I may perhaps add to a quotation, which the President makes from a speech of mine, some time in the autumn of 1873, in support of a motion, "That this House neither believes in nor desires a Conservative reaction." I seem to have compared the Conservative reaction to the "Bog of Allan," which caused consternation in the neighbourhood by unaccountably setting itself in motion, and then just, when everyone had been stirred to activity

[1] "Mr. Asquith," by J. P. Alderson (1905), Chaps. II and III.

and all kinds of precautionary measures were being taken, as unaccountably stopped. Unfortunately for my powers as a seer, within three or four months (January, 1874) the "Bog" got to work and submerged the whole political field for the space of six years.

Of my contemporaries among the undergraduates at Balliol I will only enumerate a few besides Alfred Milner and Herbert Warren—Andrew Bradley (who was elected on the same day as myself a Fellow of the College), Churton Collins, A. R. Cluer, T. Raleigh, W. H. Mallock, W. P. Ker, Joseph Solomon, Charles Gore; Arnold Toynbee and W. G. Rutherford were younger, but our times just overlapped. Outside Balliol my principal associates and friends were Herbert Paul and Henry Broadbent.

The President of Magdalen has contributed to the book which I have cited a delightfully vivid sketch of this group of ardent spirits, and of their sayings and doings, both during term-time at Oxford, and in vacation. He recalls a reading party which a number of us organized in the summer of 1875 at St. Andrews.

The party included Thomas Raleigh (afterwards Legal Member of the Viceroy's Council in India) and W. P. Ker, the most versatile of humanists, and Professor of Poetry at Oxford: both of them admirable wits, when they were once set going, but difficult to start. We used to chaff Ker afterwards that during our six weeks at St. Andrews, none of us could remember more than one occasion on which he had opened the talk. I remember years later dining in company with Raleigh at the high table of an Oxford college, which I will not name, but which possessed a professional *raconteur.* When we retired after dessert to our host's rooms, he asked us, perhaps with a little anxiety, what we thought of their show talker, adding that he was considered "the life and soul of the Common Room." Raleigh, who up to that moment had preserved through the evening unbroken silence, muttered: "In the midst of life we are in death."

In default of any other recognized form of athletic exercise, we Englishmen made acquaintance with the unknown and outlandish game of golf. The now world-famous links we often had in the afternoon almost to ourselves; and our clubs were carried for 1*s.* or 1*s.* 6*d.* a round, by — amongst other eminent professionals — young Tommy Morris, then the open champion, who died when he was only a few years over twenty, and whom some competent judges believe to have been as fine a player as any of his successors in the championship — even in these days of American superplay. He was the son and hope of "old Tom," whom golfers of a later generation can remember as the patriarch and oracle of the "Royal and Ancient" game. The parish minister of St. Andrews was Dr. Boyd, author, under the initials A. K. H. B., of a much circulated book, or series of books, "The Recreations of a Country Parson," of which one of our number (Herbert Paul, who came from an English vicarage) remarked that it was a masterpiece of misnomership, for the author was "not a parson, and did not live in the country." I was destined later on in life — unlikely as it then seemed — to be member for East Fife for more than thirty years, and often enjoyed without much political agreement the excellent company of the "Country Parson." St. Andrews was and is the only town in Scotland which still retains something of the mediæval atmosphere.

Of the contemporaries whose names I have given, none became, as I did, what is called a "professional politician." Several of them stood for Parliament (e.g. Milner) and one (Paul) sat in the House of Commons of 1906 as Member for Edinburgh. But Paul will be better remembered as one of the most brilliant and versatile among the journalists and literary men of his time, and Milner's fame was made as a civil servant and administrator, though he became a member of the Cabinet in the later stages of the Great War, and did invaluable service in bringing about in the Western theatre effective unity of command. Gore, afterwards Bishop of Oxford, was and still is the most brilliant and trusted of the leaders of the High Church party in the Church. Bradley, Churton Collins, Mallock and W. P. Ker in different fields and different degrees attained high distinction as accomplished experts in literary criticism. Rutherford was a classical scholar and teacher of a vigorous and original type, and Arnold Toynbee, *præmatura morte abreptus*, lived long enough to leave an enduring footprint on the path of social reform.

CHAPTER IV

AN INTERLUDE

BEFORE I proceed to recall some of the experiences of my active life as a professional man, I may gather together once for all, disregarding chronological sequence, some personal facts.

In the few months which preceded and immediately followed my election to a Balliol fellowship, I was, through the good offices of the Master, engaged by Lord Portsmouth to coach his eldest son Lord Lymington, who was about to leave Eton and go to Balliol. I thus obtained a glimpse of a kind of life which was new to me. The Earl of Portsmouth was a considerable landowner both in England and Ireland. He was a model landlord, a great sportsman, and though he took no active part in politics, a strong Liberal. Lord Palmerston once offered him the Garter, which he refused on the ground that he had done nothing to deserve it. He had two country houses in the south and west of England — Hurstbourne Park in Hampshire, and Eggesford in North Devon — between which my pupil and I divided our time. They were both beautiful places, in very different surroundings, and each was well provided with facilities for all manner of sport and the other interests and diversions of country life.

First and last I spent about three months in this environment, and no one could have been treated with more kindly consideration or made more thoroughly

at home. Lady Portsmouth was the sister of Lord
Carnarvon, who held and ultimately resigned the
Colonial Office in Lord Beaconsfield's Government,
and later was Viceroy of Ireland at the time of the
famous pourparlers with Parnell in the autumn of
1885. He was a frequent visitor at Hurstbourne during my residence there and was wont to speak with
great freedom of his official chief, between whom and
himself—as appears by Mr. Buckle's "Life of Disraeli"—there was not much personal cordiality. He
was a good scholar, well versed in archæology and
literature, with a somewhat precise and formal manner,
but kind and forthcoming to young people. Lady
Portsmouth was a singularly gracious and dignified
figure, and though she had her full share of domestic
burdens (being the mother of twelve children, six boys
and six girls) she never abated her intellectual and
artistic interests. Both she and her husband were much
given to hospitality.

Among their many guests I remember especially two
distinguished men, both verging on old age, and with
as little in common as it is possible to imagine, except
that while neither belonged to the ranks of the professional poets, each had acquired a reputation in that
art. One of them, Lord Houghton, who read some of
his verses aloud to the company on Sunday evening
when games were not allowed, had known everyone of
distinction in politics, society and literature for the
previous half-century, and was a fertile and picturesque raconteur. The other, known to generations of
Eton boys as William Johnson, had recently retired,
and in a whimsical mood had changed his surname to

Cory. As the author of "Ionica" he will always have a nook of his own among the more scholarly and rarefied of our poets. At the request of our hosts, he and I examined together the pupils of a local Grammar School, and thenceforward he honoured me with his friendship. He surprised his friends by marrying late in life, and came to live at Hampstead, where I also had my home. He was a most stimulating and suggestive companion for a walk or talk, with a flavour both of thought and expression which was altogether his own, and left his imprint on the minds and characters of a long succession of pupils who attained distinction in many walks of life.

In the year or two which followed I eked out my livelihood, among other ways, in examining for the Oxford and Cambridge Board at Eton, Harrow, Rugby, and other public schools. Among the boys who in this way came under my observation were Lord Curzon of Kedleston, and Sir Austen Chamberlain.

I married in August, 1877, Helen, daughter of Dr. Frederick Melland of Manchester. After fourteen years of unclouded companionship she was taken away, leaving five children, who have been to me, without exception, a constant and unfailing source of pride and happiness. There is only one gap in our ranks. The death of my eldest son Raymond, who fell in the battle of the Somme in September, 1916, left a wound which Time does not heal.

Raymond was born at Hampstead on November 6, 1878. As a small boy he went to a day-school on the edge of the Heath, where he learnt from two most excellent teachers, Miss Case and Miss Matheson, the rudiments of Latin. He spent two or three useful years at Lambrook under Mr. E. D. Mansfield, and from there won a scholarship at Winchester in 1892. He and his friend Harold Baker, who was a year senior to him, swept the board at Winchester, and in due time Raymond came out first (twenty-seven years later than his father) in the examination for the Balliol Scholarship. In the course of his University career, he won the Craven and Ireland and Derby Scholarships, and took First Class Honours in Classical Moderations, in Greats, and in Law. He was elected to a fellowship at All Souls College in 1902.

He was in due time called to the Bar, married to Katharine Horner in 1907, was doing well in his profession, and had been selected as prospective Liberal candidate for Derby, when the War broke out. He joined first the Queen's Westminsters, and subsequently the Grenadier Guards, in which regiment he became a lieutenant in the 3rd Battalion. He was pressed to join the Staff, but preferred to keep with his regiment, and fell at the head of his men in the attack of September 15, 1916.

I must leave it to others to describe the impression which he made and left upon his contemporaries and associates.

In 1924 the " Balliol College War Memorial Book, 1914–1919," in two volumes, was privately printed for the college. It contains portraits and short memorials of all the Balliol men who fell in the War. The preface states that " all the notices have been written by members of the College, except those of Basil Blackwood, Raymond Asquith and Auberon Herbert,

which were written by their friend Mr. John Buchan."
What follows is extracted from Mr. Buchan's sketch:

Raymond Asquith was beyond doubt the most remarkable figure of his Oxford generation. His great talents
were borne easily and carelessly, and he took successes as
if they were matters of small importance, the pursuit of
which could not be permitted to curtail his leisure for better
things. His manner, even as a young man, was curiously
self-possessed and urbane, as of one who was happy in society but did not give to it more than a little part of himself. Some of his contemporaries may have equalled him in
intellectual strength, but none came near the variety of his
gifts. In addition to being a fine classical scholar he had an
acute critical sense, and both in verse and prose had an uncanny gift of exact phrase. Unfortunately he has left little
behind him — only a few satires, mostly in manuscript, and,
in the hands of his friends, a number of letters which may
well be considered the best written in our time. He was
also a most accomplished speaker. At the Union his
speeches were apt to be strings of brilliant and polished
epigrams, but when he chose he could also be a formidable
debater.

When he left Oxford his lack of ambition seemed to be
more marked, and in London he was the same distinguished
and slightly detached figure which he had been at the University. After his marriage to Miss Katharine Horner in
1907 he settled down seriously to the Bar and attained a
considerable position, but it is doubtful if he would have
made one of the resounding successes of advocacy. He
was too careless of the worldly wisdom which makes smooth
the steps in a career, and he had no gift of deference
towards eminent solicitors, or of reverence towards heavy-
witted judges. Politics were a different matter. He had
every advantage in the business — voice, language, manner, orderly thought, perfect nerve and coolness. The very
fact that he sat rather loose to party creeds would have
strengthened his hands at a time when creeds were in transition. For, though he might scoff at most dogmas, he had
a great reverence for the problems behind them, and to

these problems he brought a fresh mind and a sincere good-will.

In a letter written shortly after leaving Oxford he spoke of finding life "a little barren of motives," and to his fastidiousness the ordinary rewards of success seemed scarcely worthy of a man's care. He used to speak of the "bleak futility" of ordinary politics, and of the law as "a lean casuistical business." The War brought the real man to light. He appeared to dislike emotion, not because he felt lightly, but because he felt deeply. It was no sudden sentimental fervour that swept him into the Army, but the essential nature of one who had always been shy of rhetorical professions, but was very clear about the real thing. Austerely self-respecting, he had been used to hide his emotions under the mask of indifference, and would never reveal them except in deeds. Being of the spending type in life, when he gave he did not count the cost, and of the many who did likewise few had so much to give.

In the Guards he was extraordinarily happy, and seemed to have found again the light-hearted companionship which had been the charm of Oxford. For a short time he had a post at General Head-quarters, but asked to be sent back to his battalion, for he wished no privileges, and was far happier with his men than on the Staff. He had found his twentieth year again, and death took him at the height of his powers of body and spirit. "Eld shall not make a mock of that dear head." He loved his youth, and his youth has become eternal.

When Raymond was chosen to be the Liberal candidate in succession to the veteran Sir Thomas Roe at Derby, he was brought into frequent and close association with Mr. J. H. Thomas, the sitting Labour member. In the interesting sketch of Mr. Thomas's career, published nearly ten years ago,[1] it is recorded that "their association ripened into real attachment. . . . They had a great mutual sympathy and a great deal of

[1] "From Engine-cleaner to Privy Councillor," by J. F. Moir Bussy, p. 99.

mutual understanding as to the future." "When he went to the front and was in the thick of the fighting, communications by way of keeping up the friendship frequently passed between the young lieutenant and Jim Thomas. The last letter Jim received came from the trenches shortly before the lieutenant's death, which was very sudden. It was written in lead pencil like most trench literature, and in the course of it the following passage occurred:

"I am sleeping and eating when and where a chance offers. We are now somewhere near the middle of the whirlpool, and cannot say where we may be next week. It is all very tiring and noisy, but no one can call it dull. Like most other people I have had some narrow squeaks, but am very fit and ready for anything."

Upon Mr. Thomas's own testimony I set a special value.

"If there ever was," he writes, "an illustration of right thinking in the case of a man of influence and position who could, if he had cared to do so, have made his position one of safety and comfort, but who chose rather the sphere of hard work, privation, and possible death, we see it in the action of Raymond Asquith."

CHAPTER V

READING FOR THE BAR: BOWEN AND MATHEW

WHEN I left Oxford at the end of the summer term of 1875, I came to London, took lodgings in Mount Street, and went daily to the Temple to read law as a pupil in the chambers in Brick Court of Charles Bowen.

Bowen at that time, in addition to being Attorney-General's "devil," had a large general practice, and was probably the best employed junior at the Bar. He was a remarkable man, who had from first to last a remarkable career, but he had an elusive personality, of which it is difficult, if not impossible, to describe for those who did not know him, the characteristic traits.[1]

In his school and University he had been the pride first of Rugby, and then of Balliol. There was no scholarship or prize for which he cared to compete that he did not carry off. He was a good cricketer, a first-class football player, and an athlete of conspicuous prowess. "He is the only person I ever knew to jump a cow as it stood," wrote his brother.[2] At Oxford he was President of the Union, and was elected a Fellow of Balliol while still an undergraduate. He was and always remained Jowett's favourite pupil. Many years afterwards, when I was myself a Fellow and was taking

[1] See "Lord Bowen," by Sir H. S. Cunningham (1897); and the sketch in the "Dictionary of National Biography," 1st Suppt., Vol. I, p. 238, by Sir Herbert Stephen (1901).
[2] Stephen, *l.c.*

a Sunday afternoon walk with the Master, I remember that on my asking him whom, upon the whole, he would put first for ability among his many generations of distinguished pupils, he replied without a moment's hesitation, "Charles Bowen."

His success at the Bar was not so rapid as might have been expected. Indeed he had been called ten years when, in 1871, the Tichborne Case gave him his first great chance. He was junior in that famous and long protracted litigation to Sir John Coleridge, also a Balliol man, to whom he made himself indispensable, and who rewarded him with the office of Junior Counsel to the Treasury, which is more often than not a stepping-stone to the Bench. In 1879 (two or three years after I left his chambers) Lord Cairns made him a judge of the Queen's Bench, and before long he was appointed first a Lord Justice of the Court of Appeal, and in 1893 — only a year before his premature death — a Law Lord in the House of Lords. I had by then become Home Secretary, and one of his last public services was to preside, at my request, over the committee which inquired into the Featherstone riot, and whose report, mainly if not wholly from his pen, remains the *locus classicus* as to the legal and constitutional relations between the civil and military authorities in cases of riot and unlawful assembly.

I shall not dwell at any length upon his judicial career. He was not a great Nisi Prius judge, mainly because he could not always resist the temptation to baffle and bewilder the "twelve honest men who decided the cause" by freaks of the ironic humour of which he had an inexhaustible vein. In the higher courts he was completely at home, and his unerring knowledge of law, applied by reasoning powers of equal strength and subtlety, and set off by a rare gift of felicitous expression, made him perhaps the most accomplished judge of his time. The last time I saw him was at the meeting under Lord Salisbury's chairmanship in London, after Jowett's death, in December, 1893, to consider what form the memorial to the Master should take. Among the speakers were Coleridge, Bowen, and myself — all of whom had been scholars of Balliol. Neither he nor Lord Coleridge ever spoke in public again. His death in April, 1894, while he was still under sixty, was an incalculable loss.

Bowen, with the quickest intelligence of any man at the Bar, was, when I knew him as his pupil, one of the hardest and most painstaking workers that I have ever come across. In fact he worked a great deal too hard. He was so fastidious that he could not avail himself adequately of other people's labours, though his courtesy and consideration for those, whose well-meant and often highly meritorious efforts he discarded, was unfailing and even profuse. There were few things more disheartening, when one was summoned to his inner room, than to see the "pleading," over which one had perhaps spent hours of industry and research, cancelled page after page and rewritten by his pen, or, worse still, lying in fragments in the waste-paper basket. Nor was the wound altogether salved when he dismissed you in the most mellifluous tones of his fluted voice: "My dear fellow, I cannot tell you how grateful I am to you."

To know what you must do yourself, and what you

can let others do for you, is one of the secrets of efficiency, and it was a secret which Bowen never succeeded in mastering.

Bowen had rare social and personal charm: he was one of the wittiest men of his time: his quips and sallies were unforced, and though pointed and sometimes barbed, always urbane and never venomous. He was in politics a Liberal; what he thought of the problems of "Time and Eternity" he kept to himself.

His chief antagonist in the first rank of the Junior Bar was J. C. Mathew. He was the best commercial lawyer of his day, and was the first judge to preside over the newly-founded Commercial Court. He was a Southern Irishman *pur sang* from the County Cork, and, without any advantage of connection or influence, won his way to the front of our Bar. He followed in the footsteps of his compatriot, Mr. Justice Willes, also from Cork, who became with Mr. Justice Blackburn, a Scotsman, one of the two acknowledged masters in the mid-Victorian era of the English Common Law. When promoted to the Bench they were still stuff-gownsmen, like Mathew and Bowen, and, in an earlier generation, Baron Parke.[1] Mathew was a man of wide culture and an excellent scholar, with the warmest of hearts, and from his ready and abundant humour the best of companions. He and Bowen, though for years engaged in daily rivalry, were intimate friends, and in social intercourse each goaded the other to a contest of wits. Alas! as Bowen himself said of another of the best talkers of our time, Professor Henry Smith, "the

[1] The elevation of Blackburn, who, unlike Willes, never had any considerable practice, was much criticized at the time as a Scotch job on the part of the Chancellor, Lord Campbell. But it was more than justified.

brightest conversationalist is often the most evanescent, and the *finesse* of wit, like a musical laugh, disappears with the occasion, and cannot be reproduced on paper or in print." [1]

[1] Cunningham's "Lord Bowen," p. 185, where some amusing specimens are given of Bowen's frivolous correspondence with Mathew. One remark of Mathew's may perhaps be quoted. Someone asked him after the health of a distinguished judge who had got into the habit of nodding in the afternoon. Mathew: "No occasion for alarm; I have not observed any symptoms of insomnia."

CHAPTER VI

SOME EMINENT VICTORIANS

IN one of Bulwer's later novels, he sums up his description of a leading character in some such words as these (I quote from memory): "As a man of the world he despised letters: as a man of letters he despised the world: as a representative of both, he respected himself." As a picture of the famous Master of Balliol this would be both inadequate and misleading; but it conveys a suggestion of his combination of many-sidedness and detachment. At any rate, in Landor's words, he "warmed both hands before the fire of life."

After he was settled in the Master's Lodge, it was Jowett's practice during term-time to have what would now be called "week-end parties," at which the guests were drawn from diverse quarters of the outside world. He was not specially partial to statesmen and diplomatists, though he was always delighted to have under his roof such men as Lowe, Lord Westbury, and Sir Robert Morier. But he had an intimate acquaintance with not a few of the greatest artists and writers who adorned the Victorian age. A few privileged undergraduates used to be invited to come in on Sunday nights, and it was in this way that I first had a glimpse of Tennyson and George Eliot. It is not easy for the average English reader of the twentieth century to realize the hero-worship which was given in the eighteen-seventies to this illustrious pair. Both I believe are out of fashion,

if not out of favour, with our latter-day critics, and I
am told that a similar fate is awaiting, if it has not
already befallen, another of the Victorian idols, at
whose shrine I confess that I never worshipped—
George Meredith.

Of Tennyson, I have nothing to tell that is worth recording. *Vidi tantum*—and no poet ever better looked
the part—and caught a few unconsidered scraps of his
talk.

George Eliot was a more frequent visitor, with her
husband G. H. Lewes. He had a most versatile mind,
and was one of the best and most accomplished critics
of his time. I remember Jowett asking him at table,
after the ladies had gone, whether an ordinary reader
ought to have guessed from internal evidence, that
"Adam Bede" and "The Mill on the Floss" were
written by a woman. Lewes replied that he had always
thought there was one thing which ought to have betrayed the author's sex: that no man with such fine
observation and intimate knowledge of the country and
of country life would have been so totally indifferent
to sport in all its aspects.

After dinner I was privileged to have a talk with the
Great Oracle herself—for she looked and spoke like
a Sibyl, though with all imaginable courtesy to a raw
and insignificant undergraduate. This must have been
in the year 1873 or 1874, and she asked me whether
the Church had still much hold on the intellectual élite
of young Oxford. I replied that it had very little, and
that little was on the wane. She answered: "I am
getting an old woman, and you are a very young man,
but unless my vision is at fault, you—though not I—

will live to see a great renascence of religion among thoughtful people." I asked her what Church or community would profit by it. She answered without hesitation: "The Roman Catholic Church."

That was more than fifty years ago, and it is, I think, an interesting illustration of the hazards of prophecy.

The Bagehots and Huttons and Townsends were in my young days an interesting and in some ways an important group in the literary life of London. They could not be described as a coterie or a set, but they were a disputatious tribe and rarely agreed with one another about anything except a few "fundamentals." Of the living writers they would have agreed in putting George Eliot in the front rank. I remember one night dining with Mrs. Bagehot a few weeks after the death of George Henry Lewes, which left George Eliot a widow. She told me that that morning her cook had received a letter from George Eliot's cook describing the demonstrative grief of her bereaved mistress. But, added the cook, "as they say in our part of the country, 'it's the bawling cow that misses its calf the least'": a remark which seemed to me to bear the hallmark of Mrs. Poyser's mint.

I have referred to George Meredith. Although my acquaintance with him did not begin till long after my Oxford days, it may not be inappropriate to speak of him here, in the company of two of his great Victorian contemporaries. I think I was introduced to him by Haldane, and we often used to pay him a Sunday visit at his cottage at Box Hill. I have recently read with much interest what seems to me a penetrating study of his personality and work by Mr. Priestley. I was never initiated into the inner Meredithian cult, though I have always been a great admirer of his poetry, but as a charming companion and arresting talker I put him among the first I had known. " By God," said one of the Victorian wits to him one day, " George, why don't you write like you talk?" It is true that his conversation, particularly as he grew deafer, tended to become a monologue, but it was sprinkled with gems and never bored. He was a great improvisatore and nothing could be more exhilarating than to watch him, with his splendid head and his eyes aflame, stamping up and down the room, while he extemporized at the top of his resonant voice a sonnet in perfect form on the governess's walking costume, or a dozen lines, in the blankest of Wordsworthian verse, in elucidation of Haldane's philosophy. He was a regular guest for years at our annual symposium at the " Blue Posts," and more than held his own in the most exacting company. The same gathering used also from time to time to include Edward Burne-Jones, who had a gift of delightfully perverse humour, and a rare inventiveness in phraseology and metaphor, which was entirely his own.

The years of my youth and early manhood were spent in the meridian of the golden age of Victorian literature. They witnessed, in poetry, the appearance of the best work of Tennyson, Browning, and Matthew Arnold: in fiction, some of the masterpieces of Dickens and Thackeray, and most of George Eliot, not to mention such artists as Wilkie Collins, Anthony Trollope, Charles Reade, and Charles Kingsley: while in history and biography we had with us still in full activity

Macaulay and Carlyle. The "Origin of Species" was published in my boyhood, and though in philosophy we had no one of the stature of Locke and Hume and Adam Smith, no critic, even in these days when J. S. Mill and Herbert Spencer have gone out of fashion, will question their title to a place in the long and distinguished succession of English and Scottish thinkers.

Apart from casual glimpses, the only two of these illustrious writers with whom I was brought into personal contact were Ruskin and Spencer.

When I went up in 1870 as an undergraduate to Oxford, Ruskin had just been appointed to the newly-founded Slade Professorship of Fine Art. From time to time I attended his lectures which, to accommodate the crowded attendance, were delivered in the Sheldonian Theatre. His appearance as a lecturer has been well described by his devoted pupil and biographer, E. T. Cook: "The figure of the lecturer was striking with ample gown — discarded often when its folds became too hopelessly involved — and the velvet college cap, one of the few remaining memorials of the 'gentleman commoner.' The quaintness of his costume — the light homespun tweed, the double-breasted waistcoat, the ill-fitting and old-fashioned frock-coat, the amplitude of inevitable blue tie — accurately reflected something of the quaintness of his mind and talk. . . . The blue eyes piercing from beneath thick bushy eyebrows never ceased to shine with the fire of genius."[1] Of his voice, Mallock (who was a contemporary of mine at Balliol) says in one of his transparent caricatures in the "New Republic," that it would "often hold all the

---

[1] Cook's "Life of Ruskin," Vol. II, pp. 173-4.

theatre breathless"; and that it sometimes seemed as if it "came from a disconsolate spirit hovering over the waters of Babylon and remembering Zion."[1]

Lecturing was, however, only one of the activities of this highly unconventional professor. His breakfasts at his rooms in Corpus, his "symposia" which were intended to combine "plain living and high thinking," his much derided "road-digging" experiments, were illustrations of the thoroughness with which he threw himself into the life of the place. Among his "road-diggers" were two of the most distinguished of my contemporaries at Balliol—Alfred Milner and Arnold Toynbee.[2] Of the "æsthetic" movement which was then beginning its short-lived and noxious career, and which borrowed some of its cant phrases from perversions of his writing and teaching, he had, says his biographer, an "utter loathing." We are not surprised to be told that at first Jowett's "attitude towards Ruskin was hesitating," though ultimately they became great friends.

He was undoubtedly a great and on the whole a beneficent power in the Oxford of those days. I have still a vivid recollection of seeing him more than once, in the lanes about Abingdon, alight in his buttoned frock-coat from his lumbering old-fashioned carriage,

---

[1] There was another side to the "disconsolate spirit": for instance the following — from "Præterita" — of the "conversational manners" of three Prime Ministers. "Lord Palmerston disputed no principle with me (being, I fancied, partly of the same mind with me about principles), but only feasibilities; whereas in every talk permitted me more recently by Mr. Gladstone *he* disputes *all* the principles before their application; and the application of all that get past the dispute. Disraeli differed from both in making a jest alike of principle and practice." Cook, Vol. II, p. 558.

[2] His teaching (says Mr. Cook) had "no small share in leading to the Universities' Settlements in East London and other cities" (Vol. II, p. 191).

to gather some wild-flowers that had caught his eye in the hedgerow.

My acquaintance, such at it was, with Herbert Spencer began when I was still a young barrister with much compulsory leisure. At the suggestion of some common friend, whose name I have forgotten, he wrote to me to ask if I could give him some help in the way of material for a book upon which he was engaged, in the gradual building up of the "synthetic philosophy," on the subject of political institutions. I had never been a close student of his works, but I had read enough to be sceptical of their reasoning and repelled by their jargon. However it is not for the unemployed to be over-fastidious on such a point, and a few days later the philosopher appeared at my chambers, and for some time afterwards he visited me once or twice a week. In quaintness of appearance and costume he almost rivalled Ruskin, with whom he had no other point of resemblance — physical, intellectual, or spiritual.

Happily it is not necessary for me to attempt his portrait, as the task has already been performed by competent artists who knew him much more intimately than I ever did.

Here is a sketch of the outward man by a close and fine observer of the other sex:

Memory recalls a finely sculptured head, prematurely bald, long, stiff upper lip and powerful chin, obstinately compressed mouth, small sparkling grey eyes, set close together, with a prominent Roman nose. . . . Always clad in primly neat, but quaintly unconventional garments, there was distinction, even a certain elegance, in the philosopher's punctilious manners and precise and lucid speech.

This is, however, qualified by the acknowledgment that "his elaborate explanations, couched in pedantic terms, of commonplace occurrences as exemplifications of the recondite principles of the synthetic philosophy seemed to the Philistine listener just a trifle absurd."[1]

I confess that in this connection I was one of the Philistines. Nor was I in bad company. The writer's father, Mr. Potter, a cultivated man accustomed to the companionship of friends like Huxley and Froude, when Spencer began to talk of the law of increasing heterogeneity "saw no sense in it," and exclaimed to his daughter, "Words, my dear, mere words." And when at one of Mill's select dinner parties, Spencer, at the host's instance, had descanted for a quarter of an hour, for the benefit of Grote, on the "equilibration of molecules," Fawcett, in a whisper to John Morley, asked if he understood a word of it, for, he added, "I do not."[2]

Morley himself, in a life-like sketch of the philosopher, for whom he had a genuine admiration, admits that in small, but not unimportant, things he was pedantic and neurotic. He tells of a visit that he paid to him in the company of Mr. Balfour. "We only touched from time to time on serious things, and then he would draw off in haste, as fearing cerebral agitation." What was more disquieting to Morley, who was from first to last an unshaken agnostic, was that, in his last writings, Spencer, "the head of the agnostic school," began, under the stress of "certain new speculations upon Space," following the fatal example of Mill himself, who ended as something very like a

1 "My Apprenticeship," by Beatrice Webb, p. 25.
2 Morley, "Recollections," Vol. I, p. 112.

Manichee, to falter in the faith. "It made some of the narrower or the firmer among us quake." [1]

In the early 'eighties — the time when I knew him — Spencer was engaged in a series of articles, with such titles as "The Coming Slavery" and "The Great Political Superstition," attacking, with all the fervour of an uncompromising Individualist, the Liberal party for having forsworn its faith in personal freedom. "How is it," he asked, "that Liberalism, getting more and more into power, has grown more and more coercive in its legislation?" [2] What would he have said if he had lived to see a Liberal Government introducing Old Age Pensions and National Insurance?

Spencer's "Autobiography," a work of portentous size, covering 1,000 pages, is too long for readers of only average patience, but is well worth skimming and skipping. It shows him on the whole in a human light, with a good sense of humour, an amazing range of interests, and an occasional consciousness of his own limitations. He was an ardent fisherman, and a regular billiard-player. "It is a great mistake for adults," he writes, "and especially for adults who work their brains much, to give up sports and games. The maxim on which I have acted is 'Be a boy as long as you can.'" [3] It was in this spirit that he advised G. H. Lewes and George Eliot, who were seeking health in the country, to give up reading aloud to one another in the evening, and get a billiard-table: they seem to have compromised by setting up a lawn-tennis net.

His appreciation of the great poets was severely

[1] Morley, "Recollections," Vol. I, p. 114.
[2] Beatrice Webb, p. 185.
[3] "Autobiography of Herbert Spencer," Vol. II, p. 305.

critical. After reading six books of the *Iliad* in a translation, he felt that he would rather give a large sum than read to the end. He found Dante too monotonous for his taste: " I soon begin to want change in the mode of presentation." " I am in but small measure attracted to Wordsworth . . . most of his writing is not wine but beer." [1]

I was mainly concerned in my conversations with the old philosopher, who was a model of courtesy and kindness in his dealings with younger men, in discussing the historical development of English law. His treatment of such matters was highly characteristic of his intellectual temperament and methods. He started with certain large generalizations as to the principles of evolution, which he assumed to be of universal application, and then proceeded, with infinite industry in successive fields of investigation, to amass the material facts which would illustrate and verify his theory.

In the Order of Merit, founded twenty-five years ago by King Edward, there are at the present moment (1927) the names of six distinguished men, who have presumably found a place in the ranks largely, if not entirely, on the ground of literary eminence; it is to be remembered that the Order was never intended as a badge of distinction for politicians as such. The names are, in order of seniority, those of Mr. Thomas Hardy, Sir George Trevelyan, Lord Haldane, Lord Balfour, Sir James Barrie, and Sir James Frazer; of whom two (Hardy and Barrie) may be taken to represent fiction and the drama; two (Trevelyan and

[1] "Autobiography of Herbert Spencer," Vol. I, pp. 262-3.

Frazer) history, biography and scholarly research; and two (Haldane and Balfour) speculative philosophy. No one, of course, will contend that if our most famous literary men were to be arranged in classes after the fashion of the Oxford Schools or the Tripos of Cambridge, the half-dozen who have received the Order of Merit, would necessarily constitute, still less exhaust, Class 1. It is to be observed that the list does not include any representative of the art of Poetry, except Mr. Hardy, whose primary claim in the estimation of the most enthusiastic admirer would almost certainly be based upon his achievements in the domain of creative prose.

Shortly after I became Prime Minister I wrote to Mr. Hardy to ask him if he would agree that I should submit his name to the King, and I received the following letter (given also in facsimile) in reply:

MAX GATE,
DORCHESTER,
November 5, 1908.

DEAR MR. ASQUITH, —

The honour you so generously propose to confer upon me for my defective productions in English literature is so unexpected that I am hardly able to realize all its bearings for the moment. And as the date of His Majesty's birthday is so near, and a definite reply at once would be necessary to be in time for that anniversary, I am compelled to ask that the question may stand over until next year, or the next occasion for such honours, for my consideration. Should this be impossible or inconvenient as a definite understanding I will let the renewal of the proposal or not depend upon your discretion.[1] In any case I shall have felt

---

[1] The Order of Merit was bestowed on Mr. Hardy in 1910.

it to be a privilege to have been brought by your kind thought into temporary contact with a Prime Minister whose talents and courage in acting up to principles that I share wins my admiration more and more constantly as time goes on.

> Believe me to be,
> Most faithfully yours,
> THOMAS HARDY.

Nov 5. 1908

Dear Mr Asquith:

The honour you so generously propose to confer upon me for my defective productions in English literature is so unexpected that I am hardly able to realize all its bearings for the moment. And as the date of His Majesty's birthday is so near, & a definite reply at once would be necessary to be in time for that anniversary, I am compelled to ask that the question may stand over until next year, or the next occasion for such honours, for my consideration. Should this be impossible or inconvenient as a definite understanding I will let the renewal of the proposal or not depend upon your discretion. In any case I shall have felt it to be a privilege to have been brought by your kind thought

into temporary contact with a
Prime Minister whose talents &
courage in acting up to principles
that I share wins my admiration
more & more constantly as time
goes on.

      Believe me the

        most faithfully yours

         Thomas Hardy.

CHAPTER VII

MINOR LITERARY LIGHTS

IN literature as in other forms of art the changes of fashion are rapid and baffling, and it is often difficult to understand either the extravagant admiration of one generation or the exaggerated depreciation of another. Among the English writers of my time there are a few who, one may say with confidence, are assured of that form of immortality which consists in being remembered and read by posterity. There will always be fluctuations even in the vogue of the greatest and most famous. We have seen capricious ups and downs in popular appreciation in some quite unpredictable cases. Take first a pre-Victorian writer of the highest rank, Sir Walter Scott. Mr. Gladstone used to say that he had made it a rule to read the Waverley novels through every five years. Yet though it would be ridiculous to say that Scott has been displaced, or that his works have passed (as it may be feared "The Pilgrim's Progress" has) into the class which are "taken as read," there can be no doubt that for a time he lost, not only his primacy, but his hold upon the interest and the affections, especially of the younger members of the reading public. We have seen other illustrations of the same turning and twisting of the wheel of Fortune in the vicissitudes of some of the great Victorians. Dickens himself fell for a time on lean years, and even now has to struggle hard to hold his own against the menacing inroad of the "best

sellers" and the "shockers." Nor has Tennyson been
able, wholly, to escape from the fickleness of the bookstall. But of writers of genius, such as these, we may
confidently predict that, whatever may be the passing
fashions of the hour, they will come back into their
own.

I am sometimes tempted, wandering along the by-
paths of literature, to recall the now too often neglected
names of those whom "it" altered to "fashion."

> Ah, wasteful woman, she who may
>   On her sweet self set her own price,
> Knowing he cannot choose but pay,
>   How has she cheapen'd Paradise;
> How given for nought her priceless gift,
>   How spoiled the bread and spill'd the wine,
> Which, spent with due, respective thrift,
>   Had made brutes men, and men divine.

These, which were among Ruskin's favourite lines,
are to be found in Coventry Patmore's "Angel in the
House,"[1] and are in my judgment hard to surpass for
tenderness of sentiment and felicity of phrase. Yet
the author is not, I suppose, classed higher than among
the minor Victorian poets—so exuberant was the
wealth of that prolific era.

Others who in my time have enjoyed an almost equal
measure of popularity are by now as dead as Queen
Anne, and lie in unvisited graves. I can recall at least
three noteworthy cases—Tupper, Horne, and Bailey.

Tupper, who was a contemporary at Oxford of Mr.
Gladstone, whom, by the way, he beat for a theological
essay prize, produced, before he was thirty, the first

---

[1] Prelude I ("The Prodigal") in Canto VII ("Ætna and the Moon") of Book I,
Part I of "The Angel in the House"; Patmore omitted "The Prodigal" in the
last edition of the poem, substituting "Love's Immortality."

edition of "Proverbial Philosophy," which was ultimately expanded into four series. It ran steadily
through the lifetime of a generation into fifty or sixty
editions; it was translated into French, German, and
Danish: a million copies were sold in the United
States: "Gems from Tupper" had a wide circulation;
and in my boyhood, when it was at the height of the
fashion, it was to be found lying on the drawing-room
table of countless middle-class houses in Great Britain.
Though the critics almost from the first made fun of
it, it got a firm hold on the reading public of those days,
and almost threatened to become one of the classics of
the bourgeoisie. It was, in fact, nothing better than a
collection, in the guise of "aphorisms," of pomposities
and platitudes. The following lines may serve as a fair
specimen. They are at the beginning of the discourse
"Of Tolerance."

> A wise man in a crowded street winneth his way with
>   gentleness.
> Nor rudely pusheth aside the stranger that standeth in
>   his path;
> He knoweth that blind hurry will but hinder, stirring up
>   contention against him.
> Yet holdeth he steadily right on with his face to the scope
>   of his pursuit.

Tupper himself, who was an amiable man of some
culture, outlived the popularity of "Proverbial Philosophy," and accepted from Mr. Gladstone a Civil List
pension. The book is now apparently somewhat of a
rarity, for not very long ago, when I asked my book-
seller in Oxford to sell me a copy, he was unable to find
one after a diligent search among his second-hand stock.

A similar fate has befallen a book which in its day

procured fame for its author — the "Orion" of Richard Hengist Horne. Horne, who lived till 1884, was
an eccentric man, of vagrant habits, a voluminous and
versatile writer of tragedies and poems, a friend of
Elizabeth Barrett Browning, whose "Cry of the Children" he is said to have inspired; but he was generally
known to his associates and the world as "Orion
Horne." "Orion," of which I have the original edition, was first published in 1843, and is described on the
title page as an "Epic Poem in Three Books" ("Price
one farthing"). It became immediately popular, and
went in all through eleven editions. It was not harshly
treated by the critics, and was highly praised by Edgar
Allan Poe. It is written in blank verse, of which the
following lines are a not unfavourable specimen:

> Like one uplifted in abstraction's mood
> Who sits alone and gazes in the fire,
> Watching red ruins as they fall and change
> To glorious fabrics — which forthwith dissolve,
> Or by some hideous conflict sink to nought,
> While from a black mass issues tawny smoke
> Followed by a trumpet flame.

This is better than Tupper, but not the kind of thing
to live. The public after a time turned its back on
"Orion," which is now only read by curiosity hunters,
and the declining years of the veteran author were made
easier by Lord Beaconsfield's grant of a pension.

In some ways a more tragic figure than either of these
is that of Philip James Bailey (1816–1902). He was
in the strictest sense "*homo unius libri*" — for the
whole of his literary life was given to the production
and elaboration and development of "Festus," of which
the first edition was published in 1839, when the author

was only twenty-three. It was a Bowdlerized version
of Goethe's "Faust", and was intended by Bailey to
retain the inspiration and at the same time to correct
the anti-religious tendencies of that immortal work. It
was described on its appearance by one of the hostile
journalistic critics of the day as a "plagiarism from
Goethe, with all his impiety and scarcely any of his
poetry"; and by another, with more friendly intentions: "The design of 'Festus' is excellent, and its
morals unexceptionable. The work is one of a remarkable, but of a *Christian* character."

Some other contemporary criticisms from sources of
more value are worth citing. Bulwer Lytton char-
acterized it as a "most remarkable and magnificent
production"; Harrison Ainsworth declared that
Bailey's "place will be among the first, if not the first,
of our native poets"; and "Orion Horne" was en-
raptured by its "unrepressed vigour of imagination."
A greater authority than these, Tennyson, advised Edward Fitzgerald to read it, adding, "You will most
likely find it a great bore, but there are really very
grand things in 'Festus.'" It was well received by
the public; the author devoted, as I have said, the
whole of the remaining fifty years of his active life to
the work of revision and amplification—with the result that in the eleventh or jubilee edition of 1889, the
comparatively modest original total of 11,000 lines had
been extended to 40,000. As was the case with Tupper's masterpiece, its best market was in the United
States. But it was an evanescent popularity, and in the
later years of his life Bailey, like Tupper and Horne,
was a pensioner on the Civil List.

That there are striking lines, and even good passages, in "Festus" is not to be denied: such, for instance, as the description of genius as:

> A zigzag streak of lightning in the brain.

But more characteristic of the general level of the whole is Helen's remark to Festus:

> Do! let me hear!
> Thy talk is the sweet extract of all speech,
> And holds mine ear in blissful slavery.

There were "Festus Birthday Books" and "Beauties of Festus" for a long time in circulation.

As I lately turned over the pages of these once fashionable and now forgotten writers, there came into my mind an excellent remark of Gibbon's, which is to be found in his "Autobiography":

> I adopted the tolerating maxim of the elder Pliny: *nullum esse librum tam malum, ut non ex aliqua parte prodesset.*

Another of the now faded Victorian reputations is that of Samuel Warren, whose novel "Ten Thousand a Year," after appearing in serial form in *Blackwood*, was published in 1841, had an enormous sale, and established its claim "to be one of the most popular novels of the century." His later literary efforts culminated in "The Lily and the Bee," written in honour of the Great Exhibition of 1851: of which Mr. Seccombe says that the "style suggests comparison with Martin Tupper, but it is more absurd than anything that Tupper wrote."[1] Warren practised at the Bar

[1] "Dictionary of National Biography."

with not very pronounced success; Charles Reade was one of his legal pupils. He sat for a short time in the House of Commons as member for Midhurst. In politics he was an old-fashioned Tory of the most obscurantist type, and was rewarded for his faithful partisanship in 1859, during one of the short spells of Conservative government, by being appointed to a Mastership in Lunacy (worth £2,000 a year). He seems to have dallied for a time with the Lord Chancellor's offer as inadequate to his merits: whereupon Mr. Disraeli is said to have remarked that a writ *de lunatico inquirendo* would have to be issued for Mr. Warren. He appears, however, to have proved himself quite competent for his job.

Thomas Hughes, like Samuel Warren, is known in literature as the author of a single book, also belonging to the class of so-called fiction, though no two works could be more unlike than "Tom Brown's School Days" and "Ten Thousand a Year." Hughes had no literary ambitions, and he wrote "Tom Brown" not for fame or for money, but "to do good." It was published anonymously in 1857 when the author was already thirty-five; five editions were called for in the first nine months; and it has never lost a large measure of popularity. Hughes, with Charles Kingsley and Ludlow, was one of the small band of "Christian Socialists" who sat at the feet of F. D. Maurice, and the enduring memorial of whose labours is to be found in such institutions as the Co-operative movement—on its productive, not on its distributive side—and the Working Men's College. He brought to all his work the enthusiasm of a devout and indefatigable propa-

gandist, and his later books are for the most part
short biographies of the heroes (from Alfred the Great
to Livingstone) of the special type of manly Christianity of which he was for his own generation an admirable example.   He sat for some years in the House
of Commons, where, as his friend Mr. Justin McCarthy
records,[1] "he never made much way as a speaker,"
though "the House always listened to him with close
attention."   He was a staunch upholder of the cause of
the North in the American Civil War, and received
an enthusiastic welcome in the United States on his
first visit in 1870.   In 1882 he was appointed a County
Court judge and went out of party politics, but Mr.
Llewelyn Davies tells us that "when Gladstone went
over to Home Rule for Ireland, Hughes's opposition
to that policy was touched with indignation, and he
became a vehement Liberal Unionist."   He is a remarkable instance of an author who, without any great
natural aptitude for writing, by the happy choice of a
subject which made a special appeal to English readers,
and every aspect of which he knew intimately both by
observation and by insight, has created a literary masterpiece.

There is a characteristic example of Hughes's in-
stinctive sympathies in his preface to the first English
edition of Lowell's "Biglow Papers."[2]   "In Lowell,"
he says, "the American mind has for the first time
flowered out into thoroughly original genius."   He
passes in review the earlier achievements of the "American mind": the "airy grace" of Washington Irving;
the "original power which will perhaps be better ap-

---

[1] "Reminiscences," Vol. II, p. 257.   [2] Trübner, 1880.

preciated at a later day" of Fenimore Cooper; the "dramatic power" of Mr. Hawthorne, "mixed with a certain morbidness and bad taste which debar him from ever attaining to the first rank"; the "originality" of Mr. Emerson, "coupled with a singular metallic style," producing one of the "best counterfeits of genius that has been seen for many a day." But for real genius he asserts with emphasis that the "Biglow Papers" stand alone.

Writing, I hope, with becoming diffidence, and remembering with thankful admiration the great contributions with which gifted American writers— Walt Whitman, Bret Harte, Henry and William James, Edith Wharton (to name only a few) — have, since 1880, enriched the literature of the English-speaking world, I am by no means sure that the supremacy of Lowell's masterpiece has yet been successfully assailed.

Hughes, a typical "Broad" Churchman of the mid-Victorian age, finds it expedient and even necessary to vindicate the "association of humour and Christianity." He brings into the argument the examples of Luther, of our own Latimer and Rowland Hill— he might have added Spurgeon—and, to go back to the New Testament, the "subdued humour" of St. Luke's description of the disturbances at Achaia and the famous phrase that "Gallio cared for none of those things."

One may, at any rate, hazard the opinion that satire has never, in modern times, been better or more happily applied to the democratic machine than in the two immortal stanzas in "What Mr. Robinson Thinks":

Parson Wilbur sez *he* never heerd in his life
   That th' Apostles rigged out in their swaller-tail coats
An' marched round in front of a drum an' a fife,
    To git some on 'em office an' some on 'em votes;
       But John P.
      Robinson he
Sez they didn't know everythin' down in Judee.

Wal, it's a marcy we've gut folks to tell us
   The rights an' the wrongs o' these matters, I vow —
God sends country lawyers an' other wise fellers
    To start the world's team wen it gits in a slough;
      Fer John P.
      Robinson he
Sez the world'll go right ef he hollers out Gee!

A. W. Kinglake was a man of far greater literary
faculty than either Hughes or Warren. The contemporary at Eton of Gladstone, and friend at Cambridge
of Tennyson and Thackeray, he obtained a moderate
practice at the Bar, and in 1844, after much recasting,
published his "Eothen," which became and still remains one of the classics of travel. Its second title was
"Traces of Travel brought Home from the East." It
is in many ways a unique book, and as Leslie Stephen
says,[1] as compared with the ordinary traveller's tales,
"it is more akin to Sterne's 'Sentimental Journey' and
is a delightful record of personal impressions rather
than outward facts." Kinglake sat for eleven years in
the House of Commons. He was a frequent and ambitious speaker, but the literary and rhetorical merit
of his speeches was ruined, not only by a fatal habit of
long-wordedness, but by the physical defects of a thin
voice and poor articulation. On one occasion, he con-

[1] "Dictionary of National Biography."

cluded his harangue with what Mr. Justin McCarthy describes as a "remarkably eloquent and brilliant peroration," which failed to make any impression. Sir Robert Peel (the second) asked and obtained Kinglake's permission to borrow it for himself. Accordingly the next night Peel wound up his own speech with Kinglake's peroration. "He had," writes Mr. McCarthy, "a commanding presence, splendid declamatory power, and a magnificent voice, capable of all variety of intonation and expression. He brought the House down with the sentences which, delivered by their real author the night before, had fallen dead upon the audience."[1] Probably a unique incident in the life of the House of Commons.

Meanwhile Kinglake was engaged on the great venture of his life: the "History of the Crimean War." It was conceived and executed upon a grandiose scale, and ultimately ran to eight volumes, which appeared between 1863 and 1887. Leslie Stephen, while admitting its defects of partiality and prolixity, warmly extols its literary merits: "the occasional portraits of remarkable men are admirably incisive" (was it not Kinglake who wrote that "Mr. Gladstone is a good man in the worst sense of the term"?), "the style is invariably polished to the last degree, and the narrative as lucid as it is animated."

Mr. Gladstone's judgment was, perhaps not unnaturally, far less favourable. After reading the first two volumes (1863) he writes: "Kinglake is fit to be a brilliant popular author, but quite unfit to be an historian. His book is too bad to live and too good to die. As to

Introduction to White's "Inner Life of the House of Commons."

the matter most directly within my cognisance, he is not only not too true, but so entirely void of resemblance to the truth that one asks what was really the original of his picture."[1]

It is to be feared that the eight volumes upon which so much labour and skill were expended are now rarely taken down from the shelves.

[1] Morley's "Life of Gladstone," Vol. I, p. 480.

CHAPTER VIII

BAR AND BENCH: 1876–1880

I RESUME my narrative: I was called to the Bar at Lincoln's Inn in June, 1876. As I intended to practice at the Common Law Bar I took chambers in the Temple, after a brief sojourn in Hare Court, at No. 6 Fig Tree Court, which was my professional workshop for the next six or seven years.

Lincoln's Inn from its proximity to the Chancery Courts was mainly recruited from those who were going to the Equity Bar, but from accident, or some wave of fashion, it was at this time the "nursing mother" of a number of the most eminent Common lawyers. Conspicuous instances were Charles Russell, Herschell, Edward Clarke, Webster, Bowen, Mathew, and Judah Philip Benjamin.[1] I had the honour of holding the office of Treasurer in the year 1920.

The chambers at Fig Tree Court were jointly occupied by myself and two fellow-pupils of Bowen's with whom I had made friends — Henry Cunynghame and Mark Napier. Though neither of them attained to any considerable practice at the Bar, they were both

---

[1] Amongst other great Common lawyers whom Lincoln's Inn has nurtured in the past were Chief Justices Hardwicke, Ellenborough, Denman, and Campbell, and Baron Parke (Lord Wensleydale), the most eminent Common Law judge of the early Victorian era. Erskine and Brougham, who both held the Great Seal, and the younger William Pitt — all of Lincoln's Inn — belonged also to the Common Law Bar.

Macaulay, also a Common lawyer and a member of the Northern Circuit, records with delight in his Diary (January, 1850) that he had just been made a Bencher of Lincoln's Inn. His total professional earnings had amounted to one guinea (Trevelyan's "Life," Chap. XII).

men of marked individuality, and of exceptional though diverse gifts.

Cunynghame was the son of General Sir A. Cunynghame who had recently relinquished the chief command in South Africa: his mother belonged to the Hardinge family. He was intended for the Army, passed first into Woolwich, and became a Royal Engineer. But he found his profession uncongenial, and migrated to Cambridge, where he took his degree with distinction, being second in the First Class of the Moral Sciences Tripos. He then proceeded to read for the Bar, and though he was some years older than myself we were called about the same time. He was a first-rate mathematician, an expert and ingenious economist of the school of Alfred Marshall, well versed in chemical and physical science, an artist of real natural talent, and (though he abjured the Classics) a linguist to whom the learning and speaking of strange tongues came with great facility. He made himself an accomplished lawyer, and, but for his versatility of faculties and interests, might have gone far in the profession. He acted as secretary to the Parnell and Featherstone Commissions, and while I was at the Home Office in 1894 I had the pleasure of inducing him to become Assistant Under-Secretary—a post which he filled with much advantage to the State for the best part of twenty years.

Mark Napier, one of the most lovable men I have known, was a son of Lord Napier and Ettrick, an eminent Victorian diplomatist, and had spent his early days in various foreign capitals. He was a schoolfellow of Cunynghame at Wellington, and went from there to Cambridge. He made no attempt at scholastic and academic distinctions, and it was by one of those haphazards of which his life was full that he found himself in Bowen's chambers reading for the Bar. In appearance, voice and manner, he bore little or no resemblance to the conventional type of young Englishman. He had a shrewd native intelligence, infinite courage, fine old-fashioned manners, quite exceptional physical strength and agility, a great aptitude for the mechanical arts, such as carpentry, and imperturbable sang-froid. He made a runaway marriage with a lovely and charming lady. They spent their honeymoon at the little house which I then occupied at Hampstead. It was an ideally happy union.

He did not really care much for the law, and on his rare appearances at Judges' chambers or in court he usually had a startling effect upon the tribunal. His only memorable forensic experience was when, through a chapter of accidents, he was retained to go out as junior to A. M. Broadley in 1882–3 to Cairo, to defend Arabi Pasha, and he acquitted himself admirably. His whimsical turns of thought and speech, and his inexhaustible store of humour, were a constant delight to his expectant but briefless companions, and lit up for us many a dreary hour. After some years he abandoned the Bar for the City, and ultimately became chairman of Reuters. He was in the Parliament of 1892–5, Liberal member for Roxburghshire.

When I came to the Bar a great transformation was just being effected in our legal machinery and procedure by the Judicature Acts of 1873 and 1875. They were, in substance, the joint handiwork of the two most eminent Equity lawyers of the age: Lord Chancellors Selborne and Cairns. Sir Frederick Pollock commemorated the event in a witty volume — first published in June, 1876 — entitled "Leading Cases in Verse," which though it may now and again tax the comprehension of the ordinary layman, is entitled to a place side by side with the *jeux d'esprit* of Canning and Calverley. The ideal of the great masters of Chancery learning and practice, whom I have just named, was what was called "the fusion of law and equity," and one of the means to its attainment was the abolition of the old Chancery and Common Law Courts, which had existed for centuries, each with traditions of its own, and the substitution for them of a single "Supreme Court of Judicature," consisting of a Court of Appeal and a High Court of Justice. As Pollock says, in one of his Swinburnian stanzas:

> The Courts, that were manifold, dwindle
> To divers Divisions of One.

In my judgment, after many years of practical experience, it was in the strict sense of the word a chimerical [1] ideal, and I doubt whether the administration, either of law or equity, except in matters of secondary and subordinate importance, has gained much by the change.

For some years the old Common Law Courts — Queen's Bench, Common Pleas, Exchequer — still retained their traditional names (though technically

[1] I use the word advisedly. How many of the people who talk glibly of a "Chimæra," on the platform and in the Press, are acquainted with the anatomy of that fabulous animal? (See "Iliad," VI, 181.) It is classed by Milton with those other "perverse prodigies" — the Gorgon and the Hydra ("Paradise Lost," Book II).

Divisions of the new High Court of Justice) with their separate Benches, and each with its titular Chief. In 1880 the Chiefs of the Queen's Bench and Exchequer, Cockburn and Kelly, both died, and the surviving Chief, Coleridge of the Common Pleas, became Chief Justice of England. No further appointment was made to the office of Chief Justice of the Common Pleas (which used to be called the "Attorney-General's pillow"), or of Chief Baron of the Exchequer. Henceforward there was only one Superior Court of Common Law — the Queen's Bench Division.

I am glad that my experience of the Bar goes so far back that I can still recall the faces and voices, and the judicial demeanour, of Sir Alexander Cockburn and Sir Fitzroy Kelly, who died in office at the respective ages of seventy-eight and eighty-four. Each of them had been Attorney-General, and among the half-dozen most accomplished and successful advocates of his time. Whether at the Bar, in Parliament, or on the Bench, Cockburn was by many degrees the bigger man of the two. His speech in the Don Pacifico debate in 1850 was long considered in the House of Commons as one of the most successful in living memory, and his conduct of the prosecution of the poisoner Palmer, in 1856, was unsurpassed in the advocacy of his time.[1]

I have never seen a judge, sitting, as Cockburn did, at the head of an exceptionally strong court — Wightman, Crompton, Blackburn, and Lush were from time to time among his Puisnes — who gave the same im-

---

[1] Palmer, who was in the betting world, when convicted wrote on a bit of paper to his attorney: "It was the *riding* that did it" (Ballantine: "Experiences of a Barrister's Life," 1890, p. 132).

pression of dignity and mastery. I imagine that in these qualities Lyndhurst, among the Victorian judges, was his only rival. He was an accomplished lawyer, though in black-letter learning, in the niceties of pleading, and in the intricacies either of real property or mercantile law, one or another of his Puisnes could always have given him points. But he had a nimble and assimilative mind; the knowledge of human nature which comes to an experienced man of the world; a wide acquaintance with foreign and international jurisprudence, and with both ancient and modern literature;[1] a broad outlook, which was not contracted or distorted by technicalities; and a unique command of all the resources of the best judicial eloquence.

He was not without his weakness — one of which was a love of sitting at Nisi Prius with a special jury, in cases (he was said to select them from the list) which from the character of the litigation, or the position of the parties, were likely to attract the limelight of publicity. No one who frequented the courts in the late 'seventies can forget the dramatic staging of the libel actions in which Mr. Labouchere, in his character of editor of *Truth* (first issued in 1877), was from time to time the defendant: the Chief Justice on the Bench, dignified as always, but thoroughly enjoying himself; the "twelve honest men" in the jury-box having the time of their lives; Ballantine or Parry — the veteran Serjeants—acting as counsel for the plaintiff; "Labby" in person conducting his own case from the "well" of the court: Charles Russell, still in the first stage of what

[1] At the time of his death he had nearly completed an elaborate treatise on the authorship of the Letters of Junius.

SIR GEORGE LEWIS IN A WELSH CAUSE CÉLÈBRE

(*A sketch by Sir Frank Lockwood*)

became a forensic supremacy, and Edward Clarke as
his junior, with their client George Lewis, in his
famous fur-lined coat, appearing in the same interest
for the publisher: and Finlayson, whose memory of the
courts went back for half a century, and whose stories
were a perpetual feast to the unemployed junior Bar,
reporting in wig and gown for *The Times*.

Nor was Cockburn without a touch of vanity. He
presided for the best part of a year, with Mellor and
Lush as his colleagues, over the most famous and most
absorbing of all *causes célèbres*—the trial at Bar of the
Tichborne Claimant. Cockburn's summing up—a
masterpiece in its kind—began on January 29, 1874,
the 169th day of the hearing, and occupied the best
part of twenty days. He had bestowed infinite pains
on its preparation, and it was said that he never forgave
Mr. Gladstone for his sudden dissolution of Parliament (January 26) and for thereby, to some extent,
diverting public attention from the daily instalment
of his charge, which would under happier conditions
have had the dominating place in every newspaper in
the country.

I have still a vivid recollection of attending the hearing of the case of the *Franconia*, when Cockburn presided over a court (of Crown Cases Reserved) consisting of fourteen judges. Even his authority, great and
undisputed as it was, was insufficient to restrain the
copious and often irrelevant interruptions of the argument by some of his many colleagues. I remember
hearing Benjamin, who led for the defendant, say to
Sir H. Giffard, the Solicitor-General, who appeared
for the Crown, in a loud aside: "If this goes on much

longer, Solicitor, I propose that we should agree to withdraw a judge." [1]

Perhaps Cockburn's greatest public service was rendered when he sat as the representative of Great Britain on the *Alabama* arbitration at Geneva in 1872–3. He was offered, but refused, a peerage. [2]

Chief Baron Kelly was of a very different type. He had had for many years a large and lucrative practice of the best kind at the Bar. Like Cockburn he took to politics, and was for a long time in the House of Commons, but unlike Cockburn, who was a Liberal, he was always on the Tory side, and enjoyed only brief spells of office. He was Attorney-General during Lord Derby's administration in 1858–9, and when his party again came into power in 1866, he was, much to his disappointment—for he had counted on the Wool-sack—raised to the Bench as Chief Baron of the Ex-chequer. He was already in his seventieth year, and though he had great dignity of presence and manner, and a singularly fine elocution, his faculties were soon impaired by the infirmities of age, and he became dila-

[1] "Withdrawing a juror" was in those days a common way of compromising a civil case at Nisi Prius.

The case of the *Franconia* under the name of *Reg* v. *Keyn*, is reported 2 Ex. Div. 64 (1876). The question was whether a foreign sea captain, whose ship had negligently collided with a British ship within three miles of the English coast, could be lawfully convicted at the Central Criminal Court of the manslaughter of a British subject on board the British ship. One of the fourteen judges having died before judgment was given, the remainder voted seven to six in favor of quashing the conviction: Cockburn, C. J., and Kelly, C. B., were in the majority, and Coleridge, C. J., in the minority. The Legislature then intervened, and set-tled the question for the future by an Act of Parliament. The judgment of Cock-burn, showing as it does his wide knowledge of International and of Civil Law, is still well worth reading.

This was the last decision in which two Chief Justices and a Chief Baron took part.

[2] There is some curious correspondence between the Queen and her Ministers on a previous proposal (in 1865) to make Cockburn a peer ("Letters of Queen Victoria, 1862–78," Vol. I, pp. 257–62).

tory and garrulous. Nevertheless he held on to the
end, and his annual allocution to the Lord Mayor of
London, who in those days took his oaths on November
9 in the Court of Exchequer, was always spiced with a
flavour of the Tory politics of the Eldonian era. He
had the advantage of sitting with a succession of able
Puisnes — Martin, Bramwell, Channell. One of them
— Bramwell — afterwards a Lord Justice of Appeal,
and a member of the House of Lords, was one of the
subtlest and most interesting judges before whom I have
ever had the privilege to practise. I remember him,
after a vain endeavour to check the loquacity of counsel,
shrugging his shoulders and saying: "You never
shorten anything by attempting to shorten it: on the
contrary, you lengthen it by the length of the attempt."

CHAPTER IX

RES ANGUSTA: LECTURING AND JOURNALISM

DURING my early years at the Bar, when briefs were few and the fees were small, I found it necessary to look about for supplementary resources. I had a growing family; and though my wife had a few hundreds a year of her own, and I myself for a time the income of my Fellowship (which expired in 1881), and though our domestic arrangements were of the simplest kind, there was an annual deficit to make good. I became one of the lecturers for the newly-formed London Society for the Extension of University Teaching, and delivered courses on Political Economy at Wimbledon, Clapham, and other suburbs. I may quote in this connection what I said in an address to the London School of Economics in 1922:[1] "The other day I came by chance across a bundle of the old printed syllabuses which I used to circulate week by week to my students. I confess I was amazed and humiliated to find how much I have since forgotten."

Alfred Marshall had at that time just opened at Cambridge a new chapter in the science, by the first instalment of his "Economics of Industry." As I have a congenital incapacity for, and invincible abhorrence of, mathematics, I found his geometrical methods far from helpful, and I had many animated controversies

---

[1] "Studies and Sketches," p. 141.

on the subject with Cunynghame, who was an ardent disciple of the new school. It was about this time that I made the acquaintance of Jevons, who was my neighbour at Hampstead, and whom I thought, and still think, the most stimulating and suggestive of our modern English economists.

The Society could only afford to give its lecturers a very modest stipend, and I turned my eyes in the direction of journalism. I never had any connection with the daily Press, but by a lucky accident I came across Richard Holt Hutton, joint proprietor and editor with Meredith Townsend of the *Spectator*, and was associated with their paper, first and last, for the greater part of ten years. Through their good offices I became also a contributor to the *Economist* — bereft, in 1877, of its distinguished editor, Walter Bagehot — for which I regularly wrote almost every week, until 1885, one of the two leading articles.

The *Spectator* in those days had a unique position. Townsend, at Calcutta, had made his paper, *The Friend of India*, the most interesting and powerful factor in very troubled times in the Anglo-Indian Press. Hutton, who had few if any superiors among his contemporaries — Matthew Arnold alone excepted — in the fine art of literary criticism, had been born and bred in the Unitarian tradition, but became, under the influence of F. D. Maurice, an Anglican of the Broad Church type. Matthew Arnold's well-known sarcasm at Maurice's expense, that he was always beating the bush with devout emotion and never starting the hare, did nothing to disturb Hutton — who had also an excellent sense of humour — in his sensitive, but by no means sentimental, appreciation of the mazes and mists of the Maurice philosophy and theology.

There has, I suppose, in the history of English journalism rarely, if ever, been such a partnership as that which persisted for the lifetime of a generation between Townsend and Hutton. During the whole of that era the *Spectator*, with the exception of occasional contributions from outsiders like myself, was written almost from cover to cover by the two proprietors. One of them (Townsend) occupied the lower, and the other (Hutton) the upper, floor in their dingy office in Wellington Street, just to the north of Waterloo Bridge. Ostensibly they had nothing in common: Townsend with his courtly Anglo-Indian air, tapping his snuffbox, and walking up and down his room, emitting dogmatic paradoxes: Hutton, more than short-sighted, looking out on external things through a monocle with an extra-powerful lens, and talking with the almost languid, donnish air of one who had in old days breakfasted with Crabb Robinson, and sat at the feet of Arthur Clough. I was often in and out of this curious laboratory, passing from one floor to the other, and now and again foregathering in colloquy with both of the respective occupants. There would be a free and animated clash of discussion, usually about the subjects of the forthcoming number, always ending in an *entente cordiale;* and they would return to their dens, and each set to work to hammer out in totally different styles their joint handiwork.

They shared a high ideal of journalism, and they never lacked courage. During the Civil War in America, at the risk of losing the subscriptions of much of their clientele, they never wavered in their adherence to the cause of the North.

Their general line in politics was always Liberal; Hutton, in particular, was almost a fanatical devotee of Mr. Gladstone. But when the Home Rule issue arose—and it was here that I had to part company with them—they both took from the first the Unionist side.

During those years, and it was one of the most interesting episodes in my life, I wrote for the *Spectator* upon almost every kind of topic—political, social, literary, economic,[1] and when each autumn one of the twin-brethren had to go off on his annual holiday, I was often his *locum tenens*, and assisted at the eleventh hour in "making up" the paper for the press.

When the Townsend-Hutton partnership came to an end, the *Spectator* was fortunate enough to pass under the control of my friend, Mr. St. Loe Strachey. Except upon Free Trade, I fear that in the political sphere he and I have rarely been in complete agreement. I can even remember once, probably in a bilious mood, on a platform describing the Strachey *Spectator* as a journal of "Blameless antecedents and growing infirmities." But I should like to pay my humble tribute to the high purpose, the fine temper, the urbane culture, and the unfailing wealth both of literary and political resource with which during his succession to Townsend and Hutton he has maintained the best traditions of English journalism. It was with the most sincere regret that I heard he had vacated the editorial chair.[2]

[1] Fragments from a few of these articles are reprinted in "Studies and Sketches" (1924).
[2] Mr. Strachey died after these words were written.

CHAPTER X

JUDGES AND COUNSEL

I HAD no legal connection; the office of "devil" to my late Master, Bowen, was more than adequately filled; and for my first five or six years at the Bar my practice was small, intermittent, and from a material point of view neither productive nor promising. Some part of my abundant spare time was devoted to journalism and politics: but I always gave the dominating place to my profession. I read a great deal in the library of Lincoln's Inn, and made some way in the composition of a treatise on Mercantile Law, which remains unfinished, and will never see the light of day. I diligently attended the courts, and joined the North-Eastern Circuit, where for some years I put in a fairly regular appearance at the Leeds Assizes. I was at one time a lecturer to the Incorporated Law Society, and delivered several courses, mainly on Commercial Law, to classes of budding solicitors in Chancery Lane.

The time passed in court in listening to arguments and judgments, and in watching procedure, was by no means wasted. By way of recreation — for Equity was not in my regular line — I used now and again to spend a morning in the Rolls Court in Chancery Lane, which was unique both in its output and its methods. Sir George Jessel, who sat there, was, in rapidity of apprehension and readiness of judgment, one of the greatest judges of First Instance of our own or perhaps any time. In those days the solicitor for the plaintiff could choose among the Chancery judges the one whom he wished to try his case. Jessel's list, notwithstanding his lightning-like facility in disposing of it, was always crowded. It used to be said that every solicitor who was tolerably certain that he had a good case chose the Rolls Court as a matter of course; while those who had a suspicion, or more than a suspicion, that their case was a bad one, resorted to one or another of the Vice-Chancellors: to one of them in particular, with the result that his list was easily second in bulk to Jessel's.[1]

Jessel had not only an almost uncanny quickness and sureness in threading his way through a jungle of the most complicated facts, but a memory for Case law so accurate and so retentive that he hardly needed to consult an authority. I once saw him at the end of an intricate litigation dealing with mercantile commissions in the Manchester trade, in which all the most eminent leaders of the Equity and Common Law Bars were engaged, and the hearing of which even he was unable to compress into less than four or five days, rise at the usual time for lunch, come back in half an hour, and deliver judgment off the reel, without even looking at a note. He was not perhaps so distinguished as a master of the broad principles of jurisprudence, and though his decisions were very rarely reversed, I doubt whether in these days they are often cited as illustrations, and still less as developments, of the rules of Equity.

[1] This was Malins, whose court was well worth an occasional visit, if only to watch the methods of the Bar who habitually practised there. The leaders consisted of two first-class "bruisers" — Glasse (who dominated the judge) and Higgins; and two of the primmest "high-brows" — Cotton and John Pearson. Malins had had at the Bar a considerable practice. Cairns read as a pupil in his chambers, and was persuaded by him to go to the English, not the Irish, Bar.

The Common Law Bench suffered sensible impover-
ishment from the death of Cockburn, and from the
promotion to the House of Lords or to the Court of
Appeal of the most distinguished among the Puisne
judges—Blackburn, Bramwell, and Brett. Its new
Chief, Lord Coleridge, with an impressive presence, a
silvery voice, much literary culture, a fine gift of
rhetoric, and an expert knowledge of the arts of advocacy, lacked both profound learning and the judicial
mind. He had for some years divided with Sir John
Karslake the leadership of the Western Circuit. They
were both men of imposing appearance, and in their
different way adroit and accomplished advocates. But
there the resemblance ended. They used to be called
"Handsome Jack" and "Holy John." Fitzjames
Stephen, who in robustness of intellect surpassed most
of his brethren, and who did good work as a legal historian and as a codifier, had never had more than a
very moderate general practice; and being unac-
quainted with the working of the ordinary mind, had
little weight either with witnesses or jurors. He
proved on the whole to be a disappointing judge.
Denman, who had been Senior Classic, beating for the
first place in the Tripos, Munro, perhaps the most accomplished of contemporary Cambridge scholars; and
Grove, who was in the front rank of physicists, showed
that eminence in scholarship or in science does not
necessarily bring with it great judicial qualities. Not
that I wish to suggest that the two are in any way con-
tradictory or exclusive. In my time I have known in
the Court of Appeal no fewer than three Senior Wran-
glers—Stirling, Romer, Moulton: a Senior Classic—

Kennedy:[1] and a Second Wrangler — Rigby. These were all from Cambridge, but on the same Bench there sat at least two of the most distinguished Oxford men of that era — Bowen, upon whose academic exploits I have already touched, and Davey, who had to his credit four First Classes and two University Scholarships.

Another judge of a very different calibre from these, who was appointed to the Bench in November, 1876, soon after I was called to the Bar, was Hawkins. With the two great Serjeants, Ballantine and Parry, the last distinguished survivors in an already moribund order, Hawkins had divided for some years the leadership in sensational jury trials, whether at Nisi Prius or in the Criminal Courts. He was in the Tichborne Case in all its stages. At the first trial (before Bovill, C.J.), much to his chagrin, Coleridge took advantage of his precedence as Solicitor-General to cross-examine the Claimant. Hawkins led for the prosecution in the subsequent criminal trial at Bar. He had great gifts as an advocate (I heard him myself in one of the last of his "big" cases — the St. Leonards Will) particularly in the handling of witnesses, but possessed only a slender modicum of law. As a criminal judge he at first had a reputation for exceptional severity, but being at heart good-natured and humane, he gradually passed to what some critics, of whom I was not one, thought the opposite extreme. In Civil cases he was the opposite of a good judge. He delighted in mischievous tricks, sometimes of an almost monkeyish kind: he had

---

[1] Those who are curious in such matters may like to be reminded that Moulton and Kennedy headed their two Triposes in the same year, 1868. In that year the 9th Wrangler was Buckley (now Lord Wrenbury), who was also for some years a Lord Justice of Appeal.

a morbid dread, not altogether without reason, of being reversed on appeal : and in his later days on the Bench he became intolerably prolix and verbose. He was a member of the Jockey Club, and his sporting tastes, and the many anecdotes of which he was the more or less legendary hero,[1] made him a popular figure with the man-in-the-street. On his retirement he was given a peerage, and, as Lord Brampton, from time to time took part in the judicial business of the House of Lords. He amassed a considerable fortune, and gave a substantial share of it to the Roman Catholic Church, to which late in life he became a convert.

To turn from the Bench to the Bar, the leaders in the Common Law Courts in the years with which I am now dealing (1877 to 1883) were Holker, Henry James, Hardinge Giffard (afterwards Lord Chancellor Halsbury), and Henry Matthews (afterwards Home Secretary, and Lord Llandaff) : and among the younger men, Charles Russell, Herschell and Webster. On the commercial side the lead was divided between Butt, Watkin Williams and an abler and more learned man than either, though an indifferent advocate, Arthur Cohen, who by the caprice of fortune was never promoted to the Bench. All the men whose names I have just mentioned were members of the House of Commons — most of them on the Liberal side.

Of Henry James, to whom, of them all, I was myself under the greatest personal obligations, I have already given a sketch in my book " Fifty Years of British Parliament." Holker's predominant position was, at first sight, difficult to understand. He came from Lanca-

---

[1] He was known in the higher strata of the criminal classes as "the Old Un."

shire; like James, he had never been to Oxford or Cambridge: he was a big, unwieldy, sleepy-looking man,
with none of the arts or graces of oratory, and with a
deceptive appearance of clumsiness and even of lethargy.
But he became the acknowledged leader of the Northern
Circuit, where with Lancashire juries he was an almost
invincible winner of verdicts; and when he acquired
a London practice, he soon showed that he was equally
formidable in attack and defence. He had an extraordinary endowment of intuition and tact, both with
witnesses and juries, which was the secret of his success.
I have always thought that he was the nearest reproduction in our time of Scarlett,[1] the most adroit and most
successful of English advocates, with the single exception of Erskine. His health began to be unequal to
the grinding competition of the Bar, and in 1882 Mr.
Gladstone, who had only known him in the House of
Commons as the Tory Attorney-General of Lord
Beaconsfield's Government,[2] paid him the unique compliment of making him a Lord Justice of Appeal. He
died only a few months after his appointment, and
though he had already made his mark, he had no adequate opportunity of proving his judicial competence.

Hardinge Giffard, who in the end occupied the
Woolsack for a longer time than any Lord Chancellor
since Lord Eldon, though he had, like so many of the
profession, little success in the House of Commons, was

[1] Brougham, who was without doubt the first forensic and political orator of
his day, went the Northern Circuit, where he was often pitted against and worsted
by Scarlett. At the end of a long Assize one onlooker said to another: "How is
it that Mr. Scarlett succeeds so often against a much cleverer man like Mr. Brougham?" "Oh," was the innocent reply, "because Mr. Scarlett is almost always
on the right side."

[2] Disraeli used, when some legal point arose in debate, to say to the Chief
Whip: "Send for the Hippopotamus."

in his later years at the Bar quite in the forefront of the leading advocates. He had graduated at the Old Bailey and on the South Wales Circuit, and in standing was a contemporary of Sir Henry James and Sir Harry Poland. He was not supposed to be a laborious student of his briefs, but the quickness with which he foresaw and apprehended points in the actual conduct of a case, his skill in the cross-examination, and in that still more difficult art, the re-examination of witnesses, together with a considerable faculty of effective rhetoric, made him a formidable antagonist in the handling of a jury. On the Bench his long experience as Chancellor in time gave him exceptional weight and authority in the judicial work of the Privy Council and the House of Lords. He cannot be classed as a lawyer with the two great Lord Chancellors who preceded him — Selborne and Cairns. His methods were more akin to those of his successor Lord Loreburn; always patient and courteous with counsel, his mind was quickly made up; he had no taste for first principles or dialectical refinements; but without in any way departing from or ignoring settled principles of law, he kept his attention fixed on the justice and merits of the particular case.

His exercise of judicial patronage provoked not a little criticism, some of it in my opinion well founded; but there was never any suggestion that it was biased by unworthy motives or illegitimate influences.

Of the younger men whom I have named above, two — Richard Webster and Charles Russell — both rose to be heads of the Bar. It is difficult to conceive two more diverse types. Webster had taken a respectable degree at Cambridge, where his chief distinction

Mr. Justice L. Smith

Lord Justice Hannen

THE PARNELL COMMISSION, 1888

From "Vanity Fair" Cartoons by "Spy"

Mr. Justice Day

was gained in long-distance races on the running path. He was a man of the most unwearying industry, of prodigiously strong physique, with an exuberant geniality of manners, which though not insincere was apt to be a little overdone. He used to call his juniors by their Christian names as soon as he had ascertained what they were. He amassed in a very short time an enormous practice and was a great favourite with the solicitors, though neither his speaking nor his examination of witnesses rose much, if at all, above the level of mediocrity. But he was, after his own fashion, an adroit and resourceful antagonist, possessing in a supreme degree (as I have more than once experienced to my cost) the art of the cuttle-fish which darkens the waters. He was seen perhaps to the least advantage in the Parnell Commission, and his acceptance while Attorney-General of *The Times* brief in that famous inquiry struck a death blow at the custom which up till then allowed the Law Officers of the Crown to take private practice. Webster was the most blameless of men — a sound Tory, a good Churchman, and amiable and benevolent in all the relations of life.

Charles Russell, whom for real genius I put in a class by himself among the advocates of my time, was an Irish Catholic, born and brought up in Ulster, where he started practice as a solicitor. He came to London, was called to the English Bar, and settled down for a time at Liverpool, where he soon became a busy junior in the local Passage Court and at the Assizes. He took silk early, acquired a commanding practice on the Northern Circuit, and rose rapidly to the effective leadership of the Common Law Bar. He was a good, without being exactly a profound lawyer, and had an autocratic manner, and when he pleased a rough tongue, which made a consultation with him an ordeal to which few solicitors or junior counsel, however eminent, looked forward without a certain degree of apprehension. For myself, I delight to acknowledge that though I was his junior in not a few of his most important cases, I hardly ever heard from him an angry, or even an impatient, word.

The only time when I can recall anything in the nature of a "breeze" between us was once during the Parnell Commission. The case of *The Times* had at last dragged to an end, and the court rose for a few days to give Russell time to get ready his opening speech for the defence. The forgery of the Pigott letters had already been exposed, and there was nothing to be done but, so far as one could, to make mincemeat of the rest of the case—a dreary and unappetizing task. With immense industry I performed my duty as a junior by collating and analyzing and tabulating the evidence of the long procession of resident magistrates and district inspectors who had succeeded one another in the witness-box; and, armed with my *dossier*, went to spend Saturday to Monday with my chief at his country house at Tadworth.

On Saturday evening he insisted on our playing cards, for real, though small stakes, with the governess and his two small daughters, and it was not until half-way through Sunday morning that I could induce him to talk about the case. I produced with some complacency the fruits of my industry, and when I had got— say to the County Kerry—I observed that his attention was wandering, and I paused. He turned upon me with ferocity, half genuine, half assumed: "My dear Asquith, I am disappointed with you. I am greatly disappointed with you. What concern have I with these petty details of speeches and outrages? I intend

"Henry accept my heartfelt thanks"

'Le Caron it is but your due'

Slow more.
Curtain

SIR HENRY JAMES AND LE CARON
(*A sketch by Sir Frank Lockwood*)

to deal with the matter on broad historic imaginative lines, and to ignore this trumpery farrago of gossip and lies." As the "farrago" was the main thing that at this stage two, at any rate, of the three judges cared about, and intended to report upon, I got him at last to consent, in some interlude in his speech, to read out my tables and get them on the notes. The speech, when it did come, was a fine performance: a review of the dealings of England with Ireland, and especially with Irish land: "a great speech worthy of a great occasion," as after its peroration the President, Sir James Hannen, wrote on a slip of paper which he handed down from the Bench.

Two other reminiscences of Russell's part in this unique inquiry I must put on record. The one is purely personal to myself. After a long wrangle as to whether *The Times* counsel were entitled to call expert witnesses to handwriting before producing evidence as to how they got possession of the letters — a point which was decided against them by the court — Mr. Macdonald, the manager, was at last put into the box, and told the amazing tale of the purchase of the forgeries, which still remains almost unique in the annals of infantine simplicity and malevolent credulity. As he was one of the principal witnesses, it would of course naturally have fallen to Russell to cross-examine him; and I was never more surprised in my life than when, just as the court rose for lunch, he turned to me and said: "I am tired: you must take charge of this fellow." I protested, but in vain, and I was left to the critical task of conducting the cross-examination: a task all the more formidable because my leader, the greatest cross-examiner at the English Bar, sat there throughout and listened. I got on to what proved to be an effective and even a destructive line of attack, and in the course of a couple of hours or so made the largest step in advance that I ever took in my forensic career. Russell, who throughout had not interrupted by suggestion or otherwise, was unmeasured in his appreciation of every successful point, and when I finished almost overwhelmed me with the generosity of his praises and his congratulations. It was a moment that will never fade from my memory, and up to his death we remained the most attached and devoted friends.

ON THE HUNDREDTH DAY OF THE PARNELL COMMISSION
(*A sketch by Sir Frank Lockwood*)

The other point which is worthy of recall relates to Russell's own cross-examination, not of one, but of a score of witnesses, which was as great a feat of advocacy as I or anyone living can remember. Our solicitor, Sir George Lewis, one of the acutest and most resourceful men who had ever practised the law, had done everything that ingenuity and industry could achieve in preparing the ground for us. But of a large mass of the witnesses who were called — magistrates, inspectors, constables, informers — we knew absolutely nothing, when one after another they entered the box. Time after time I have seen Russell, with a blank sheet of paper before him, feel his way, by question after question, until he had got right inside the man's mind, and then proceed, more often than not, to reduce his evidence to the flimsiest of cobwebs, or to demolish it altogether. His cross-examination of Pigott, brilliant as it was, was a relatively easy task; for we knew beforehand almost everything that was to be known of the speckled career of that needy renegade. When Pigott dined with Labouchere on the eve of his flight to Spain, he was asked by his host what he thought of Russell as a cross-examiner. "Not bad," Pigott replied, "but you must remember what materials he had!" Almost anyone can cross-examine if he is supplied with adequate "materials"; but I have seen no one who could rival Charles Russell, when he had nothing to go upon but his own intuition and flair.

The methods by which he achieved the first position in the most competitive of all professions were not at all of the conventional kind which are commended and illustrated in such a volume as Mr. Smile's "Self-Help." He was, though capable of intense concentration, not an exceptionally industrious man. He had many interests outside his profession: two in particular which absorbed a good deal of his time — sport (especially horse-racing and cards) and politics. He was for many years a member of the House of Commons, where, despite strenuous efforts, he never achieved a reputation comparable to that which he enjoyed in the

LORD RUSSELL OF KILLOWEN

From the painting by J. S. Sargent, R.A., in the National Portrait Gallery. Copyright photograph: National Portrait Gallery.

courts, and he developed into an almost ubiquitous platform speaker. When he became Lord Chief Justice, he succeeded by a strong effort of will in controlling his natural impatience, and made a careful and admirable judge.

Nature had been lavish in endowing him with the external adjuncts of a great advocate — an imposing presence, fine features, "an eye like Mars to threaten or command," and a powerful and flexible voice which could strike any note in the gamut of forensic oratory. To these he added the artifices of an accomplished actor; the snuff-box, the bandana handkerchief, the pince-nez, were all called into service, and played their part in a varied and formidable apparatus. The whole was wielded and controlled by the power, which swayed witnesses and juries alike, of a dominating personality. *Quare* — as Quintilian says of Cicero — *non immerito ab hominibus aetatis suae regnare in judiciis dictus est.*[1]

Sargent's portrait of him in his judicial robes is one of the most life-like and impressive even of that great artist's masterpieces.

[1] "Institutio Oratoria," X, 112.

CHAPTER XI

PROGRESS AT THE BAR: 1883–1885

IN the course of 1883, the promotion of A. L. Smith to a judgeship rendered vacant the "blue ribbon" of the junior Bar—the office of Junior Counsel to the Treasury, or "Attorney-General's devil." Sir Henry James, who was then Attorney-General, selected as Smith's successor R. S. Wright—an event which indirectly had a great effect on my personal fortunes.

Wright, like Bowen, was a Balliol man, and was one of the soundest classical scholars of his time. He was all his life a special favourite of Jowett, who died in his house. He became a Fellow of Oriel, and edited the "Golden Treasury of Ancient Greek Poetry," which was, and is, one of the best of anthologies. His success at the Bar was not rapid, and though his practice by this time had grown to considerable dimensions, and was of a high class, it was not of a kind that took him very much into court. He was a bachelor, and lived in the Temple on the floor above his business chambers. He was one of the best-hearted and most generous of men, though abrupt in speech and angular and peppery in manner. He had some strange habits. He used to rise very early to begin his day's work; as soon as the newspapers were on sale, he emerged into Fleet Street and bought one; and punctually at 8 o'clock he walked down the Strand to Pall Mall and breakfasted at the Reform Club. He returned to his chambers by 9, and, unless he had to go into court, spent the rest of the day there, with a tall hat on his head and a brier pipe in his mouth. He was an indefatigable worker and smoker, and at the end of the day walked again to his club where he dined, and was back at the Temple and in bed before 10 o'clock. He was rarely seen in any kind of society, but he was fond of country sports, especially of shooting. He bought a property in Hampshire where he built himself a house (without shutters or blinds), and every Sunday morning held what purported to be a "democratic" conference with his labourers, to settle the agricultural programme for the following week. In politics he was an ardent Radical, and twice stood unsuccessfully for Parliament.

He belonged to a much earlier Balliol generation than my own: indeed, I hardly knew him; and I was not a little surprised when, soon after his appointment, he sent for me and asked if I would "devil" for him. I migrated — without any pangs of regret — from Fig Tree Court, and from that time till Wright's promotion to the Bench (1883–90) I shared his chambers at 1 Paper Buildings, where, except during the time that I was Home Secretary, I continued my practice till I retired from the Bar at the end of 1905. For a time my work was that of a "devil," pure and simple, but Wright's clients gradually got to know me and to give me work; they included the solicitors to some of the great railway companies; and by the end of 1885–6 I had the nucleus of a substantial and growing practice of my own.

One of the chief items in my heavy debt of gratitude to Wright, was his introduction of me to the Attorney-General, Sir Henry James, which came about in a curious fashion.[1] I had always been a keen politician, and was an early and active member of the Eighty Club. It was through association with it that I first formed one of the most intimate and valuable friendships of my life—that with R. B. Haldane, who was at the Chancery Bar, and just beginning to "devil" for Horace Davey. One of the troublesome and embarrassing domestic problems with which at this time Mr. Gladstone's Government had to deal was the Bradlaugh case: a controversy which revealed in the political world unsuspected depths of bigotry and hypocrisy, and was exploited for all it was worth by Lord Randolph Churchill and his newly-formed Fourth Party. In 1883 the Government attempted to settle the matter by an Affirmation Bill, and Mr. Gladstone instructed the Attorney-General to help him in getting up the legal and historical side of the case. James applied to Wright, who asked me to go over the ground and prepare a memorandum for the Prime Minister. Naturally I devoted much time and care to the task, and when my MS. was completed it gave great satisfaction, first to the Attorney-General and then to Mr. Gladstone himself. James kept the MS., and more than ten years afterwards he gave it as a wedding present to my wife.

From that time onwards I was a frequent visitor and worker at the Attorney-General's room in the Law Courts. My associates there were two other young barristers of strongly contrasted types, both of whom afterwards attained distinction: Alfred Lyttelton, the

---

[1] My debt to James I acknowledged at the dinner at which I was entertained by the Bar on July 10, 1908, and he sent me a few days afterwards the letter reproduced at page 101.

41. CADOGAN SQUARE. S.W.

July 13. 1908

My dear Prime Minister

You are generally very
accurate in your statements
On Friday you were not so -
You said that you owed me
a debt which could never be
repaid -
If ever there was a debt

it was repaid - amply - nine
times repaid by the letter a
copy of which you used at the Bar
dinner.

They are words that will
ever be cherished in my memory

Ever yours

[signature]

Please do not reply

ideal of a public school and University man; and W. O. Danckwerts, who, though of Danish or Hanoverian extraction, came from the Cape, and was in appearance the embodiment of the average Englishman's idea of a Dutch Boer. He was a painstaking and already an exceptionally learned lawyer, and, with many amiable qualities, the most pertinacious and dogmatic of mankind. I have seen Henry James, half in fun and half in earnest, drive him from the room amid a cataract of statutes and law reports, Danckwerts slowly retreating, and arguing the whole way at the top of his voice, until he was well outside in the corridor. James's good temper was unfailing and he was always both appreciative and considerate[1] to those who helped him. He had by nature the tastes of a man of pleasure, and he never married; but he was ambitious, and working in the double harness of law and politics, he brought to both not only very serviceable talents, but an immense capacity for taking pains. He was, I think, Mr. Gladstone's favourite law officer.

As Attorney-General it fell to his share to draft and to pilot through the House of Commons the Corrupt Practices Act of 1883, a complicated and technical measure which in many important respects provided a new code of electoral law. He suggested to me that I should prepare a short manual, to guide election agents and others through the intricacies of the new system; and accordingly I became responsible for a little volume — "An Election Guide" — which was published for me in 1884 by the Liberal Central Association. It

[1] Sir Algernon West used to say of Mr. Gladstone, whose devoted private secretary he was for many years, that he was "an appreciative" but not "a considerate master."

is probably long since obsolete, but for some years it had a fair circulation, and indirectly it helped me professionally: for after the general election of 1885 there was a crop of election petitions, in most of which I was retained as one of the counsel for the Liberal candidate.

CHAPTER XII

FORENSIC EXPERIENCES

IT will be convenient here, in defiance of chronological order, to give some more pages, in sequence to those which have preceded, to my forensic career.

I took the professionally imprudent step of standing for Parliament while still a junior at the Bar in July, 1886. I was elected, and continued to be a member of the House of Commons for the same constituency (East Fife) from that date until 1918. The double life which this involved imposed what would seem to our degenerate successors a heavy physical burden, as the House in those days kept late hours, and we frequently did not get home until two, or even four, in the morning. But the little group to which I belonged was young and vigorous; the veterans set us a good example; and the cant about the perils of "overwork," and the need for frequent "rest and change," had not yet come into vogue.

The most important case in which I was engaged as a junior was the inquiry (1888-9) before the Parnell Commission, of which I have already given an account in "Fifty Years of British Parliament," and to which I refer again in Chapter X of this book. My normal practice was almost entirely on the civil side in London, and I soon discontinued going circuit. My excursions into the criminal courts were few and far between,

but I can recall one or two occasions when I found myself at the Old Bailey. One was in 1887, when I de-
fended my friend and fellow-member of the House of
Commons, Cunninghame Graham, who was indicted
jointly with Mr. John Burns on a charge of "unlawful
assembly," their alleged offence being that, in defiance
of an ill-judged prohibition of the Commissioner of
Police, sanctioned by the Home Secretary, Henry
Matthews, they had attempted to hold a public meeting
in Trafalgar Square. I then for the first time made the
acquaintance of Mr. Burns—afterwards for many
years my colleague in the Cabinet—who conducted his
own defence with vigour and adroitness. Both defend-
ants were found guilty by the jury, and were sentenced
by Mr. Justice Charles to six weeks' imprisonment.

It happened that one of my first administrative acts,
when I became Home Secretary myself five years later,
was to deal with this very matter. There was no doubt
that the practice of assembling a crowd, composed for
the most part of idle and unemployed people, in and
about the Square, on any day and at any hour, under
the guise of holding a "meeting," had degenerated
into an intolerable public nuisance. But there was not
sufficient reason, as I said at the time, why "the law-
abiding people of London" should be "permanently
excluded at all times, however convenient, under any
conditions however reasonable, and for any purpose
however legitimate, from this accustomed place of
meeting." I took advantage therefore of an Act of
1844, which vested in the Crown the property in the
soil of the Square, to lay it down for the future that on
Saturday afternoons, Sundays, and Bank Holidays,

meetings would be allowed of which notice had been given to the police, which obeyed their instructions, and which dispersed before nightfall. This regulation has been observed ever since, and has worked with perfect smoothness and success.

The only other appearance at the Central Criminal Court of which I have a vivid recollection was when I was retained to prosecute the publisher of the English translations of Zola's novels, for obscenity. In those days the law, which has since been altered, required that all the matters complained of should be set out verbatim in the indictment. I accordingly spent the best part of a fortnight in the Long Vacation, with scissors and a pot of paste at hand, in a diligent quest for the most objectionable passages in M. Zola's voluminous works.[1] All of these excerpts were, in due course, solemnly engrossed upon a piece of parchment, which I presume is still preserved among the files of the Old Bailey. There was no public trial, as the defendant pleaded guilty, and was sentenced to a fine of £100.

There is one other incident in my career at the Junior Bar which is perhaps worth recording. I continued to do occasional "devilling" for Sir Henry James, after he ceased to be Attorney-General in the summer of 1885. In the autumn of that year, the first of the two great personal tragedies in my political experience, of which the Divorce Court has provided the *mise en scène,* was brought upon the stage. A Liberal member of Parliament, Mr. Donald Crawford, filed a petition

---

[1] A French paper, commenting on the case, referred to "*la pudeur effarouchée de l'avocat Asquith.*"

for the dissolution of his marriage on the ground of his wife's adultery with Sir Charles Dilke.

It is not easy at this distance of time to see things in the proportions which they then assumed. Dilke was at that moment one of the most conspicuous figures in the public arena. It is not too much to say that in the betting ring of politics he was, in the event of anything happening to Mr. Gladstone, one of the first favourites, if not the first, for the succession to the Liberal leadership. He had started his career — at a time when old-fashioned Radicals, like Mr. Bright, were not only Monarchists, but ardent and vocal in their loyalty to Queen Victoria — as a militant Republican, who went from platform to platform denouncing the bloated Civil List of a sovereign who was rarely seen by her subjects, and who, as he alleged, claimed exemption from income tax. He even challenged the opinion of the House of Commons on the subject, and with the backing of a blue-blooded young Radical, Auberon Herbert, went to a division in which, apart from the tellers, they mustered two votes. The Queen, who was not in these matters a placable woman, was mortally offended. Dilke stood aside from Cabinet rank, in favour of his friend Chamberlain, when the Liberal Government of 1880 was in process of formation. He became a most efficient Under-Secretary at the Foreign Office, and afterwards President of the Local Government Board[1] with a seat in the Cabinet. He showed not only marvellous industry and matchless knowledge of detail, but much parliamentary dexterity, in carry-

---

[1] When seeking re-election in December, 1882, on his admission to the Cabinet, he admitted that in his "political infancy" he was "perhaps rather scatter-brained."

ing through the Redistribution Bill of 1884-5, on the basis of single-member constituencies.[1]   He was by nature a dull and ineffective speaker, but he acquired fluency, and an adequate equipment of debating capacity, by long practice and experience.   He developed in fact, as has not infrequently happened, into a House of Commons "superstition"; and though, in competition with men of the brilliance of Harcourt and Chamberlain, he seemed like a cab-horse among thoroughbreds, he was, as I have said, in the judgment of many shrewd political "tipsters" well in the running for the contingent leadership.

When the divorce proceedings were instituted, Dilke very wisely retained as his leading counsel Sir Henry James and Mr. Charles Russell, both of them his close political and personal friends, and the two most accomplished advocates at the Common Law Bar.   Mr. Crawford's case against his wife depended entirely upon her own confession to him, which, though damning to herself, was, of course, in law no evidence against Dilke.   I was present (as James's "devil") at the consultation at which the proper conduct of the case, when it should come into court, was discussed. Dilke had from the first professed his innocence, and we had none of us any reason to doubt his word.   There was, as I have said, technically no evidence against him. Was there, then, any reason why he should go into the witness-box and deny the charge on oath?   The two eminent counsel, with their unrivalled experience, were

---

[1] At the end of the Committee stage, Dilke was reported to have said to a Liberal colleague: "I have left the Tories not more than twelve seats in London." In the first general election which followed, in November, 1885, London returned thirty-six Tories to twenty-six Liberals.

both decidedly of opinion that there was not. Mr. Chamberlain, who also was present as Dilke's oldest and most trusted friend, inclined to the opposite view. He pointed out that no one outside the legal world would understand how, if Mr. Crawford got a divorce on the ground of his wife's adultery with Sir Charles Dilke, the same court should hold at the same time that there was not a shred of evidence against Sir Charles. This was exactly what eventually happened, when the case came on before Mr. Justice Butt (also an old friend of Dilke's). Mr. Crawford got his decree, and Sir Charles, who had not gone into the box, was dismissed from the suit.

Mr. Chamberlain's instinct was right, and the two great counsel proved to have committed an error in forensic judgment. The public took the politician's and not the lawyer's view: the unofficial *Censor Morum* of those days, Mr. Stead of the *Pall Mall Gazette*, insisted that further inquiry was needed to vindicate the purity of our public men; Dilke was himself persuaded to press for the intervention of the Queen's Proctor: the inquiry took place, and his career was blasted.

There were many who still believed that he was a wronged man: amongst them the miners of the Forest of Dean, who some years later returned him as their member to the House of Commons, and Mr. Stead was warned that, if he ventured into the constituency on his threatened purity crusade, he would be thrown down the first disused mine-shaft that offered itself for the purpose.

Dilke, with the unfailing support and sympathy of a talented and devoted wife, showed undefeated courage, and plodded along as a laborious and useful private member. He was bitterly disappointed when, notwithstanding the championship of his claims by King Edward, "C.-B." declined in 1905 to include him in his administration. His constituents stood by him with unwavering fidelity to the end. But the loss of his wife struck him a mortal blow, and he died in 1911.

I was encouraged by the growth of my practice, and by a certain amount of reputation which I had acquired by my cross-examination of one of the principal witnesses in the Parnell Commission,[1] to apply for "silk": always a hazardous step, and especially so for one who had not been called more than twelve years. There have been not a few tragic instances of men who had enjoyed a large and lucrative junior practice failing entirely to make their way "within the Bar." I took the plunge, however, largely at the urgent prompting of Haldane, who had determined to join in the same adventure.

Both our names appeared in the list of new Queen's Counsel created by Lord Halsbury in February, 1890: which also included Cripps and Lawson Walton. It has probably never happened before or since that, as events turned out, one batch of "new silks" contained (prospectively) a Prime Minister and Chancellor of the Exchequer, a Lord Chancellor, an Attorney-General, and a Lord President of the Council. Nor had any of the four whom I have mentioned to wait long for a remunerative share of the leading work of the different courts.

I was not dissatisfied with my professional prospects

---

[1] See *ante*, Chapter X.

when, little more than two years after I had become a
Queen's Counsel, I was confronted with the necessity
for taking a still more formidable decision. I had been
selected in August, 1892, to move the Liberal amendment to the Address, which defeated Lord Salisbury's
Government, and Mr. Gladstone offered me the post
of Home Secretary in his new Administration. Acceptance meant the abandonment, for the time at any
rate — perhaps for all time — of my profession; for a
high place in the Cabinet, it is true: but in a Cabinet
which could only count, at the best, upon a composite
and precarious majority of forty in the House of Commons. I was just approaching my fortieth birthday;
my five children were all very young; and they and I
had, the year before, sustained a terrible blow in the loss
of the most devoted and unselfish of mothers and wives.

Once again I took the plunge. Of the three years
which followed, in the political and personal sphere,
I defer what I have to say. When in July, 1895, the
elections went against us, and a Unionist Government,
with a large and homogeneous majority, was installed
in power, I found myself, not only out of office, but
with the most dubious and remote prospect of regain-
ing the rewards of political ambition. I therefore
resolved to return to the Bar — a step for which, in the
case of an ex-Cabinet Minister, who was *ipso facto* a
Privy Councillor, there were, I believe, no precedents
— not without consulting and receiving the approval
of my old master and friend, Sir Henry James, who,
now become Lord James of Hereford, was a member
of the new Cabinet.

For the next ten years (1895–1905) I was, notwithstanding many distracting and sometimes absorbing political activities, one of the leaders of the Common Law Bar. I was rarely concerned in the more sensational class of litigation which excites the man-in-the-street, and is exploited by the Press. My practice was, however, of a varied kind, and one of its most interesting fields was in the Judicial Committee of the Privy Council, which is the ultimate Court of Appeal from all the outlying parts of the Empire. I was much engaged in Indian appeals, where for some years Haldane and I almost divided the lead. We used to have as "juniors"— amongst many other able lawyers— two remarkable men, each of whom, in the chronology of the calendar, might almost have been our father— Vaughan Hawkins and J. D. Mayne; both of them authors of standard legal textbooks—Hawkins on "Wills," Mayne on "Damages." Hawkins, who had been Senior Classic at Cambridge, was one of the most learned and accomplished Equity lawyers of his day. Mayne had early in life migrated to India, where he became an acknowledged authority both on Hindu and Mohammedan law. Neither of them ever took "silk": Hawkins because he had no gift of advocacy; Mayne, a master of incisive and cynical speech, because, after spending the best part of a lifetime in India, he had no unsatisfied ambitions here at home. We had the great advantage of appearing constantly before one of the best tribunals of our time.

Lord Westbury, who had a judicial intellect, and a mordant wit, second to none in the Victorian era, after his resignation of the Chancellorship was fond of sitting in the Judicial Committee, of which judges and ex-judges who have been made Privy Councillors from all parts of the Empire are *ex officio* members. He once pressed Sir William Erle, who had presided with the greatest distinction as Chief Justice over the old Court of Common Pleas, to come occasionally and sit with him. "No," said Erle, "I am old, and deaf, and stupid." To which Westbury replied: "My dear fellow, what does that matter? I am old: X is deaf: Y is stupid. Yet we make an excellent tribunal."

That was before my time: and in our days there could be no greater privilege to an advocate, whatever were the merits of his case, than to be able to argue it before a Bench of which Watson, Herschell, and Macnaghten were members.

Shortly after my return to the Bar in 1895 I was engaged in two cases of great interest to the racing world — Hawke *v.* Dunn, and Powell *v.* Kempton Park Race Course Company. The point at issue in both was the same — whether an unroofed enclosure adjoining a race-course, and resorted to upon payment for admission by bookmakers and the general public for betting purposes, was a "place kept and used for betting" within the meaning of the penal provisions of the Betting Act, 1853. To a layman the question may not seem a recondite one, and the answer fairly obvious; but it excited an exceptional diversity of judicial opinion. It was argued first and last before five different courts; of the two opposing views one was upheld by thirteen judges, and the other by eight; and the ultimate decision of the House of Lords (that the Act had not been infringed) was only given by a majority, among the two dissentients being Lord Davey, one of the most eminent lawyers of the time. I may be prejudiced from having argued on the losing side, but I confess I have always thought the decision wrong.

I remember the case mainly because of an amusing incident which occurred during the hearing in the House of Lords where I was for the appellant. There was an unprecedented number of Law Lords present— no fewer than ten—and partly from their interest in the subject matter, and partly from a bad habit which some of the most distinguished among them had acquired of thinking aloud, they were so much occupied in a continuous cross-fire of interrogations and retorts, addressed for the most part not to counsel but to one another, that at the end of the first day's argument I doubt whether I had completed a single sentence. The next morning the same kind of thing went on, and the House having to rise for the day because of a Cabinet meeting, at half-past one, when it was nearing a quarter past the Lord Chancellor, Lord Halsbury, who presided, suggested to me, very considerately, that perhaps I might like to break off then, and resume my argument the next morning. I expressed my acknowledgments, I hope with becoming gratitude and respect; but I added that it would not take me more than a quarter of an hour to finish what I had to say, if I could have the time to myself. They all laughed with the utmost good humour; except for my own voice, absolute silence reigned in the chamber till the clock pointed to the half-hour, by which time I had made and completed my point.

Among my forensic contemporaries there are two whom I must single out for special mention, both be-

SIR RICHARD WEBSTER AND PIGOTT

(A sketch by Sir Frank Lockwood)

cause of their own qualities and because they were
among my closest personal friends—Frank Lockwood
and Rufus Isaacs.

Frank Lockwood came from Yorkshire: a fine up-standing figure of a man, with great natural gifts of voice, gesture, and facial expression. He spent more

(A sketch by Sir Frank Lockwood)

of his time at Cambridge in amateur acting than in the pursuit of learning, and I believe at one time seriously thought of going on to the stage, for which he had many

JOSEPH CHAMBERLAIN AND G. J. GOSCHEN
(*A sketch by Sir Frank Lockwood*)

H.T.
26 June 1890

With every wish to
do my duty to the House
& the Country I can't take
off any this more

W. H. SMITH

(*A sketch by Sir Frank Lockwood*)

SIR FRANK LOCKWOOD
From the "Vanity Fair" Cartoon by "Spy"

aptitudes. He could have made his living in another branch of art—that of caricature—in which in my judgment he excelled all his contemporaries, amateur or professional. His observation and invention, whether of persons or situations, was intuitive, and in rapidity of execution, with the fewest possible strokes of pen or pencil, I have never known his equal. In court, or in the House of Commons, he would jot down on the margin of his brief or of the order paper with lightning-like rapidity the humours of the scene, and his notebooks during the Parnell Commission contained a whole gallery of small masterpieces in pen-and-ink. Among his favourite victims, of whom sketches are reproduced in these pages, were Webster, R. T. Reid, Goschen and W. H. Smith.

I first made his acquaintance when I joined the North-Eastern Circuit, where he had already acquired a considerable practice, mostly on the criminal side, at the West Riding Sessions and the Leeds Assizes. Without any pretensions to being a lawyer in the technical sense, his overflowing fund of humour, his readiness in retort, and his skill in cross-examination, made him a favourite and highly successful advocate. On one occasion he strayed into the Rolls Court with a small "Consent" brief, and Sir George Jessel, observing him, and amazed at his intrusion into such unfamiliar precincts, exclaimed: "Well, Mr. Lockwood, what are *you* here for?" Lockwood, affecting to look at the fee marked on his brief: "I regret to say, my Lord, for two and one."

He had a prosperous life: took "silk"; got into Parliament and became Solicitor-General in Lord Rosebery's Government. To the infinite grief of his friends, of whom I was one of the most intimate, he died prematurely in the full tide of what we all thought to be his inexhaustible vitality. He had a charming and generous nature, and there was no more popular man either at the Bar or in the House of Commons.

Lockwood was my senior at the Bar; Rufus Isaacs (now Lord Reading) was a good many years my junior. His career is one of the most romantic of our time. At the age of seventeen he went to sea as ship's boy in a tramp steamer; then tried the Stock Exchange, where, through no fault of his own, he was unfortunate; read for the Bar, and very soon after his call had acquired a large and lucrative practice; went into Parliament, was the first Attorney-General to enter the Cabinet, and in due course became Lord Chief Justice of England. He was British Ambassador at Washington during a critical period, and finally was appointed Viceroy of India, whence he has recently returned after a strenuous and highly successful term of office, which has been fitly recognized by the grant of a marquisate.

Although there is a considerable disparity in our ages I soon became closely associated with Rufus Isaacs both in professional and political work. He was a powerful advocate, most formidable perhaps in mercantile cases where knowledge of the practices and usages of business is invaluable. In the Cabinet he was a very useful counsellor — level-headed, not to be " rattled," with a shrewd and resourceful judgment, and never lacking in courage. It has been given to few men in our time to play so many diverse parts, and it may be said of him that the higher he has been tried the better he has emerged from the ordeal.

Politics brought my forensic career to an end in December, 1905, when I entered Campbell-Bannerman's Cabinet as Chancellor of the Exchequer. On personal and professional grounds, Mr. Balfour's sudden and unforeseen resignation came upon me at a very inopportune moment. I had just received a retainer on behalf of some members of the family of the ex-Khedive to go to Egypt—with a brief marked 10,000 guineas—to represent them in a litigation as to the Daira estates in the Egyptian courts. I was looking forward to spending my Christmas at Cairo, and as it was calculated that the case would not last more than a fortnight or three weeks, I should have been back in time for my political and legal work at home. It was, as may be imagined, with much reluctance that I was forced to abandon my voyage and return my brief. There are people, I know, who think that the "spoils of office" offer an irresistible allurement to adventurous and ambitious politicians: my own experience, which is by no means unique, is that the pursuit of politics is apt to involve a man in heavy material loss.

I will conclude this restrospect with a brief reference to the last case in which I ever appeared at the Bar. It was also the last in which I found myself associated, either as colleague or adversary, with Sir Edward Carson. It was a Revenue dispute relating to Income Tax, and Carson, though the resignation of the Government had been announced, still held his office as Solicitor-General and argued for the Crown. I, on the other hand, represented the aggrieved taxpayer, and

as rumour had already assigned to me the office of
Chancellor of the Exchequer in the new administration, my learned friend indulged in some good-hu-
moured sarcasms at my anomalous position in asking
the court to cut down my own prospective revenue. I
forget which way the case, not of much importance,
was decided, nor was it one that called for any special
exercise of forensic skill, but I always regarded Carson
as an exceptionally dangerous antagonist. His early
professional experience had been gained entirely in
Ireland; indeed he had been an Irish Law officer before he was called to the English Bar. But he rapidly
acquired a commanding position here, and after the
elevation of another Irishman, Charles Russell, to the
Bench, he was in my opinion unsurpassed as an advocate in the handling of witnesses and in the presentation
of a case to a jury. I must add that though at the Bar,
as in politics, we were almost invariably on opposite
sides, I always found him not only a most honourable
antagonist but charming and considerate in every personal relation.

CHAPTER XIII

MY FIRST ELECTION

I MUST now turn to my novitiate in the other great profession which has been the main occupation of my working life — that of politics.

I had taken part as a skirmisher, and more or less as a free-lance, in the great Gladstonian uprising, for such in effect it was, of 1880; though, as I have explained, I was not yet in a position to become a candidate. One of the incidental results of that memorable struggle was the formation of a club, mainly recruited from the young men of the party, which, in honour of the electoral victory it was intended to commemorate, received the patronymic of the Eighty Club. The club, which had no local habitation and no staff except a secretary, was happily constituted in personnel from the beginning. It was a body of itinerant missionaries, and not a few of those who in later years gained distinction in the House of Commons graduated on its platforms. Haldane was, I think, its first secretary. It gave its members much needed initiation both in team-work and in what Mr. Disraeli called, in his early campaigning days, "standing on one's own head." It was good dialectial exercise, for example, in the years 1883–5 for a young Liberal gladiator, evening after evening, to defend the dispatch, the recall, and the "rescue," of General Gordon. This was one of the main controversial themes of the general election of 1885; but the arena had been considerably enlarged when in the following year Home Rule became the authorized party cry, and we had to demonstrate our title, as against some of our old comrades in arms, now disguised in their Unionist war-paint, to the true Liberal succession.

Haldane, at the election of 1885, had annexed without serious bloodshed one of the new county constituencies in the south of Scotland — Haddington or East Lothian. The Parliament then elected was one of the shortest on record, and when it was dissolved as early as June, 1886, he urged me to follow his example, and undertake a foray in the same quarter (East Fife) on my own account. Our cases were dissimilar in almost every particular but one — that we were both barristers of the English Bar, which was not in itself a passport to the representation of a Scottish county. For he was not only a Scotsman, but had made himself already a known and respected figure in his county, while I was an Englishman, a "carpet-bagger," and totally unversed in the indigenous Scottish art of "heckling." There is in East Fife a small town called Auchtermuchty where hand-loom weaving then still survived, and I can well remember standing for more than an hour, after my first speech, while the old weavers in the audience put me mercilessly through every item of their Shorter Catechism of the Radical faith. It was by no means plain sailing, and when with my agent I returned from our nightly quota of village meetings, there was often little to encourage us in the survey of our evening's adventures. I can recall our once inducing the local baker — a strong Tory, as it turned out — to take the chair. There were perhaps a dozen men in the room, and when I had done my best to light the heather, after a prolonged pause the village doctor rose and in a tone of icy courtesy proceeded to move that "Mr. Asquith is *not* a fit or proper person to represent this constituency." The "flesher," whose mind dwelt exclusively on the impending massacre of the Ulster Protestants, was at last induced to second the resolution, which was then declared by the chairman to be carried unanimously.

Happily for me the contest lasted little more than a week, at the end of which I was elected at the head of the poll (2,862 votes against 2,487), and from that day I was for thirty-two years consistently returned for East Fife. Years later, when Mr. Birrell had joined me in the "Kingdom of Fife," of which he sat for the West Division, we were both staying with Haldane at Raith as the guests of our friend, Ronald Ferguson, now Lord Novar. We strolled up one morning to an elevation on his property which commands a fine view of the Firth of Forth and the adjacent territory. We all admired the prospect, but the only articulate ejaculation came from Birrell: "What a grateful thought, that there is not an acre in this vast and varied landscape which is not represented at Westminster by a London barrister!"

For a number of years Birrell and I sat as colleagues, never without a contested election, in which he always had a much larger majority against his Tory opponent than I had against mine. Birrell used to tell against himself a remark made to him by one of his staunchest supporters: "I canna reckon how it is, Mr. Birrell, that ye always hold your seat so easily, while *a really clever man*, like Mr. Asquith, only gets in with the greatest difficulty."

There are few departments in our public life in which I have witnessed more changes than in that of electioneering. There can be no question that corruption, direct and even indirect, and "undue influence" have been substantially diminished, and in many, if not most, parts of the country may be said to have entirely disappeared. This is no doubt partly due to the establishment of secret voting, and partly to Sir Henry James's Corrupt Practices Act of 1883, which made any election expenditure, even for legitimate purposes, which exceeded the prescribed scale, illegal and a ground for the avoidance of the election by petition. It is true that the excellent provisions of this statute are frequently evaded in practice, but the risks which attend any pronounced and substantial excess are too great to be faced by any agent who knows his business. Moreover, the enormous increase in the size of the electorate, particularly since the admission of women to the suffrage, has made any attempt to debauch a constituency by the expenditure of money a practical impossibility. I remember in the old days being counsel at the trial of a petition in an East Anglian borough which returned two members, with an electorate of very moderate dimensions and pretty evenly divided between the two political parties. Little more than a handful of votes was needed to turn the scale, and in the hour or two before the close of the poll there was quite a brisk market in the public-houses at a tariff of from 2s. 6d. to 2s. a head. My unfortunate clients, two of the most blameless of mankind, had been returned at the head of the poll, but as, after a trial which lasted for nearly three weeks, a single payment to a voter at the market rate was traced to an undoubted agent, they were both unseated. This, of course, might happen now; but there has been since 1885 a continuous and significant decline in the number of petitions after a general election, with the incidental result that the members of the Bar who specialized in this branch of practice (and of whom I myself, in the laxer days of the past, was one) have been deprived of what every few years used to be a lucrative windfall.

I was first returned to the House of Commons in 1886, and I fought my last contested election in 1924. In the forty years, or thereabouts, that intervened, what may be called " the mechanism of electioneering," particularly in rural constituencies, had been largely transformed by the introduction of motor transport. My first constituency was, when I went there in 1886, cut off by arms of the sea both on the north and the south from the rest of East Scotland — the Tay Bridge having been blown down and the Forth Bridge still incomplete. The constituency covered a large area, with a mixed population — agriculture, fishing, workers in small factories, and in a few mines — all living in scattered villages. There was no central town, Cupar and St. Andrews belonging to a separate group (the St. Andrews Burghs) which had a parliamentary representative of its own. The result was that the candidate had to visit and make speeches at some thirty different places, and as the railway was geographically useless, he had to rely entirely on the horse-drawn vehicles of the time. This was very hampering to his activities, particularly when, as was my case, he was a "carpet-bagger," on whom the electors had never set eyes before, and who had arrived late on the scene. In the course of twenty years the motor-car revolutionized the conditions, and enabled one every day to cover twice the distance in half the time.

The lairds of Fife, with two or three exceptions, were in those days Tories of the most reactionary and fossilized type, and among the clergy of the Established Church of Scotland in the villages and small towns I doubt whether I had, from first to last, more than half a dozen supporters. In the University city of St. Andrews, which, as I have said, was in a constituency of its own, there was among the professors always a considerable Liberal element, which included two successive principals—Donaldson, a fine scholar who had been tutor to Lord Rosebury; and Herkless, an ecclesiastical historian of repute, who despite his orders in the Established Church used to come to my meetings and give me valuable platform help. East Fife was in the fullest sense a democratic constituency. In some of the smaller towns the old industry of hand-loom weaving of linen, which was carried on in the cottages and was rapidly dying out, had not yet been completely superseded by the power-driven factory. The hand-loom weavers, who used to take it in turns to read newspapers and books aloud while the others worked, were for the most part advanced in years, and not a few of them had belonged to the Chartist movement in their youth. They had as a body a large and varied store of political and historical knowledge, and being without any respect of persons, or any bowels of mercy for ignorance and inexperience, they were the finest masters of the art of "heckling"— now fallen into decrepitude — whom even Scotland has produced.

I had a most devoted and capable agent, Mr. Ketchen, a solicitor and banker at Elie, to whom and to his son (now Keeper of the Register of Sasines in Edinburgh) I was, so long as they were able to serve me, indebted for the admirable organization which enabled us for many years to emerge from a succession of electoral contests with ever-growing majorities. Ketchen was one of the shrewdest of mankind, with an independent position of his own in the county, and on the best of terms with men of all parties and creeds. As an illustration of one of the changes which in the course of forty years have come over Scottish ideas and habits, I may recall a piece of advice which he gave me in 1886. After a strenuous week, I proposed to go over to Edinburgh on Sunday morning to spend the day there. The only way in those days of getting across the Forth was to take the steamer from Burntisland to Granton, which started soon after cock-crow. Ketchen was horrified, not so much in his character of adherent and, I think, elder of the Free Church, but of prudent and vigilant election agent: "My dear sir," he exclaimed, "I would rather pay down £100 than that it should be known that you had used the ferry on the Sabbath Day!"

The opponent whom I fought and beat in 1886 was a sitting member, Mr. Boyd Kinnear, a local laird and a writer of some repute, who, belonging to the Radical wing of the party, had followed Mr. Chamberlain in voting against the second reading of Mr. Gladstone's first Home Rule Bill, and stood as a Liberal Unionist. He had been returned with a large majority at the head of the poll less than twelve months before, in a contest in which he was bitterly opposed by the Tories, who now obeyed with wry faces and in reduced numbers the summons to give him their votes. At the declaration of the poll it was found that I had a small but adequate majority. In my subsequent contests in Fife, it was always a straight fight between Liberal and Tory: the Labour vote (in those days not relatively a large one) was cast for the Liberal candidate. This was the case till the election of December, 1918, when, to the infinite and equal surprise of both my friends and my opponents, I succumbed (under the guise of an anti-patriot) to the Coalition between Mr. Lloyd George and Mr. Bonar Law, which assassinated the Liberal party. It was the first time since the Reform Act of 1832 that the County of Fife had returned a Tory as its representative.

CHAPTER XIV

PARLIAMENTARY NOVITIATE

MY maiden speech in the House of Commons was delivered in my second session on March 24, 1887. It was on the third night of a full-dress debate in which all the leaders took a share, on a Government motion, then still unusual in form, that precedence over all other business should be given to the first Order, which happened to be the Irish Crimes Bill in charge of Mr. Balfour. Mr. Balfour had not at that time been longer at the Chief Secretary's office than a very few weeks, and he was still in what may be described as the callow stage, from which, during the course of a single session, he emerged as one of the most formidable and accomplished debaters in the House of Commons. Charles James Fox, when he was once asked how he had developed from being one of the worst, to being the best, speaker in the House, replied: "By speaking every night on every subject."

The conventional tremors attached by tradition to a "maiden," and often even more painfully to a second, speech have been vividly depicted by one of the most expert of parliamentary performers. Disraeli's description of the first interview of the young Coningsby with his awe-inspiring relative, Lord Monmouth, is the *locus classicus* on the subject:

"Milord is ready to receive you," said the valet. Coningsby sprang forward with that desperation which the scaffold requires. His face was pale, his hand was moist, his heart beat with tumult.   Music, artillery, the roar of cannon, and the blare of trumpets may urge a man on to a forlorn hope; ambition, one's constituents, the hell of previous failure, may prevail on us to do a more desperate thing; speak in the House of Commons; but there are some situations in life, such for instance as entering the room of a dentist, when the prostration of the nervous system is absolute.

As often happens in such cases the ordeal is in truth often worse in prospect than in actual retrospect.   In my own case the theme was a comparatively easy one. When you had got into your own stride it more or less carried you along, and when I sat down I was the happy recipient from Mr. Chamberlain of a friendly compliment.   Two or three of the leading topics may be allowed a fragmentary resuscitation.[1]   I fully accepted the doctrine that it was the duty of the executive, at all times and in all places, to enforce the law, whether it was good or bad, without discrimination of persons. Though a loyal member of my party I did not think that the fact that a Liberal Government had committed what I conceived to be a colossal and disastrous mistake in 1881 was any reason why, at the instance of a Conservative Government, the same blunder should be repeated in 1887.   Ireland was for the time being freer as a whole from crime than at almost any date in her history.   Such crime as there was, was mainly in the south and west, where the standard of rent was abnormally high, where reductions had been most unreasonably refused, and where evictions had been most frequent in number and cruel in character.   As to boycotting, it was one of those impalpable things which legislation could not reach: so far I agreed with Lord

[1] The whole speech is to be found in "Speeches by the Earl of Oxford" (1927).

Salisbury. But to my mind there was a remedy, and only one remedy, for it, which was to alter the conditions out of which it sprang. Nothing at any rate could be gained or hoped from setting up a system which was neither resolutely repressive nor frankly popular —one of those half-hearted compromises which history had marked with the brand of political imposture.

In the immediately following months (1887-8), the schism in the Liberal party widened out into an irreparable breach. Its principal organizations—the National Liberal Federation, the Eighty Club, and the National Liberal Club—though two of them were of Mr. Chamberlain's parentage—declared themselves definitely for Home Rule on Gladstonian lines. Lord Hartington, with the co-operation of Mr. Bright, Mr. Chamberlain, Mr. Goschen, and other eminent "Liberal Unionists" (as they came for a time to be called) started a separate party machinery. Perhaps the actual date of formal division may be put at the annual meeting of the National Liberal Federation at Nottingham on October 18, 1887, at which Mr. Gladstone himself was present. I had the honour of being selected as one of the speakers. Nothing that I said aroused more general assent than my statement that the limits of reasonable and practicable concession had been reached. "It was a very good thing to do what they could to recover the lost sheep. Henry IV had said that Paris was worth a Mass. But they might pay too high a price even for the capitulation of Birmingham."

There was a good deal of skirmishing in the House of Commons in 1888, in which I took a fairly active part in the early stages of the Parnell Commission Bill

—an extra-constitutional measure, which was not accepted without grave misgiving by some of the most weighty authorities on both sides of the House. Subsequently the venue of the Irish controversy was largely shifted to the floor of the court, and after the Pigott forgeries had been exposed, to the platforms of England and Scotland. My own parliamentary incursions in debate were, as was inevitable, mainly given to Ireland. But I took two opportunities of emphasizing other heads of overdue Liberal reform which had no direct relation to Home Rule: the payment of members, and the removal of religious disabilities, as a disqualification for any minister of the Crown. Of the first of these changes, it is not necessary now to say more than, though at the time it was denounced as fatal to the freedom and independence of the House of Commons, it has been annually passed for many years with the same ease and absence of objection as an Expiring Laws Continuance Act. Whatever may be the party preponderant for the time being, no Government of any complexion would venture to omit it from its sessional programme. The object of the other Bill, which was introduced by Mr. Gladstone himself, was to enable Roman Catholics to hold the offices of Lord Chancellor of England and of Lord Chancellor of Ireland.

The Liberal position as it was fought by the party as a whole at the ensuing election in June, 1892, may be compendiously summarized from my election address.

The address begins as follows:

The country has been governed since 1886 by a Coalition resting upon the support of a composite majority. Its policy has been so constituted as to give effect to the reactionary views of the Tories who form the bulk of its supporters, both in Parliament and in the country, and at the same time to conciliate the dwindling scruples and to smooth the downward path of a small contingent of deserters from the Liberal camp.

Its essential Toryism has been prominently manifested in the enactment of a permanent coercive law for Ireland, and in the proposal to create, at the expense of the taxpayers, a new vested interest in public-house licences. On the other hand, the measures on the faith of which the Coalition have sought, and seek, to establish a title to Liberal support have been half-hearted, superficial, and incomplete: Local Government Acts for England and Scotland which make no provision for parochial self-government or for the popular control of the police, a Land Purchase Act for Ireland whose operation depends upon the will of the individual landlord, and the Small Holdings Act of the present year which its authors have deprived of real and effective validity by the deliberate omission of compulsory powers.

The claim of Ireland to legislate for and administer her local concerns no longer occasions alarm or bewilderment. . . .

The real security for permanent political union between Great Britain and Ireland is perceived to be in the indissoluble community of their social and material interests. . . . The case of Ireland is one of paramount urgency . . . but the attention of the next Parliament must be given from the first to British concerns also. . . . I am one of those who believe that the collective action of the community may and ought to be employed positively as well as negatively; to raise as well as to level; to equalize opportunities no less than to curtail privileges; to make the freedom of the individual a reality and not a pretence.

The remainder of the address cites a number of specific reforms ranging over a wide area, such, for example, as the abolition of plural voting, and the ending of a hereditary second chamber.

This syllabus may be taken as, on the whole, a fair and representative summary of the immediate aims of the rank and file of the Liberal party—especially of that section of it which had a definite leaning to the "Left"—on the eve of the general election of 1892. It will be observed that (1) notwithstanding the electoral set-back which had to be faced as the inevitable result of the split in the Irish party, and of its consequences in Great Britain, Irish Home Rule was still given the front place in the electoral "manifesto"; and (2) that there was full recognition of the need for a concurrent prosecution of such radical reforms in the sphere of domestic legislation and administration in Great Britain as had come to be compendiously described as the Newcastle Programme.

During my first six years in the House of Commons I worked in close association with a small group of friends, almost all, if not all, of whom were under forty years of age: Haldane, Edward Grey, Sydney Buxton, Arthur Acland, and Tom Ellis. All but Acland and Ellis still survive. I refer elsewhere to our activities, and our relations with the grave and reverend occupants of the front bench. While in the main good party men, we displayed from time to time independent tendencies, and were regarded in those days as more or less advanced Radicals. Some adventurous spirits —in particular Mrs. Green, the widow of the historian, and Miss Beatrice Potter (about to become Mrs. Sidney Webb) —thought the experiment worth trying of bringing us into relation with the young Intelligentsia of the Socialist party, which was then to be found in the Fabian Society. The following extract

from Miss Potter's journal describes one of these con-
frontations. It is dated May 31, 1891, when the Parliament of 1886 was drawing near its end:

We had a queer party at Alice Green's: five of the young
Radicals — Asquith, Haldane, Grey, Buxton, and Acland
— to meet five Fabians — Massingham, Clarke, Olivier,
Shaw, and S. W(ebb), with Alice and myself. It was not
successful; though not quite a failure, since all were pleasant
and cordial. Asquith spoilt it. He was determined that it
should not go. Haldane made himself most pleasant, and
is really playing up: but the machine of the Liberal party
is slow to move.[1]

I regret that my memory of this little gathering is
of the vaguest. I was certainly not conscious of the
sinister and blighting influence which the writer at-
tributes to me, though I think it very likely that I
showed that, so far as I was concerned, I was determined that "It" — if it meant more than friendly *rapprochement* for the free interchange of views — "should
not go."

[1] "My Apprenticeship," Beatrice Webb, p. 412.

CHAPTER XV

SOCIAL RELATIONS OF POLITICIANS

GIBBON spent eight years in the House of Commons, without opening his mouth. He sat for a short time in a subordinate office on the Treasury bench, but he gives a vivid picture of the life of a back-bencher: not indeed a typical back-bencher of any time; for this one was a man of genius and an artist in language, who yet shared the frailties and disabilities of his fellow-members.

This is his own summary of his experiences:

After a fleeting illusive hope, prudence condemned me to acquiesce in the humble station of a mute. I was not armed by nature and education with the intrepid energy of mind and voice,

Vincentem strepitus, et natum rebus agendis.

Timidity was fortified by pride, and even the success of my pen discouraged the trial of my voice. But I assisted at the debates of a free assembly; I listened to the attack and defence of eloquence and reason; I had a near prospect of the characters, views, and passions of the first men of the age. . . . The eight sessions that I sat in Parliament were a school of civil prudence, the first and most essential virtue of an historian.

Before I come to my own transformation in 1892 from the status of a private to that of an official member, I may say something of my experiences and impressions during the six years that I sat on the back benches.

The Liberal Unionists, though they hardened as

years went on into thick and thin supporters of the
Tory Government, sat on the Opposition side of the
House interspersed with their old comrades, the
"Gladstonians." They had an organization and whips
of their own, one of them being a burly Radical, W. S.
Caine. He was best known as a temperance advocate,
and even after the split used to find a seat as near as
might be to his old leader, Sir Wilfrid Lawson, who
was a convinced and defiant Home Ruler. Caine was
a born wire-puller of the "hail-fellow-well-met" type,
and a general favourite with us all, though Labouchere
in one of his pasquinades in *Truth* had branded him as
a "genial ruffian." It was, when such controversies
as those over the Crimes Bill and the Parnell Commission were raging furiously, a severe trial of the
patience and temper of the back-benchers of both the
Liberal wings, to be sitting as they often did cheek
by jowl. It speaks well for the average standard of
parliamentary manners in those days that what are now
called "scenes" were—except when the Nationalists
were out for an evening on the warpath—of infrequent
occurrence.

The Front Opposition bench presented a curious
spectacle. Mr. Gladstone sat opposite the box in the
leader's place, with Sir W. Harcourt or Mr. John
Morley on his left to act as a kind of buffer. Occupying the seats nearest the gangway, were the Liberal
Unionist chiefs—Lord Hartington, Mr. Chamberlain,
Sir Henry James, Mr. Heneage. On the other side of
Mr. Gladstone were the old colleagues who had remained faithful to him. It took some time to get accustomed to the sight of these eminent gentlemen, all

of whom had held office under Mr. Gladstone a year or two before, taking their turns at the same box to engage in mortal combat with one another. Lord Hartington, who carried the most weight with the House of any of the dissentients, was removed from the scene by the death of his father in 1891, and thereafter Mr. Chamberlain was the acknowledged leader of the band.

It may be noted that both the Speaker (Mr. Peel) and the Chairman of Ways and Means (Mr. Courtney) were Liberal Unionists.

The Home Rule controversy had led to a good deal of social boycotting and blackballing at clubs. Mr. Gladstone, and in a minor degree his avowed followers, were for the time in the blackest books of what is called in London " Society." [1]   But all this affected, or infected, only a limited number of people, and the *camaraderie* of the House of Commons was on the whole well preserved. Mr. J. E. Ellis, a much-respected Liberal member of uncompromising principle, who used to sit on the bleakest altitudes of the back benches, in an interesting letter to his wife describes how on the introduction of the Home Rule Bill on April 8, 1886, he found himself close to Mr. Trevelyan, who had just resigned from Mr. Gladstone's Cabinet:

I sat next but one to Mr. Trevelyan. . . . I was glad to hear him say how much (in his opinion) good humour had grown during the last fifteen years. He remarked it would have been almost impossible then for anyone dissenting, as he did, from the policy of the Government, and having resigned so recently, to come and sit amongst its staunch adherents. [2]

[1] Mr. Page, the American Ambassador, reports a similar state of things in 1913. "Life and Letters," Vol. I, p. 145.
[2] "The Life of John Edward Ellis," A. Tilney Bassett, p. 67.

A PAGE FROM "THE OLD CHESHIRE CHEESE" VISITORS' BOOK

The social and personal relationship of political opponents is an old theme upon which much has been written. There are two schools of opinion: those who think that friendly and, still more, familiar intercourse between the combatants when they are off the battlefield impairs the sincerity of public life; and those who think that political differences may without any lack of honesty be ignored in private. Mr. Bright seems to have belonged to the one school, and Mr. Chamberlain to the other.

"John Bright," says his biographer, Mr. G. M. Trevelyan, "always tended towards the sterner view of familiarity between political opponents, namely that it is difficult to attack in public a man with whom the orator consorts much in private."[1] Mr. Bright's practice does not seem to have been so severe as his precept: there are several indications in Mr. Buckle's "Life" that he cultivated in private friendly relations with Disraeli.

Mr. Chamberlain expressed the other view at the Milner dinner, over which I presided, in March, 1897 — a function in which the leading politicians of both parties participated either in person or by letter. Mr. Chamberlain said in the course of his speech:

We fight our political battles in this country with great energy and sometimes perhaps with too much vehemence. But fortunately there is a large space in the field of politics, and a still greater space in our social life, which is altogether free from any taint of party bitterness; and foreigners have told me that what has struck them most in their experience of this country is the fact that political opponents, even in the bitterest controversy, can still remain firm personal friends.

[1] "Life of John Bright," p. 358.

There was never any social intercourse except of a perfunctory and quasi-official character between Gladstone and Disraeli. No two men were ever born less capable of understanding each other. Towards Lord Salisbury, on the other hand, Mr. Gladstone seems to have always entertained friendly feelings and was several times his guest.

Lord Bryce, in his "Studies in Contemporary Biography,"[1] records that "in 1890 he [Mr. Gladstone] remarked to me apropos of some attack, 'I have never felt angry at what Salisbury has said about me. His mother was very kind to me when I was quite a young man, and I remember Salisbury as a little fellow in a red frock rolling about on the ottoman.'"

Another example of friendly relationship between opposing gladiators in our own time is furnished by the case of Sir W. Harcourt and Mr. Balfour. Harcourt in a speech at Holloway, July 7, 1896, prefaced an attack on the proceedings of Mr. Balfour by saying: "We respect Mr. Balfour's ability, and we appreciate and reciprocate his courtesy, and it will be an ill day for the House of Commons when those engaged in the honourable contests of parliamentary conflict are incapable of mutual regard and the delight

> In the stern joy that warriors feel
> In foemen worthy of their steel."[2]

"I enclose a most charming letter from dear A. Balfour," Harcourt wrote in January, 1903, to his son. "No wonder everyone loves him."[3]

[1] Page 456.
[2] "Life of Harcourt," Gardiner, Vol. II, p. 410.
[3] *Ibid.*, Vol. II, 591.

Mr. Balfour said of Harcourt at his death:

In the utmost height of party controversy, when feeling was running strongly, when he himself perhaps was taking, as was his wont, a leading place in the fighting line, he never allowed party differences to mar the perfection of personal friendship. . . . I am proud to say that he honoured me with his friendship for many years, and never was that friendship clouded even when our political differences were in their most acute stage.

I have always belonged myself, in practice, to the laxer of the two schools, and I trust that it may continue to maintain, without sacrifice either of principle or of combative energy, one of the characteristic traditions of our public life.

CHAPTER XVI

TWO IRISH ORATORS [1]

(LORD OXFORD INTENDED ALSO TO WRITE IMPRESSIONS OF JOHN
DILLON, WILLIAM O'BRIEN, AND POSSIBLY MR. HEALY)

THERE has never in my experience been a section
or group in the House of Commons — outside
the traditional parties, Liberal and Conservative — which had the same command of the most varied
parliamentary resources as the Nationalists under the
leadership of Parnell.

One of its most notable figures, for a time, was John
O'Connor Power. He was a man of humble extraction, and is said to have been born in the workhouse at
Ballinasloe. He started life as a house painter: was
drawn into the Fenian organization, at whose secret
meetings he soon became a favourite orator; and rose
to be an important member of the Supreme Council.
Mr. William O'Brien depicts him as a man who, having "walked for years under the shadow of the gal-
lows," was "gifted with a common sense keen enough
and fearless enough to guide him in the evolution from
the impracticable to a wise and patriotic possibilism." [2]
In this new phase of his career he helped to bring about
a concordat between the extreme men and the Home
Rule Federation in 1873. In the following year (1874)
he was elected member of Parliament for Mayo " after

---

[1] I am indebted for some of the particulars in this sketch to the kindness of
my old friend, Mr. T. P. O'Connor, the Father of the House of Commons.
[2] "Recollections," pp. 139–140.

a fierce fight between the Church and the Fenians and the young party which Parnell was bringing into existence." [1]   In the House of Commons he soon won his way to the front, not only by his exceptional gifts of speech, but by the impression which he gave of a powerful and sincere personality.   He was an active associate of Parnell in the invention and development of the tactics of obstruction, and in the debates on the South Africa Bill and the abolition of flogging in the Army. He was deputed by a meeting of " advanced Nationalists " in Dublin in 1876 to go to the United States in company with Parnell to present an address to President Grant of congratulation on the centenary of American independence.

In the early days of the stormy and momentous session of 1881, there is the following entry in Sir Henry Lucy's " Diary ":

Mr. O'Connor Power gave fresh illustration of the fact already established, that below the very first rank in which so few stand, he is one of the most graceful and powerful debaters the House possesses.   Either by skill, or more probably by force of character, he has impressed the House with a sense of his moderation and fairness. [2]

He appears to have been a man of irritable temperament and something of *a mauvais coucheur*, and fell foul of two of the most powerful persons in the left wing of the Nationalist party — Biggar, and Patrick Egan the treasurer of the Land League.   He broke loose from Parnell's leadership at the beginning of the session of 1884, on the ground, amongst others, that it " had imposed upon his country the most stringent

[1] T. P. O'Connor.
[2] "Diary of Two Parliaments: The Gladstone Parliament, 1880–1885," p. 108.

and hateful coercive code ever imposed upon any people." Thenceforward he stood aloof, and became a
parliamentary free-lance, whose incursions into debate
were far from welcome to his old associates. But he
never lost his hold upon the House.

He drifted gradually into the Liberal ranks, and
stood unsuccessfully for English constituencies at Ken-
nington in 1885, and ten years later for South Bristol.
He was pursued as a renegade and traitor with relent-
less hostility by his old party, though some of them —
such as Michael Davitt, T. P. O'Connor, and perhaps
Parnell himself — would have been glad to see him,
one of the ablest and most dexterous parliamentarians,
back in their ranks. He appeared fitfully from time
to time at St. Patrick's Day banquets, and other outside
gatherings, where he spoke with all his old eloquence
and effect, but (as Mr. O'Connor says) "it was a heart-
break to him not to be in the House of Commons,"
which he was never able to re-enter.

He was, I believe, the real author of a phrase which
was sometimes attributed to me, that the Liberal Unionists were "the mules of politics: without pride of an-
cestry, or hope of posterity."

One of the most gifted of the Nationalist leaders was
Thomas Sexton, who was certainly at one time their
most finished and powerful speaker. He was a man of
undistinguished appearance, and of retiring manners,
and I never succeeded in establishing with him more
than a superficial acquaintance. Mr. Justin McCarthy
rated him at his best as second only to Gladstone among
the orators and debaters of the time, and declares that
in private conversation he was " even more brilliant than

in public debate." He adds: "Mr. Sexton is of all men the most unsocial in the ordinary sense of the word. . . . He never dines out. He never goes out to luncheon. . . . When the session was over he would disappear, and his friends would know nothing more of him for a time." [1]

When I entered the House of Commons he had already made his reputation, and was a recognized master of debate. He was first returned to the House at the general election of 1880, and would seem to have entered it with all his natural faculties already fully developed. Lord Eversley, then Mr. Shaw Lefevre, an "old parliamentary hand," describes the impression made upon him by one of Sexton's early speeches in the session of 1881, in the debate on the introduction of Mr. Forster's Irish Coercion Bill, which lasted all through the night, the following day, and the next night. [2]

Mr. Sexton spoke for nearly three hours, between 2 and 5 o'clock in the early morning. I was one of the six or seven English members who were present, and heard the whole of it. I had rarely listened to a more closely reasoned, eloquent and cogent speech. There was no reiteration, and scarcely a word was redundant. It was a presage of many speeches of the same quality from Mr. Sexton, which gained him so great an influence in his party and so high a reputation in the House.

I have followed Mr. Shaw Lefevre's example, and remained in a half-empty House to listen to the whole of one of Sexton's almost interminable harangues. To anyone interested in the technique of speaking he was an instructive study. I have never known him at a loss

[1] "Reminiscences," Vol. II, pp. 381–7. [2] "Gladstone and Ireland," p. 139.

for the appropriate word: the structure of his sentences was impeccable; and he had a large range of national moods. He was not epigrammatic or humorous; though there was abundant ease and occasional felicity, I cannot recall any specially brilliant or striking phrase; he was rarely loud or over-emphatic; but the stream of orderly and lucid argument, its level surface lashed now and again by gusts of passionate invective, would flow on, sometimes for hours, unhasting, unresting, without a pause, or any apparent prospect of its ever running dry. There was little or no sign of preparation, but for House of Commons purposes he would undoubtedly, even in his best days, have been more effective if he could have curbed and chastened his native fluency.

Mr. Gladstone's estimate of his powers is noteworthy. Writing from the House of Commons to Lady Frederick Cavendish, shortly after her husband's assassination (May, 1882), he says: "Sexton just now returned to the subject, with much approval from the House. Nothing could be better either in feeling or in grace: the man is little short of a master."[1]

His taste, however, was by no means faultless. He gave great offence to the House by a speech in which, in repelling Bright's charge against the Irish members of being disloyal to the Crown, he declared that "licentiousness of language with regard to his opponents had been the main characteristic of Bright's life, and his career and age, instead of bringing him dignity or reserve, had only weakened his judgment."[2] Mr. Gladstone, the next year, wrote to Mr. Bright, with whom

---

[1] Morley, Vol. III, 69.   [2] July 28, 1885.

he was now at issue over Home Rule: "The offences of Nationalists have been great; the worst of them, I frankly say, was committed against *you* by Sexton in a well-known speech."[1]

As time went on his oratory was more and more infected by what Sir Henry Lucy called the "fatal blight of fluency." Already in 1888 that acute observer writes of him: "Occasional passages in his voluminous discourses are flashes of heaven-born eloquence. But they are so smothered in verbiage that they have no chance either to burn or to illumine."[2] This became increasingly the case; his rising to take part in debate more often than not emptied the House; and when he retired in 1896, he had ceased to be a parliamentary force.

Mr. William O'Brien's estimate of Sexton is at once friendly and discriminating:[3]

When the darts of that provoking toreador, Mr. Healy, eventually made the arena distasteful to him and caused his withdrawal from parliamentary life, his old colleagues were lost in wonder and incredulity at the decision that reduced those magnificent oratorical gifts to silence, and exchanged the theatre of his glory and, as it seemed, of his fondest interest, for the obscure successes of a commercial career. If he has not left a deeper impression on the history of his generation, the fact can only be attributed to the nervous sensibilities which are so often the penalty of fine talents, to the superabundance of words which sometimes watered off his best arguments into diffuseness, and perhaps to an excess of that logical rigidity which sometimes made him overlook the practical effect of principles and figures in real life, through an almost morbidly clear view of the abstract demands of right reasoning and stern finance.

[1] Trevelyan's "Life of John Bright," p. 452.
[2] 'Diary of Salisbury Parliament," p. 141.
[3] "Recollections," pp. 251–3.

CHAPTER XVII

CABINET OFFICE: 1892–1895

I HAVE described elsewhere [1] the circumstances, personal and political, in which I became Home Secretary in Mr. Gladstone's Government in August, 1892, and have said something of the multifarious duties which the holder of that office has to keep under his control. In the eighteenth century there were only two Secretaries of State—one for the South and one for the North; their functions were of the most disparate kind; each always had a seat even in the small Cabinets of those days. They were rarely commoners (though the elder Pitt is an exception) and were always figures of high consideration, sometimes from the personal qualities of the temporary incumbent, but more often from his being the spokesman and figurehead of one of the competing aristocratic groups between whom the "spoils of office" were distributed.

From Walpole onwards, the First Lord of the Treasury and the Chancellor of the Exchequer (two offices, but often held by a single person) were the nucleus of the Cabinet. The Lord Chancellor was always an indispensable adjunct; and in the next degree the Lord President of Council and Lord Privy Seal. If to this group the two Secretaries of State be added, you have all the normal constituent members, six or seven in number, of an eighteenth-century Cabinet. The pre-

[1] "Fifty Years of British Parliament."

cise composition of the Cabinet on these lines was by
no means invariable. Sir Robert Walpole's contained
but a single commoner, Sir C. Wager, who was First
Lord of the Admiralty. Many years later the younger
Pitt admitted his brother, Lord Chatham, who held
the same office, to Cabinet rank. But the total number
of the Cabinet rarely exceeded seven or eight until after
the coalition with the dissentient Whigs in 1794.

During the nineteenth century, partly through the
necessity of providing for the Peelites, the average of
the aggregate members steadily increased.

In France, since the establishment of the Third Republic, as soon as Royalism had passed from a national
danger to a constitutional impossibility, we have witnessed a rapid transition from the two- or three-party
system, which on the whole has held its ground in Great
Britain, to the experiment of government by parliamentary groups. They vary from time to time in composition and number, and, with the exception of the
extremists of the Right and Left, shift and re-shift
without any intelligible relation to specific principles,
or even definite programmes. The result is written in
the baffling annals of small and precarious majorities,
of incalculable combinations, and of constant ministerial instability.

The climax was reached in the recent financial chaos
in which no one remembers the names, or even the number, of the statesmen who were called upon to form and
to disband Cabinets, and which witnessed every possible permutation in the personnel of government, until
every one available was swallowed up, for the time
being, in the *Grand Ministère* of M. Poincaré.

With their usual felicity the French have found the *mot juste* for the occasion, and have invented or adapted the word *dosage* to describe the process by which, if possible, each group, and at any rate every manageable group, in the Chamber is represented by a portfolio of its own.[1]

In the Cabinet, when I was first admitted to it, the Secretaries of State, who had now risen in number from two to five, all had seats as a matter of course. *Inter se,* no one of them had precedence over the others, though it was customary in any formal enumeration to put the Home Secretary's name first. Nor among Ministers generally was there any question of what the French call *dosage:* up to this date all the members of a Cabinet still belonged in form and in substance to the same political " group."

Even in the trying days which followed the Boer War and the " Khaki " election, though many nicknames were from time to time interchanged, there was no serious movement—as there had been in the case of Home Rule—to dissolve the old party ties or to abandon the old party nomenclature. It was feared by some of the more ardent partisans on the Liberal side, and hoped by more than a fraction of their Tory antagonists, that the old sores would sooner or later break out; but nothing of the kind happened, and the Cabinet which held office from 1905 down to the outbreak of the Great War in 1914 was probably one of the most harmonious in our history.

---

[1] The so-called *Grand Ministère* of Gambetta in 1881 was an abortive attempt by the greatest French statesman then living to procure something like parliamentary fusion in a chaos of groups. Like the prodigy, Marcellus at Rome, it was doomed to a short life, and came to an end after three months.

It would be tedious to repeat the narrative which I have given in a previous book[1] of the life of the Liberal Government which, first under Mr. Gladstone and then under Lord Rosebery, held office from 1892 to 1895. I may, however, add to what I have said there of my own work as Minister of Justice at the Home Office a brief account of two incidents.

One of them—the Featherstone Riot—aroused considerable controversy at the time, and earned for me for some years in the rhetoric of the Labour platform the designation of "Asquith the Murderer." It came about as follows. A miners' coal strike had been for some time going on at or near Featherstone in the West Riding of Yorkshire. Its progress was marked by growing disturbances, which developed into organized violence and arson. The local magistrates, with whom the responsibility for the preservation of peace and the protection of property primarily rests, were soon brought to the end of their resources; they tried in vain to supplement their own police by borrowing from adjoining areas; and at last, in response to their repeated appeals to the Home Office, I sanctioned their applying for the necessary help from the military forces in the neighbourhood, whose legal duty it is, according to the Common Law of England, as citizens, to come to the aid of the civil power in such an emergency.

Their intervention put an end to the whole disturbance within forty-eight hours. A magistrate was present with the troops; he made no fewer than seven appeals to the crowd, who were armed with sticks and bludgeons, to discontinue the work of destruction, much

[1] "Fifty Years of British Parliament."

valuable property being already ablaze; the Riot Act was read; a bayonet charge was unavailingly made; and as the defensive position held by the small detachment of soldiers (fewer than thirty men) was becoming untenable, and the complete destruction of the colliery was imminent, the magistrate gave orders to the commander to fire. Two men on the fringe of the crowd were unfortunately killed.

As I was not satisfied, after a careful study of the evidence given at the two inquests, that all the facts had been adequately investigated, I took the unusual course of appointing a Special Commission to examine and report upon the whole affair. The commissioners whom I nominated were Lord Bowen, one of the most eminent of the judicial members of the House of Lords, Sir Albert Rollit, a solicitor of wide experience and a Conservative M.P., and Mr. Haldane, then a Liberal member, and afterwards Lord Chancellor.

No one disputed the impartiality and competence of the Commission, and after an exhaustive inquiry at Wakefield they made a Report, setting out in detail all the facts, defining in a passage which has become a classic in our law, the respective duties of the civil and military powers in such cases, and completely justifying in every respect the action both of the magistrates and of the officers and rank and file of the soldiers. The matter was then fully debated in the House of Commons, when I challenged in vain my accusers to prefer and make good any charge which they thought fit to make.

It took years, however, to dissipate the legend, assiduously circulated, mainly by ejaculations from the back benches of so-called "Labour" meetings, that I had sent down the soldiers deliberately to help the owners in the dispute and to thin the ranks of the strikers.

I had already incurred considerable odium in another quarter, to which in the then distribution of parties it was, on the face of it, not politic, or at any rate tactful, at that moment to give offence. Mr. Redmond, the parliamentary head of the small surviving band of Parnellites, brought forward an amendment to the Address, which he no doubt calculated would be equally embarrassing both to his anti-Parnellite rivals and to Mr. Gladstone and his colleagues, who were not to be forgiven for their "desertion" of "The Lost Leader" in the hour of his need. He demanded a reconsideration of the sentences upon a number of "Irish dynamiters" who were still lying in penal servitude, for conspiring, and in some cases actually attempting, to cause by explosives and infernal machines wholesale destruction of life and property in some of our great urban centres. I gave the cases, separately and collectively, the most minute attention: not because I had any doubt on the point of principle — viz. whether, when a railway station, for example, crowded with innocent wayfarers, is wantonly blown to pieces, it makes a difference that the murderers were or might have been actuated by "political" motives — but because I realized that in charges of this kind the evidence, coming as it often does from tainted quarters, is peculiarly open to suspicion.

The result of my examination was that I was left without a shadow of doubt as to the guilt, or as to the propriety of the conviction and sentence, of any one of the prisoners. I reviewed all the cases in a long speech in the House of Commons, to which I may fairly say that no answer was possible. It was a hard ordeal for our anti-Parnellite friends to have to support the Government, and their leader, Mr. Justin McCarthy, an amiable and highly accomplished man whom the gods might have reserved for less troubled waters, felt moved to complain that I had "shut the gates of mercy with a clang." Mr. John Morley, who was charged with the delicate task of shepherding our allies, while entirely agreeing that I had taken the only possible line, remarked to me rather grimly the next day that perhaps I might have been a little less "*cassant.*"

For the purpose of these Memories I will refer to only two of the speeches which were made on the Home Rule Bill of 1893: Sir Edward Clarke's on the First Reading, and my own on the Second.

Clarke was one of the very few great forensic advocates of our own, or indeed of any, time who have succeeded in the House of Commons. While he was still a young man, and a junior at the Bar, his sensational capture for the Conservatives of a seat in the old Radical stronghold of Southwark at a by-election in February, 1880, was one of the main causes which prompted Lord Beaconsfield to dissolve Parliament in the following month. Oddly enough, at the ensuing general election, in April, Clarke lost the seat which he had so recently won. He found speedy consolation in July, 1880, at Plymouth, which he represented for twenty years. He soon made his mark in the House of Commons, and from 1886 to 1892 he was Solicitor-

General in Lord Salisbury's Government. It was a signal testimony to the position which he had attained that when the Front Opposition Bench, which had on it speakers of such ability as Balfour, Goschen and Hicks Beach, came to decide which of their number was to follow Mr. Gladstone, in the debate on the introduction of the new Home Rule Bill, their choice should have fallen upon Clarke.

There could hardly ever have been a more difficult parliamentary task. Not only was Mr. Gladstone still the greatest living master of the art of exposition, but no one outside the Cabinet could form any trustworthy forecast of what he was going to say. On the crucial question, for instance, of the relations of the Irish members and the Imperial Parliament, was he going for retention or exclusion? And if for retention, was it to be absolute, and for all purposes? Or intermittent, and only for some? The spokesman of the Opposition must be prepared, on the spur of the moment, to deal with any of the possible solutions of the problem which the Government might be going to present. Add to this, that he must have to begin his speech in the most depressing of all parliamentary conditions — the exodus of at least half the House to the Lobby, to discuss among themselves the Prime Minister's statement.

Clarke, however, was undismayed at the prospect and undertook the part assigned to him. I listened to every word of his speech, delivered for the most part in a half-empty House, and I agree with Lord George Hamilton that "it was one of the best debating performances" witnessed in our time. Lord George tells us that, in reply to his congratulations the next day,

Clarke said: "It was a tremendous brain-strain, and for the first time in my life I had, after speaking, a severe headache for an hour or two."[1]

Let me add two or three words here on the subject of Clarke's subsequent parliamentary career, recommending to all who are not already familiar with the book his interesting autobiography: "The Story of My Life."

When the Unionist Government was formed in 1895, he declined the Solicitor-Generalship, refusing to submit to the conditions proposed as to the abandonment or limitation of private practice. In 1897 Lord Salisbury offered him the Mastership of the Rolls, which he also refused, on the ground that "a purely judicial office would shut me out from that part of the work of my life which gives me most interest and pleasure" (*i.e.* parliamentary life). He has since said publicly that "no opportunity of accepting a judicial position" was given him later. The reason no doubt was his avowed hostility to the policy of the Government which led to the Boer War. In the debates on the subject in 1899–1900 he crossed swords with Mr. Chamberlain, and certainly did not get the worst of the encounter. He did not stand at the "Khaki" election of 1900, and though in January, 1906, he attained one of the ambitions of his life by being returned at the top of the poll for the City of London, the Tariff Reformers made his seat uncomfortable, and he resigned in May of that year for reasons of health.

Happily he is still in the full enjoyment of a green old age, and when a dinner was given to me in Lincoln's

[1] "Parliamentary Reminiscences and Reflections, 1886–1906," p. 210.

Inn Hall by the Bench and Bar, on my being raised to the peerage, Clarke kindly undertook, and performed with all his old grace and felicity of speech, the duty of proposing my health.

My name appeared on the back of the Home Rule Bill, and I took part in the debate on the Second Reading on April 14, 1893. I endeavoured to meet the main points which had emerged, and which now belong for the most part to the dust-bin of history. I dealt especially with the claim put forward by a section of the Province of Ulster, which at that time repudiated separate treatment, and yet insisted that because a majority of its inhabitants objected to Home Rule the rest of Ireland, which wanted it, should not have it. Mr. Balfour had recently crossed St. George's Channel to stimulate and stiffen the forces of potential resistance, and, with perhaps undue levity, I described his appeals as the "conditional incitements of an academic anarchist." The leading Unionist journal was good enough to say the next morning that I had "made perhaps as good a case for my clients as anyone who has yet spoken on the same side": a criticism which I quote because, through all the stages of this controversy for the next twenty years, my interventions and arguments were, after the conventional fashion of epic poetry, always disposed of by Unionist critics with the same epithet—"forensic."

The session of 1893, which lasted well into 1894, was almost exclusively taken up with the Home Rule Bill, and other Government measures which failed to survive the destructive activities of the House of Lords. It furnished the materials for the first chapter in the annals of "ploughing the sands," which is the fittest description of the legislative efforts—with the notable exception of Sir W. Harcourt's great Budget of 1894 —of Mr. Gladstone's last and Lord Rosebery's only administration. It was what is called an object lesson in the difficulties of attempting to carry on government without an independent majority in the House of Commons. It terminated in the resignation and final demission of office by Mr. Gladstone. He left his life work only half done: unfinished but not wasted. He had, years before, unconsciously selected his own epitaph:

Exoriare aliquis nostris ex ossibus ultor.

As I said at the time, March, 1894: "Under the glorious weight of years spent in the service of great causes and high ideals he has laid down the bow which none but himself could bend." But neither I nor any other prophet could have foreseen whence the Avenger was in due time to appear. Mr. Gladstone would no doubt have quoted once more from his favourite Virgil:

Quod minime reris, Graia pandetur ab urbe.[1]

No one, it was conceded on all hands, could fill Mr. Gladstone's place, but I was one of the majority of his late colleagues who held that in all the circumstances Lord Rosebery was best fitted for the succession. There are great and obvious drawbacks, under a constitution such as ours, which does not allow a Minister to speak in both Chambers, in having the head of the Government in the House of Lords. Since Lord Salisbury gave up office in 1902, the experiment has never been

[1] Æneid, VI, 96.

repeated; the latest and in some ways a crucial case of its disuse being the preference shown by the rank and file of the Tory party for Mr. Baldwin over Lord Curzon in 1923. But, in 1894, the only commoner on the Liberal side who had, from length of service and pre-eminence of talent, a *prima facie* claim to the Prime Ministership, Sir William Harcourt, was ineligible: not because he was disliked or distrusted, but because he was believed by those who had worked with him not to possess some of the qualities which are essential for the command of a not very seaworthy vessel, doomed to navigate its course, more or less without compass or chart, through waters both deep and shallow, strewn with perils seen and unseen.

The choice of Lord Rosebery certainly did not imply any preponderance, even for the moment, of the "Whig" element in the Cabinet. On the contrary, Lord Rosebery was a prime favourite with some of the most democratic sections of the party: especially in London, where his chairmanship, both tactful and driving, of the first County Council had secured for him the whole-hearted confidence of the Progressives. His candidature was known to have the warm approval of Mr. John Morley, and was endorsed by what were then considered some of the principal of the Radical organs in the Press. Moreover, it was not long before it became apparent that on what was rapidly becoming the dominant issue of the immediate future — the relations between the two Houses of Parliament — he was ready to take a more active, and indeed a more aggressive, line than either Sir William Harcourt, or even Mr. Morley himself. From the platform campaign which he carried on with vigour in the early months of his headship, they both—Harcourt in particular—stood almost ostentatiously aloof.[1]　There cropped up from time to time questions of Foreign Policy—for the most part of minor importance—on which differences arose in the Cabinet, but those differences did not follow sectional lines.　Although I was generally classified as a thorough-going "Roseberyite," I more than once in those matters took Harcourt's side.

The personnel of the Cabinet remained very much as Mr. Gladstone had left it, the principal changes being the accession of Lord Kimberley to the Foreign Office and of Henry Fowler to the India Office.　No one who was there will say that it was a pleasant Cabinet to sit in.　But considering the internal relations between one or two of its leading members, and the fortuitous majorities upon which it had to depend for its existence from day to day,[2] it made on the whole a very presentable appearance in the House of Commons.　Harcourt's own Budget, which absorbed practically the whole of the session of 1894, was one of the most remarkable personal *tours de force* since the palmy days of Mr. Gladstone.　Fowler created for himself a reputation as a parliamentary debater of the first class by his speech on the Indian cotton duties.　I myself—except for an occasional bout with Mr. Chamberlain—was occupied during the session of 1895 in the mornings in piloting my Factories and

[1] See Gardiner's "Life of Harcourt."
[2] It was defeated during the first week of its life by an amendment to the Address moved by one of its own supporters.

18 94. Marriage solemnized at *the Parish Church* of *S¹. George Hanover Square* in the County of *London*

No.	When Married.	Name and Surname.	Age.	Condition.	Rank or Profession.	Residence at the time of Marriage.	Father's Name and Surname.	Rank or Profession of Father.
817	May 10 1894	Herbert Henry Asquith	41 years	Widower	Secretary of State	127 Imperial Street	Joseph Dixon Asquith	Manufacturer
		Margaret Emma Alice Tennant	30 years	Spinster	—	40 Grosvenor Square	Charles Tennant Baronet	Baronet

Married in the *Parish Church* ———— according to the Rites and Ceremonies of the Established Church, by ———— or after Banns by me,
Randall T. Rogers;
H¹. Thursford
Chambers

This Marriage was solemnized between us, { Herbert Henry Asquith / Margaret Emma Alice Tennant }

in the Presence of us, { A. K. James Ralfour / Charles Tennant / H. H. Thursford / Ribblesdale / M¹. M°Cann }

Workshops Bill among the shallows of a Grand Committee, and for the rest of the day and part of the night in heaving through, inch by inch and almost word by word, the earlier clauses of the Bill for the Disestablishment of the Welsh Church. The short interludes, when other Bills were on, were generally taken up in interchanging amenities with deputations from the Welsh members, who did not always speak with the same tongue. The last evening that we spent in Committee we finished with a Government majority of seven.

The next day a snap vote in a thin House on a side issue directed against Campbell-Bannerman, who was the most popular member of the administration, brought our labours and our official life to an end.

After all, it was not altogether a case of "ploughing the sands." The fundamental principles of Harcourt's "confiscatory" Budget are now an integral part of our fiscal system, and the disestablished Welsh Church, the much compassionated victim of "sacrilege" and "spoliation," is pursuing with growing efficiency its independent life.

On this subject I may introduce here a letter from Dr. Gore, then Canon of Westminster, dated March 23, 1895:

I cannot refrain — though I am not wholly on your side in the matter — from expressing my gratitude as a Churchman for your speech on Thursday night on the Welsh Disestablishment Bill. What it is right to do is a difficult question and I will not inflict my views on you, but I am sure you deserve the gratitude of Churchmen for the pains you were at to grasp and state the idea of the Church in its relation to the State. You seemed to me to distinguish the Church and the Establishment in a way that left nothing to be desired. We haven't met for many years, but I thought you would forgive my writing this.

*   *   *   *   *

In chronological sequence this is the place to record that I was married for the second time in May, 1894, to Margot, youngest daughter of Sir Charles Tennant. My life has since that date been lived in full partnership with her, and all our experiences, both of joy and sorrow — and there has been a large measure of both — have been shared in common. By force of circumstances we have seemed to live much in the glare of publicity, but our true life has been elsewhere.

CHAPTER XVIII

MR. GLADSTONE AND THE QUEEN

MR. GLADSTONE'S growing physical disabilities had compelled him, in his final months of office, to withdraw to some extent from active daily participation in the rough and tumble of parliamentary conflict. But, as was said of one of our most illustrious generals, the knowledge that he was in command, and might at any moment appear in the field of battle, meant more, both to his followers and his antagonists, than the addition of many battalions to the roll-call of his rank and file. Since the removal of Lord Beaconsfield, he was the one man of genius left in British politics. But unlike Lord Beaconsfield, who in his later years enjoyed in an exceptional degree the sympathy and even the affection of Queen Victoria, Mr. Gladstone, the most loyal of Ministers, had to the end of his official life the misfortune to be on terms of almost chronic friction with the Sovereign.

I will cite one or two illustrations from his correspondence with me while I was Home Secretary.

The first is on a small question of Honours, the particulars of which I forget.

BLACKCRAIG,
18 *Sept.*, '92.

MY DEAR ASQUITH,—

Once when Palmerston had been put out I commended in speaking to Graham his conduct in Opposition as being moderate, when Graham replied to me, "His bones are sore." My bones are still sore, since the Queen laid me on my back for my birthday list of Knights and made me cut out a fair percentage. I think, however, with you that the case is good, but I should wish to reserve it for three or perhaps four weeks when there would I think still be time for accomplishing the business before the expiry of this year.

Yours sincerely,
W. E. Gladstone.

The second is of more historical importance, showing as it does the Queen's invincible repugnance to Home Rule and to any form of Disestablishment. It referred to the following letter from Queen Victoria to Mr. Gladstone:

Windsor Castle,
25 Feb., 1893.

The Queen was much surprised to find on reading the report of the debate in the House of Commons on Thursday night that, what Mr. Gladstone did not sufficiently explain, and therefore led her to suppose was only a Bill for suspending claims founded on vested Church interests in Wales, — was, as Mr. Asquith admitted, the first step towards the disestablishment and disendowment of the Church of England!!

There is no "Church of Wales," and therefore this measure is in reality directed against the whole Church! The Queen thinks Mr. Gladstone cannot have fully considered this, and she must say this is a very serious step and one which she cannot help contemplating with great alarm.

She now recognizes the force of the protest of the deputation of Convocation received on Thursday in their address, in the answer to which she was advised to ignore the remonstrance of the Bishops and Clergy against this calamitous proceeding.

Surely Mr. Gladstone cannot be aware of the strong feeling of uneasiness and apprehension which the Home Rule Bill produces, and to add this measure to it is most unfortunate. Had the Queen known the real intention of the

Government she would not have passed over in silence the protest of the Bishops and Clergy.

The Queen trusts Mr. Gladstone may yet pause before taking so disastrous a step as to attempt to disestablish part of the English Church of which she is the Head, and of which she always thought Mr. Gladstone was a loyal member.

Of this curious fulmination Mr. Gladstone sent me a copy in a characteristic letter:

10 DOWNING STREET,
WHITEHALL.
Feb. 26, '93.

Secret.

MY DEAR ASQUITH, —

The enclosed is in no way formidable except that it will entail on me the necessity of writing rather a long letter.

Can you supply me with any explanation, such as it would be useful to submit, on the reference to you in the second page? It is not a matter of necessity, but I thought it possible you might like to say something.[1]

Her Majesty's studies have not yet carried her out of the delusive belief that she is still by law the "head" of the Church of England.

Yours sincerely,
W. E. GLADSTONE.

It is well known that Mr. Gladstone was ready at any rate to defer his resignation, and to advise a dissolution of Parliament, in order to try conclusions at once in the electoral arena on the issues which had already arisen between the House of Lords and the Liberal party. His colleagues were, so far as my recollection goes, though the matter was never brought formally

---

[1] I no doubt pointed out in reply that Her Majesty's reference to what I was alleged to have said was founded on a complete misapprehension.

before the Cabinet, unanimously opposed to an immediate dissolution. Such a step would be universally construed as an indication, whatever might be the result of the polls, that Mr. Gladstone's leadership was coming to a close, while the Harcourt budget, which was to be the chief legislative feature of 1894, and with which it was confidently and correctly predicted that the House of Lords would not venture to interfere, would have to be sacrificed. There was certainly no disposition in any quarter to underestimate the gravity of his loss both to the party and the State; nor any want of consideration to him personally in the weeks of negotiation, indecision, and carefully preserved secrecy, which preceded the final disclosure.

I still think that his colleagues were right in differing from their venerable leader.

I cannot deny myself the pleasure of inserting here the reply which Mr. Gladstone was good enough to make to my letter of regret and sympathy. As a matter of interest it is also reproduced in facsimile:

10 DOWNING STREET,

WHITEHALL.

Mch. 5, '94.

MY DEAR ASQUITH, —

I cannot sufficiently thank you for the letter which you have added to the other touching utterances I have received from my colleagues, whom I cannot yet quite bring myself (as I must soon) to call my late colleagues.

It is in one sense a satisfaction to me to feel daily the solidity of the ground on which my resignation has been based: because it prevents all necessity from moving onwards in mind to that other ground which by the calendar and the clock we are fast approaching.

The future is in my mind a clouded picture: but I am glad that the prolongation of my political life has given me an opportunity of helping the arrangements under which you have taken your stand in political life.   I well remember the impression made upon me by your speech at the Eighty Club, the first time I ever saw or heard you.   It has since been, of course, deepened and confirmed.   Great problems are before us: and I know no one more likely to face them, as I hope and believe, not only with a manly strength, but with a determined integrity of mind.

I most earnestly hope that you may be enabled to fulfil your part, which will certainly be an arduous one.

Believe me,
Ever sincerely yours,
W. E. GLADSTONE.

My dear Asquith

I cannot suffici-
ently thank you for the
letter which you have
added to the other touching
utterances I have received
from my colleagues, whom
I cannot yet quite bring
myself (as I must soon) to
call my late colleagues.

It is no more than a satisfaction to me to feel deeply

the solidity of the ground
on which my resignation
has been based : because
it prevents all necessity
from moving onwards in
enmity to that other ground
which by the calendar.
and the clock we are just
approaching.
the future is in my view
a clouded future : but I
am glad that the prolonga
tion of my political life has
given me an opportunity

of helping the arrange-
ments under which you have
taken your stand in political life. I cannot forget how
the impression made upon me
by your speech at the Eighty
Club, the first time I was,
saw or heard you. It has
since been, of course, deepened & confirmed. Great
problems are before us: and
I know no one more likely
to face them, as I hope and believe,
not only with a manly
strength, but with a determined integrity of mind.

I most earnestly hope that you may be enabled to fulfil your part, which will certainly be an arduous one. Believe me

Ever sincerely yours

W. E. Gladstone

CHAPTER XIX

1895–1905

L ORD ROSEBERY'S resignation, in June, 1895, was followed by the formation, for the first time, of a Coalition Government between the Tories and the Liberal Unionists. Both leaders and rank and file had now, after ten years of close and daily co-operation, overcome the shyness and even suspicion which hovered over and to some extent embarrassed their first *rapprochement.* Each had gradually learned to forgive and forget; and the formal union between Lord Salisbury and Mr. Balfour on the one side, and Lord Hartington and Mr. Chamberlain on the other, was nothing more than the regularization and registration of an accomplished fact. There was no need for wedding-bells, or even for the ceremonial ode which Lord Salisbury's newly created Poet Laureate, Alfred Austin, would have been only too happy to supply. The dissolution was disastrous to the Liberals,[1] who by the resignation of their own Government had invited and even courted defeat. Harcourt, who, like Morley, had lost his seat, and found refuge in one of the " Celtic fringes," maintained an unruffled front, but there was, for a brief interlude, the nearest approach that I can remember, with the exception of the months succeeding King Edward's death, to a truce in controversial politics, until the outbreak of the War.

1 The new House of Commons was composed of 411 Unionists, 177 Liberals, and 82 Nationalists: a Unionist majority of 152.

I had survived the electoral storm, and even — like Campbell-Bannerman — managed to increase my majority; but it was necessary to find *de quoi vivre*, and as I have said I resolved to return to the practice of my old profession. I had been away from it for three years — a serious gap — but my interest in its problems and struggles was unabated, and before long I recovered the ground which in my absence I had necessarily lost. My old leader and chief, Charles Russell, now Lord Russell of Killowen, had become Lord Chief Justice and head of the Common Law Bench. Clarke and Carson had established their title as the most formidable advocates at Nisi Prius Bar. In the Privy Council and the Railway Commission I found that the competitors who were most to be feared were Haldane and C. A. Cripps (afterwards Lord Parmoor).

I have nothing to add to what I have written elsewhere on the Jameson Raid, and the proceedings and report of the House of Commons Committee of Inquiry; or upon the resignation, in October, 1896, by Lord Rosebery of the leadership of the Liberal party, to be succeeded after a short interval by the abdication of Sir William Harcourt, with the acquiescence and sympathy of Mr. John Morley. The fortunes of the Campbell-Bannerman regime which followed are unique in our party history: in the course of little more than five years it witnessed both the apparent disruption of the Liberals, and their achievement of an unexampled electoral victory at the polls.

Little noticed at the time, and even less remembered now, is an incident which perhaps may be regarded as, in Horatio's words, a "prologue to the omen coming on."

The issue between Free Trade and Protection had long been considered in this country as a thing of the past. Protection, as an item in the Tory programme, had been abandoned by Lord Derby as far back as 1851. Disraeli had the sagacity to leave it to "dumb forgetfulness" in an unvisited grave.

A small band of Tory "Die-hards" (as they would now be called) in the 'eighties, headed by Mr. James Lowther, Mr. Ecroyd, and Colonel Howard Vincent, sought to revive it under the guise of "Fair Trade," on the pretext that our leading industries were being "murdered" inch by inch by foreign competition. They received for a long time no encouragement from the Front Bench, and not very much from the rank and file of their party. Lord Randolph Churchill, still in his mutinous days, and casting about to find a constructive creed for his "Tory Democracy," dallied with the heresy in his famous Blackpool speech. But it was the most half-hearted and short-lived of flirtations, and henceforward he seems to have left it severely alone. Mr. Chamberlain, who was then at the head of the Board of Trade, was wont from time to time to honour it with a contemptuous mention, as he expounded the orthodox doctrines of the highest and driest Free Trade in their most austere and uncompromising garb. At a later date and after the Liberal rupture, he had seemed to view with some favour the idea of "Imperial Zollverein," but as I said at Leicester in the autumn of 1896, it was apparently a *ballon d'essai* which "in light-hearted fashion he had thrown

into the air to see which way the wind would carry it."
A few weeks before I spoke, Mr. Balfour at Sheffield
had taken the opportunity to make a magisterial pro-
nouncement exposing the ignorance of Howard Vincent and his associates of the elementary economics of
international trade. As I pointed out in commenting
at Leicester upon this discourse, while Mr. Balfour
had lucidly "explained the A B C of Free Trade" for
the edification of his followers, there was no mistaking
the growing sympathy which was by this time being
manifested in influential quarters in the Conservative
party in favour of some form, veiled or unveiled, of
Protection.

This note of warning passed almost entirely un-
heeded.

The South African War, and the controversies to
which it led, had curious and unforeseeable effects upon
the development of domestic politics.

For a time the war was undoubtedly an asset of considerable value in the balance-sheet of the Government
of the day. The blunderings of pre-war diplomacy,
and the absence of pre-war preparation, were forgiven
when the early disasters in the field were repaired by
the success of our arms. Mr. Chamberlain and Lord
Milner seemed to be firmly established in popular
favour.

The Liberal party, on the other hand, was broken
into fragments. Mr. Gladstone was gone; his two
successors in the leadership (if successors they can be
called) had one after the other resigned; another of the
most respected of its "elder statesmen," Mr. John
Morley, though he did not conceal his views, was hold-

ing aloof from active politics; and the new leader, Campbell-Bannerman, who had the good-will of all sections, spent many anxious months in the effort to damp down, if he could not extinguish, the combustible elements around him which were constantly threatening to break into flame. The dangerous practice of coining nicknames was already coming into fashion. Harcourt, Morley, and ultimately Campbell-Bannerman himself, were labelled as " pro-Boers"; Rosebery, Grey, Fowler and myself as "Imperialists." Not a few of the portents which herald disruption were discerned by the Tadpoles and Tapers of the day in the political firmament, and it seemed to them there was a risk that the schism of 1886 was going to be repeated.

The Government took advantage in 1900 of what must be admitted to have been a tempting situation. They dissolved Parliament. If the " Khaki " election did not fulfil the expectation of its promoters—for it left the relative numbers of the two great parties practically unchanged—yet it seemed to assure the Government of an extended lease of power for another five or six years. And this turned out to be their undoing. For it led them to introduce reactionary domestic legislation, particularly in regard to education, which was profoundly unpalatable to the Liberal-Unionist side of the partnership. And it gave Mr. Chamberlain, as the now recognized Empire-builder-in-Chief to the Coalition, the opportunity of raising the flag of Imperial Preference, which had an equally disintegrating effect upon his Tory associates.

This was bad enough, but worse was to follow. Almost in the twinkling of an eye it became apparent that the Liberal party had been gratuitously presented with the one specific which was most certain to salve its wounds and to re-establish its unity. The lately warring sections fraternized, without difficulty or delay, in a cause which both by their tradition and their convictions commanded their united allegiance. *Quinquennium Mirabile.*

CHAPTER XX
PERSONAL SKETCHES

I HAVE now reached the end of the Unionist regime which lasted in effect from 1886 to 1906. The protracted death-bed scene, and the final convulsions, I have already endeavoured to depict in my previous book.

This may therefore be an appropriate halting-place to say something of a few of the personages with whom, in the struggles which preceded the downfall of the Coalition, I was in contact or collision.[1]

The greatest personal loss sustained by the House of Commons in the interval between the removal of Mr. Gladstone and the resignation of the Coalition (1905) was undoubtedly that of Sir William Harcourt. He had ceased for some years to be an official leader, but the keenness of his interest in the shifting fortunes of the party fray did not lose its edge, and the zest for life which never left him to the last was agreeably stimulated and varied by his succession to the family estate. Though by nature and habit a man of contention, his happiest hours were spent in the company of his devoted son and daughter-in-law and their children at Nuneham. *Sunt risus rerum:* and he used to exclaim with humorous bitterness that in his old age his sins had found him out. The author of the Budget of 1894 was called upon to pay death duties on his own extended scale; and the uncompromising opponent of

---

[1] Various sketches are included here which, if Lord Oxford had lived to complete the book, might have been subject to other arrangement. The Executors.

the new Education Act found himself burdened at Nuneham as the principal landowner in the parish, with the main cost of the upkeep of a denominational school! The old warrior had the most enviable of ends: he passed quietly away in his sleep, without the pangs of parting, or any of the disabilities of infirmity and disease.

SIR CHARLES DILKE

Another conspicuous parliamentary figure was that of Sir Charles Dilke who continued to be an active member of the House of Commons for some years after the downfall of the Unionist regime. It was under his chairmanship, and at a meeting of his constituents at Cinderford in the Forest of Dean (October 8, 1903), that I opened the counter-campaign to that which Mr. Chamberlain had started two days before at Glasgow in the great fiscal war. His last important public service was his presidency of the Committee of the Commons, which in 1906 reported in favour of the differentiation of earned and unearned income for purposes of income tax.

Dilke was out of the House during all the early years of my own membership, and I was not a personal witness of any of the steps by which, despite some not inconsiderable natural disadvantages, he had built up for himself a great parliamentary position. He was never up to the last an agreeable speaker to listen to, and though, as he showed in his " Prince Florestan of Monaco," not without a vein of humour and sarcasm,[1]

[1] He was even credited with the authorship of the "Fight in Dame Europa's School" — an anonymous *jeu d'esprit* which had a large circulation in the early days of the Franco-German War of 1870-1.

his memory was over-stocked with detail, and there was a lack of the sense of proportion in his voluminous encyclopædia of political knowledge. He was, moreover, too apt to assume that his audience had the same intimate knowledge as himself of the by-ways of history and the technique of administration. This often gave an air of pedantry to really good stuff. For example, speaking to his constituents at Chelsea, he once said:[1] "For expressing an opinion favourable to Continental disarmament he would perhaps be styled by the Conservatives a partisan of 'peace at any price.' He would, however, comfort himself with the recollection that, so far as he knew, that phrase was first used *in a memorandum by F. Von Gentz in* 1815, in which the words were contemptuously applied to the opinions of Lord Castlereagh and the Duke of Wellington a few months before Waterloo."

The personal and political friendships which for so many years united Mr. Chamberlain and Sir Charles Dilke is one of the most pleasing and touching incidents of our times. Dilke—who had in the spring of 1880 a more commanding parliamentary position, as well as much longer experience—was more than content that Chamberlain should take his place in the new Gladstone Cabinet. Later, when the cloud descended upon Dilke which for the rest of his life overshadowed his career, Chamberlain's faithful and chivalrous devotion never failed him for a moment. It may be recalled that Morley, speaking in the House of Commons on February 8, 1904, said of Chamberlain that "he possesses in

[1] February, 1882 — Jennings's "Anecdotal History."

a most marked and peculiar degree the genius of friendship."

The new-comers whom the fiscal controversy helped
to bring into prominence—Mr. Bonar Law, Lord
Hugh Cecil and Mr. Winston Churchill—were drawn
from the Conservative ranks. Lord Hugh and Mr.
Churchill happily still adorn the House of Commons
and keep alive its best traditions as a debating assembly.

BONAR LAW

Mr. Bonar Law's career came to a premature close,
after he had attained and held for not more than two
hundred days the office of Prime Minister. I was
never on terms of intimacy with him, though we sat for
a time together in the first Coalition Cabinet in the
War. I remember well his maiden speech, which
earned him without any delay a subordinate place in
the moribund Ministry of Mr. Balfour. Throughout
the fiscal fight his resourceful sophistries, as I thought
them, made him a formidable antagonist. But that in
the mutations of politics he was destined to become the
head of a Government seemed as unlikely then as
twenty-five years earlier it would have seemed to predict
a similar future for Sir Henry Campbell-Bannerman.

He was a man of considerable personality, as he
showed when he upset the Coalition Government of
Mr. Lloyd George, at the temporary sacrifice, at any
rate, of the co-operation of some old and intimate colleagues. He returned from the "Tranquillity" general
election with an adequate majority, and if he had lived
history might have taken a different turn.

ARTHUR ACLAND

Arthur Acland came of one of the oldest landowning families in England with traditions of various forms of public service, and he received the conventional education of boys of his class at Rugby and Christ Church. In the schools at Oxford he took a couple of "seconds," and though he seems to have organized in his own college for economic and political discussions a small body of undergraduates and young dons which went by the name of the "Inner Circle," he was not widely known in the University, and I believe never took part in the debates at the Union.

He was from the first deeply interested in economic questions, especially in their Labour aspect. He took Orders, but soon unfrocked himself, and as Steward of Christ Church and then as Bursar of Balliol gained first-hand knowledge of the administrative side of the business of landowning. In 1885 when the extended county franchise came into operation, he stood for the newly created mining constituency of Rotherham, and retained his seat there during the whole of his parliamentary life.

I had never known him at Oxford, belonging myself to the next academic generation; and it was not till six or more months after his entrance into the House of Commons that I met him there as a fellow-member in the brief autumn session of 1886. I forget how and when we first drew together, but certainly from the early part of the session of 1887 we were on terms not only of political intimacy but of close personal friendship. Of our little group, which Morley has described

in his "Recollections" more impartially than I am
able to do, Acland was in age the senior member and
I suppose that, according to the calendar, Sydney Buxton and I came next. Haldane occupied the *via media*,
and Edward Grey and Tom Ellis were the juniors.
The oldest among us was barely forty. During the six
years of that Parliament (1886–92) we sat together,
talked together, generally worked together, and as a
rule, to which spasms of individuality now and again
provided occasional exceptions, we voted together.
Each of us made his own contribution to the common
stock: but we all acknowledged in Arthur Acland our
corporate conscience. As Morley truly says of us, we
were a "working alliance, not a school," and we "took
our politics to heart."[1] "To Acland," he adds, "be-
longs special credit for keeping in touch with the
labour people and their mind." As I have said elsewhere, when in 1890 the prospect of a Liberal administration seemed imminent, we of the "new blood"
hoped to see Acland its Chief Whip.

When in 1892 Mr. Gladstone formed his last Government, Acland was admitted to the Cabinet. Our
legislative opportunities were severely circumscribed
by the smallness of the Government majority, and the
vigilant and uncompromising hostility of the House of
Lords. But within those limits, Acland gave abundant
proofs of a high order of administrative talent, and left
an enduring impress of his strong personality on his
own office of Education. Harcourt, probably the most
ruthless economist who has ever presided over the Exchequer, writes to him (January, 1893) :

[1] "Recollections," Vol. I, pp. 323–4.

I have just sanctioned an additional £250,000, or there-abouts, for your department, and here you are, like Oliver, asking for more. There are sixteen of us, and at your present allowance of increment that will add just £4,000,000 to the Estimates.

He made free education a reality, and raised the age of compulsory attendance at school; but the most controversial of his administrative acts was his circular about school buildings, which were in many districts insanitary and unsuitable, directing his inspectors to report on them with a view to structural improvement. This was a plain and necessary step towards the attainment of educational efficiency, but it was treated in the clerical world, in which the "unfrocked" Minister was regarded with the same suspicion as later, for a similar reason, was M. Combes in France, as a blow specially aimed at the denominational schools and "religious" education. According to one of the most assiduous of their parliamentary champions, Sir Arthur Griffith-Boscawen, it was the "direct cause of that 'intolerable strain' which nearly paralyzed the Voluntary Schools, and led up to the unfortunate legislation of 1902."[1]

Acland was the least self-advertising of men. Though a clear and vigorous speaker, he made no pretence to oratory, and had a natural abhorrence for all forms of clap-trap. It is amusing to find that one of his platform utterances once aroused the apprehension of King Edward, then Prince of Wales. "When one of the junior Ministers, Mr. Arthur Acland, fulminated against the peers in a speech at Portsmouth (1893), the Prince wrote to his old Oxford correspondent, Sir

[1] "Fourteen Years in Parliament," p. 58.

Henry Acland, the speaker's uncle: 'It is a pity he should imitate the Bombastes Furioso style of an older colleague of his.' Bombastes Furioso was the Prince's sobriquet for Sir William Harcourt."[1] This must have been a unique and very uncharacteristic indiscretion on Acland's part.

During the dreary and protracted debates in the Committee stage of the Home Rule Bill in 1893, Acland used to provide dinner every night for Morley and myself in his small official room somewhere in the bowels of the House of Commons. He was the best of company, with a wide range of knowledge and a ready sense of humour, and we used to resent the summonses of the division bell, which too often spoilt our dinner and interrupted our talk.

Lord Morley has left a vivid and indeed picturesque narrative of the circumstances which preceded and accompanied Lord Rosebery's succession to Mr. Gladstone in the office of Prime Minister.[2] The choice of Rosebery in preference to Harcourt was in accordance (he says) with the " dominant view of the leading junta inside the Cabinet—I mean Spencer, Asquith, Acland, and myself." I only refer to the matter here as illustrating the influence and authority which in the course of less than two years Acland had acquired with his colleagues.

In the dissolution which followed the fall of the Rosebery Government, Acland was re-elected for his old seat. But his health, which had always been uncertain, made the daily routine of the House of Com-

[1] "Biography of King Edward," by Sidney Lee, p. 533.
[2] "Recollections," Vol. II, pp. 1–23.

mons irksome to him, and he retired in 1899 from parliamentary life. He did not, however, lose touch with politics or with his old colleagues, and Mr. Balfour's reactionary Education Bill of 1902 brought him back into active participation in our council. After the Liberal victory at the election of 1906, he rendered from outside invaluable assistance to the new Government on such matters as education and land. He refused a peerage in 1908.

During the War he brought out an anthology from the patriotic poetry of Wordsworth, with an illuminating introduction of his own.

There have been few men in my lifetime whom it was a greater privilege to know, or with whom it was an equal pleasure to work. He had quick intuitions and a resolute tenacity of purpose which was often a useful goad to comrades of a more lethargic temperament; and his social sympathies, like those of Arnold Toynbee, were deep and keen without any taint of sentimentalism or cant.

LORD COURTNEY

Leonard Courtney was a Cornishman, who began life in his youth as a clerk in the Bolithos' Bank. While thus engaged during the day for five and a half years, he read classics and mathematics in the evening with a Cambridge graduate. Winning a sizarship at St. John's he was enabled to go to Cambridge, where his mathematical powers brought him to the front and he graduated as Second Wrangler in 1855. He came to London, was called to the Bar, wrote on political economy, and became a professional journalist. He joined the staff of *The Times* in 1864, and from that date to his retirement he is said to have contributed to the paper some 3,000 articles. Those were the palmy days of the Delane editorship, and it does credit to both the parties concerned that a man of Courtney's strong individuality and advanced views should not have been galled by the harness which, as a constant leader-writer in the great organ of the *juste milieu*, he had to wear. He ceased his connection with it when at a by-election in 1876 he was elected for Liskeard, and took his seat in the House of Commons as a member of the Radical group.

When Mr. Gladstone formed his second administration in April, 1880, he offered a minor post in it to Courtney, who refused, as he desired to establish his position in the House as a private member free from the trammels of office. But his entry into official life was not long delayed, and between 1881 and 1884 he held successively the Under-Secretaryship of the Home and Colonial Offices and the Secretaryship of the Treasury. He was of too independent a character to be a model colleague, as he showed on at least two occasions, in the course of the debates on the Franchise and Redistribution Bills in 1884. First he refused to vote against a woman suffrage amendment to the Franchise Bill, in company with Dilke and Fawcett, who were also members of the Government. This act of insubordination perturbed the Prime Minister, but was passed over. But a little later in the same year his loyalty to the other of the two causes to which he gave lifelong devotion—proportional representation—which was not provided for in the Redistribution Bill led him to resign his office. He was never afterwards a member of a Government.

Courtney was pre-eminently a House of Commons man, and no one was more versed in its rules and procedure. In the session of 1885, he frequently took the place of the Chairman of Committees, and was from the first not lacking in self-confidence. "One Friday night," wrote his wife in her journal, "he came home in great spirits, having called half the House to order, including the Grand Old Man. The Prime Minister took it very well, and afterwards expressed his admiration to Mr. Rathbone."[1] In the following year, when Mr. Gladstone, with whom he was always a favourite, was again in office, he was, though not a Home Ruler, appointed Chairman at the instance of the Government. At the election in July, 1886, he stood as a Liberal Unionist, and when the new Parliament met he was re-appointed Chairman — an office which he held during the first six years of my parliamentary life.

The office of Chairman is as difficult as — in some ways more difficult than — that of Speaker. It requires a clear head, a quick and nimble mind, the power of taking and sticking to instant decisions, an equable temper, a large stock of patience, and a measure of personal authority. In these qualities Courtney was not excelled by any among the series of Chairmen whom I have known and watched at their work. He was certainly no respecter of persons. Lady Courtney records another illustration in May, 1887: "He distinguished himself by refusing Mr. W. H. Smith (leader of the House) the closure. . . . A few days later he called

[1] "Life of Lord Courtney," by Gooch, p. 252.

Gladstone to order in the middle of a wrangle between the two front benches, and made him sit down." I have myself seen him, when Mr. Gladstone rose to take part in debate, pass him over and call upon some obscure member on the back benches. No one can say of him that he ever courted popularity. Rarely has there been a man whose exterior was so appropriate a garment for his character and temperament, and some of Lockwood's best caricatures, jotted down on the margin of the Order paper, were devoted to different aspects and angles of "Mr. Courtney in the Chair."

When the Liberals came in with their modest majority, after the election of 1892, Courtney, though still a stiff anti-Home Ruler, gave a general support to the rest of their programme. In March, 1895, Peel resigned the Speakership, and Harcourt, with the consent of his colleagues, offered to nominate Courtney for the post. He was a member of the Liberal Unionist party, and not at all loved by our Irish allies. But he was undoubtedly better fitted by his qualifications and experience than anyone else in the House for the Chair, which, strange to say, was, at the moment, coveted by Campbell-Bannerman. A strong opposition to his candidature, however, speedily developed on the Opposition side, not only among the Conservatives, who were bent on the appointment of Sir M. W. Ridley, but among Courtney's Liberal Unionist colleagues, including Mr. Chamberlain. It was the attitude of the Liberal Unionists which led him ultimately to decline to stand, and the Government were for a time almost at their wits' end for a suitable candidate. Mr. S. Whitbread — the *vir pietate gravis* of the House — refused to be put in nomination. According to Lord Ullswater, in "A Speaker's Commentaries,"[1] "the story went that Mr. Labouchere, sitting one day next to Mr. Herbert Leon, saw a good-looking man passing up the floor of the House, and inquired who he was. He was informed that it was Mr. Gully, Q.C., a leader of the Northern Circuit. 'Then that is the man for us,' said Labouchere; and he thereupon busied himself in promoting his candidature." However that may be, Gully became the Government candidate and just succeeded in beating Ridley. Mr. Balfour chaffed Sir W. Harcourt on his nomination: "Strange that you should want to put in the Chair a man that neither you nor I know by sight."

In 1896 Courtney was attacked by one of the most grievous of human afflictions — eye trouble; and he was never able to read again. He bore the calamity with unflinching courage, and did not in any way relax his interests or his activities in public affairs. He was generally an impressive and often a formidable speaker. His attack on the report of the Jameson Raid Committee had the effect of provoking Chamberlain beyond measure. Lady Courtney describes the scene in her journal: "I sat in Mrs. Gully's gallery between Mrs. Asquith and Mrs. Labouchere. The former was loud in praise of L. [Courtney] and Lady Frances Balfour spoke of it as his greatest effort this session. Anyhow, it simply infuriated Chamberlain, who made a very clever and biting speech, turning almost entirely to L., and hissing out his words at him almost like a snake."[2]

[1] Vol. I, p. 254.   [2] "Life of Lord Courtney," p. 348.

Courtney still sat among the Liberal Unionists below the gangway on the Government side, but when the South African War broke out his declared revolt against the Ministerial policy made him an "Outlander" among his old associates, and at the "Khaki" election in 1900 he was defeated. Six years later, though still an opponent of Home Rule, he stood for Edinburgh as a Liberal. He was once more defeated, and on Campbell-Bannerman's advice was raised to the peerage.

He spoke from time to time in the House of Lords, but his energies were mainly given to working outside for woman suffrage and proportional representation, and the other causes, such as the protection of the Eastern Christians, which engaged his special sympathies.

There was something angular about Courtney, and it is true, as Lord Ullswater says, that he did not suffer fools gladly. He never sat in a Cabinet: indeed his whole official life was confined to the holding for some four years of subordinate posts in the Government. He had not the temperament of a good party man, and was never able to subscribe to the whole creed of his political associates, or to repeat, without reservations and with becoming fervour, their favourite formulæ. In a sense he was an eclectic, but where the fortunes of his own chosen causes were concerned he was not far from being a fanatic. He was an isolated figure, but he won the respect of all whose respect was worth having.[1]

[1] His sister-in-law, Mrs. Sidney Webb, has put on record her impressions of him soon after he entered the family: "He brought to bear on our discussions a massive intelligence and an amazing memory, combined with the intellectual integrity and personal disinterestedness of a Superman" ("My Apprenticeship," pp. 175-6).

LORD BRYCE

If I were asked who among the persons directly or indirectly engaged in politics in our time was the best educated, I should be disposed to single out James Bryce. Acton, who was only incidentally a politician, had an even wider range of reading, and an equally tenacious and comprehensive memory. Lecky's knowledge, though it covered a large and varied field, was much more specialized, and the same was true of one who was a better artist, with greater gifts of presentation than either of them—John Morley. No man in these days can take all knowledge for his province, but Bryce came as near to being what may be called a universal specialist as any of his contemporaries. He was an excellent classical scholar who had won the Craven at Oxford. He moved with freedom among most of the modern languages, which are more than dialects, and which have a literature and history worth knowing. He was an historian who was equally at home in the mediæval and modern worlds: his "Holy Roman Empire" and "American Commonwealth" are textbooks which may be supplemented but are not likely to be superseded. He was a geographer, who had seen with his own eyes most of the countries of the world. Though not a mathematician or a physicist, he had quite a competent knowledge of such sciences as botany, geology and anthropology, and—if science it can be called—of jurisprudence. He was up to the end of a long and active life, a large part of which was given to the severely practical tasks of politics, administra-

tion, and even diplomacy, adding every day to his ac-
cumulated store of accurate and well-assorted knowledge. Though not the master of a distinguished style
either in writing or speech, he had the gift of lucid exposition, never overlaid with decoration or with pedantry. And what he knew in any of the many fields of
research over which his interests and his studies had
roamed was always accessible, both to himself and other
people. The American philosopher, William James,
once said in a vein of good-natured irony: "To Bryce
all facts are born free and equal."

He was by birth an Ulsterman, but of direct Scottish
extraction, won great distinction at Glasgow University and Oxford, was for years a Professor of Law, both
at Oxford and Manchester, and was a member or correspondent of the most famous of the learned societies
of Europe and America. He was in fact, from the
standpoint of culture, *totus teres atque rotundus.*

He was a good many years my senior, but I enjoyed
his friendship, and co-operated with him as a fellow-
worker and a colleague in some of the most strenuous
adventures of public life. He gave me valuable help
in the guerrilla warfare which was carried on against
the Welsh Church Bill.

At the time of the Boer War, and during the controversies which it raised in the Liberal party, Bryce
sided throughout with Campbell-Bannerman. When
the Liberal Cabinet was formed in December, 1905,
it was, I think, a not unnatural disappointment to him
that he was not offered a post of greater status in the
official hierarchy than that of Chief Secretary for Ireland. But he never betrayed any such feeling, and dur-

ing his short tenure of the office he tackled his job with indefatigable industry, and kept on the best of terms with the Irish.   No one could wish for a more loyal or steadfast comrade in counsel or in action.

In political history Bryce will be remembered mainly for two things.   The first was the enthusiastic interest which he shared with Mr. Gladstone in all efforts to emancipate and protect the Christian victims of Turkish misrule.   The other was his lifelong effort, by writing, speech and action, to attain a better common understanding between the democracies of Great Britain and the United States.   Soon after the advent of the Campbell-Bannerman Government, he was asked by the Prime Minister to undertake the Embassy at Washington, and though the holding of such a post cut him off from direct contact with English political life, he did not hesitate to accept.   His appointment was hailed with acclamation in America, and during his ambassadorship there he may almost be said to have become a national institution.   He probably knew as much of the genesis and structure of American government in all its aspects as any citizen of the United States.   I once heard him, when Theodore Roosevelt was on a visit here, and we lunched with a small party at Sir Edward Grey's, severely correct the ex-President, who, in the looseness of conversation, had lapsed into a mistake over some of the intricacies of the American constitution.

He was, when he suddenly passed away, an old man according to the calendar, but he had suffered no abatement either of faculties or interests: for he was one of those who never grow old.

LORD WOLVERHAMPTON

(Henry Fowler)

Fowler had already been six years in the House of Commons, and had served for a short time as Under-Secretary at the Home Office under Sir William Harcourt in the second administration of Mr. Gladstone, and as Secretary to the Treasury in the third, when I entered Parliament in 1886. His place was on the front Opposition bench, while we newcomers sat behind and aloft, and it was some time before I was brought into real contact with him, probably through the good offices of John Morley. Our acquaintance gradually ripened into friendship, and he became a regular guest at the annual dinner in Elm Park Gardens on the eve of the session, at which Morley entertained and admonished his younger and more mutinous friends.

Fowler was the son of a well-known Wesleyan minister, and although in later years he was sometimes to be found worshipping with Anglicans, he was from first to last a loyal Methodist. It was a source of pride to his denomination that he was the first Wesleyan to enter the Cabinet and to be created a peer. He began his professional life as a solicitor in Wolverhampton, and almost from the first took an active and ultimately a leading part in the municipal life of the town. Its senior member in the House of Commons was, and had been almost from time immemorial, Charles Villiers — the pioneer before Cobden and Bright of Free Trade and later a member of Lord Palmerston's last Cabinet. It was said that during the last twenty years of his parliamentary life Villiers never visited Wolverhampton, declining even to attend the unveiling of a statue which the faithful borough had erected in his honour. The fidelity of his constituents, however, never wavered, and at elections he used to be returned automatically at the head of the poll. Wolverhampton was then a two-membered constituency, and at the general election of 1880, Fowler, who was an ideal "local" candidate, was nominated by the Liberals as their second string, and became Villiers' colleague in the House of Commons.

He took his place below the gangway and was reckoned among the Radicals, and when three years afterwards Morley entered the House, he sat by or near him. Fowler was never at heart a Radical, nor perhaps was Morley, but the friendship between them, notwithstanding occasional political divergences and marked differences of temperament and outlook, persisted to the end. He soon became, as his daughter tells us, a House of Commons man in the fullest and most unqualified sense.

His enthusiasm for the House of Commons knew no abatement, even when matured by long years of familiarity and experience. He never left his first love in spirit; and even on the day when he took his seat in "another place," great though he felt the honour, glad though he was at the distinction as a crown to his labours, yet he alone knew with what a tender and yearning regret he realized that his House of Commons life was over, and the familiar green benches would know him no more.[1]

He gradually became a master of the technique of parliamentary procedure, and was never more at home

[1] "The Life of Lord Wolverhampton," p. 130.

than when, towards the close of his active life, in the first year of Campbell-Bannerman's Government, he was entrusted with the task of piloting through the House a set of new rules.

It is true, as his biographer says, that he "was never one of Mr. Gladstone's favourites"[1] and that he always felt that his great leader gave a somewhat niggardly acknowledgment of his "indisputable claims." But his own explanation of the "lack of sympathy" between them — that he was not a Churchman, but a leading member of a nonconforming church — was singularly wide of the mark, and is sufficiently refuted by Mr. Gladstone's partiality for, and close intimacy with, Morley. *"Nulla salus extra Ecclesiam"* was a maxim which Mr. Gladstone never applied to political relationships, and if he had allowed such considerations to influence him he would certainly have *prima facie* given the preference to an orthodox Wesleyan over an undisguised agnostic. Curiously enough — for at first sight no two men seemed to have less in common — Fowler's personal allegiance seems for a long time to have been given to Sir William Harcourt.[2]

He took an active and useful part in the Opposition campaigns between 1886 and 1892, and when the last Gladstone administration was formed he appears to have had great expectations. "You will be disappointed," said Morley, who had access to the inner sanctum, "but I have done all that I could." Fowler asked but one question: "Is it the Cabinet?" "Of course, but——" He was offered a post — the Local

---

[1] "Life," p. 132.　　　　[2] *Ibid.*, p. 175.

Government Board—which was not then considered as in the first rank, though it had been accepted by Chamberlain in the administration of 1886. "This," says his daughter, "was one of the hardest blows he ever received, and it was one that he stood up to the best." [1] It gave him, however, the opportunity of showing his quality by carrying the Parish Councils Bill— a most intricate and technical measure—through the House of Commons; and on the formation of the Rosebery administration in 1894, when Lord Kimberley went to the Foreign Office, Fowler succeeded him as Secretary of State for India.

In 1895 he made his famous speech on the Indian cotton duties, and scored for the Government—then in troubled waters—a signal victory over the Opposition. Sir Arthur Godley (now Lord Kilbracken), the Permanent Under-Secretary for India, wrote of it at the time: "It saved the Government: it produced an admirable effect in India: and it was a great personal triumph."

Fowler was inclined to be somewhat sensitive as to his personal and official dignity. Probably by accident, he was for a considerable time not invited to "dine and sleep" at any of the Queen's country residences, and I remember his complaining to me one day with some bitterness of what he called the "Windsor boycott." All the more keen was his gratification when he became (as he did in time) one of the Queen's personal favourites among her Ministers, and though not fond of animals, he showed much attachment to a collie dog which he had brought back as a memorial of one of his visits

[1] "Life," pp. 253–4.

October 12/08.

My dear Prime Minister,

From your letter
just received. I quite
understand that
as Lord Wolverhampton
is so anxious to
take the office of
President of the Council
you have no other
alternative but to
recommend him
to me for that post
in which I agree
but all the same
much regret that
he gives up the

Chancellorship of the
Duchy of Lancaster!

I should prefer upon
the recommendation
that Lord Fitz maurice
should succeed Lord
Wolverton myself, with
a seat in the Cabinet —
And continuing to
represent the Foreign
Office in the House
of Lords — (though
no longer Under Secretary)

Believe me,
Very sincerely yours
Palmerston

to Balmoral. It gave him real pleasure to be made a G.C.S.I. when the Government fell.

In the dissensions which troubled the Liberal party during and after the Boer War, Fowler was an ardent Liberal Imperialist, and became with Sir Edward Grey and myself a vice-president of the Liberal League, of which the president was Lord Rosebery. Lord Rosebery (says Fowler's daughter) "fulfilled my father's personal ideal of Liberal leadership perhaps more than any other man." [1]

He was now growing old and was no longer an active combatant either in the House or on the platform. When the Campbell-Bannerman Government was formed in 1905, it was at his own request that he was given a light post, that of Chancellor of the Duchy. When I took over the reins in 1908, he became a viscount at the same time as his old friend Morley, and a little later he was made President of the Council. [2] He conducted the Old Age Pensions Bill in the House of Lords. It was not easy to reconcile him to the view that age and growing infirmity counselled retirement, and his daughter is kind enough to pay me an over-generous tribute for the manner in which I reluctantly discharged a most unwelcome task. [3]

I have given elsewhere a brief estimate of Fowler's personality and career. [4] He was, as I have said there, "in many ways a remarkable man." He was good all round, and specially good in finance: an excellent

[1] "Life," p. 469.
[2] The letter from King Edward VII, reproduced on pp. 201–202, has reference to this appointment.
[3] "Life," p. 673.
[4] "Fifty Years of British Parliament."

friend, and a most loyal colleague, for whom I always cherished feelings of warm affection.

LORD CHAPLIN

Henry Chaplin was known to his contemporaries in the world of sport and fashion as "The Squire," and no one ever looked the part to greater perfection. He began life as the owner of broad acres with a large rent roll, and became one of the best of horsemen, a devotee of racing in the days when gambling was at its zenith, and owner of the famous and sensational Derby winner, Hermit, whose subsequent success as a sire of the stud provided Chaplin for years, after he had exhausted his patrimony, with a handsome annual income. His interest in the hunting field and the turf remained unabated to the end of his life, and our personal friendship, which had lasted through thirty years of unremitting political hostility, was cemented when, during the War, I agreed as Prime Minister, at his suggestion, to the setting up of a National Breeding Stud in Ireland.[1]

But his main ambition in life was to be taken seriously as a politician. He entered the House of Commons when quite a young man as member for Lincolnshire in 1868, and, with the exception of a single year, he sat there continuously until 1916, when he was raised to the peerage. He was already a well-seasoned member of eighteen years' standing when I was first elected, and during the half-century, for it was little less, of his parliamentary life he was always a conspicuous figure.

[1] The experiment has, I believe, been very successful, both from the point of view of the taxpayer and of the breeding of the best thoroughbred stock.

He made his maiden speech on the Irish Church Bill in April, 1869, and Mr. Gladstone, who followed him, expressed "the sense of pleasure with which he had heard an able and at the same time frank, ingenuous, and manly statement of opinion, and one of such a character as to show the House that the man who made it is a real addition to the intellectual and moral worth and strength of Parliament." This magnificent compliment from the Prime Minister gave immediate prominence to the young member, though it must be added that in a sense it was his undoing.

From that time onwards his speeches were framed upon what he conceived to be the Gladstonian model. Macaulay, who suffered in his day from a tribe of imitators, says somewhere in his characteristic way: "I believe my style to be a good style, but it is very near being a very bad style indeed." That is in a sense true of Mr. Gladstone's oratory. It was superb, and in many ways unique, but it required a more skilful copyist than Chaplin to make an imitation of it tolerable. The involutions, the periphrases, the parentheses, the reservations, the circumlocutions, were all more or less faithfully reproduced, but—in Burke's phrase—they were "the nodosities of the oak without its strength." Lord Ullswater describes Chaplin as "quite the last of the exponents of the old-time style of oratory."[1] Nevertheless for some years, at any rate, he was an acceptable and even a favourite speaker. Mr. Disraeli shortly before he left the House of Commons wrote to Lady Bradford (July 30, 1875): "I am very glad Harry C. [Chaplin] was not at Goodwood. He has

[1] "A Speaker's Commentaries," Vol. II, p. 84.

never left my side, and his aid has been invaluable. He is a natural orator and a debater too. He is the best speaker in the House of Commons, or will be. Mark my words." [1]

An amazing forecast from such an accomplished and experienced critic.

The admiration of his early efforts was not confined to eminent politicians like Gladstone and Disraeli; it seems to have been shared by the chief journalist of the day — Mr. Delane of *The Times*. In a speech made in the House of Lords on the Irish Free State Bill in March, 1922, Viscount Chaplin, as he had now become, relates the incident as follows:

Viscount CHAPLIN [2] said that his first speech in the House of Commons was made fifty-four years ago, and was on the question of the plantation of Ulster. The following year he made a speech on the land question, and next day when he was crossing the lobby — he was ashamed to say, to get a drink at the bar — a gentleman whom he had never seen before accosted him and said: "I am Mr. Delane, Editor of *The Times*. My object in introducing myself to you is to tell you that you made a speech last night on the Irish Land Bill that *The Times* wants." Mr. Delane added that he would always report him at any length he liked.

When I entered the House, Disraeli's rosy vision had already been dispelled, and though Chaplin was, as he always remained, one of the House's favourites, the audience which listened to his copious rotundities came there, especially the younger men, as much for amusement as instruction. There were, however, occasions when he exhausted the patience of the House, as,

[1] "Life of Disraeli," Vol. V, p. 387.
[2] House of Lords, March 28, 1922, on the Irish Free State Bill.

for instance, on my amendment to the Address in 1892, when for some strange reason he was chosen to wind up the debate on behalf of the Government. Lord George Hamilton in his "Parliamentary Reminiscences"[1] gives a lively picture of the scene:

For some reason or other which at that time was not very intelligible, it was considered necessary to spin out this debate for four nights. . . . I went out of London before the concluding date of the debate, and during my absence a letter requesting me to sum up the debate on our side missed me. Harry Chaplin, being in town, had to take my place, and lucky it was that he did so. I never have been of any use in talking against time. Chaplin was gifted with rare fluency of speech, and as a rule could spin out his talk to any length. On the night in question it was from a tactical point of view most desirable that we should poll our full strength, but certain of our party were slack, and at 9.30 we were considerably short of our full numbers. The Opposition was fully aware of this.

Chaplin was our last speaker, and he had a most difficult task for more than an hour and a half in talking against continuous interruptions and jeers. But he held his own gallantly, and though constantly gravelled for want of matter, he still continued to talk. At 10.50 all but two of our men had arrived, and these two were at last located and found to be playing billiards at the Carlton. This was known to the Opposition, and the noise redoubled. Poor Chaplin, at the last gasp of endless perorations, was informed, "Five minutes more, old boy, and it will be all right," and so he held on. In came the two culprits, and amidst the vociferous applause of both sides he sat down, having most successfully discharged the unpleasant duty imposed upon him.

The orator's gigantic frame, his ruddy cheeks and yellow hair, his immaculate costume with its frock-coat of a special cut, the eye-glass firmly fixed in one eye

---

[1] "Parliamentary Reminiscences, 1886–1906," pp. 202–3.

from which in his more impressive moments it was carefully removed, the pivot-like movements of his body, with now and again a sweeping gesture of the arm after the Gladstonian model — all these combined to produce a familiar picture which lives in the memories of generations of members of Parliament.

He was made Chancellor of the Duchy in the " Caretaker" Government of 1885, and was only not a member of Lord Salisbury's second administration because — according to Mr. Churchill — he thought the post offered him below his claims. "In July, 1886, Mr. Chaplin indignantly declined the Presidency of the Local Government Board, because the offer was unaccompanied by a seat in the Cabinet."[1] Two or three years later he entered the Cabinet as the first President of the Board of Agriculture, and in the Unionist Government formed after the general election of 1895 he was for five years President of the Local Government Board. In the reshuffled Government after the "Khaki" election, much to his chagrin, he was not given a place.

He was a painstaking Minister, always accessible and genial, but his methods were not suited to the rapid dispatch of business, and singularly ill-adapted to the conduct of a contentious Bill through Committee. An amusing illustration is to be found in Sir Arthur Griffith-Boscawen's "Fourteen Years in Parliament": the Bill to which he refers is the Agricultural Relief Bill, 1896:[2]

Mr. Chaplin's conduct of the Bill in Committee was not always happy. He made really great speeches on the small-

[1] "Lord Randolph Churchill," Vol. II, p. 126.   [2] P. 98.

est amendments, so much so that it was remarked that he seemed to consider it not a Rating but a pero-rating Bill. . . . I remember on one occasion Sir William Harcourt arose and dexterously turned one of the clauses of the Bill inside out, making it look particularly ridiculous. Mr. Chaplin responded in a great speech, which left the House very much where it was before. When he sat down the following conversation was overheard on the Treasury Bench.

Mr. CHAPLIN: "Was that all right, Arthur?"

Mr. BALFOUR: "Excellent, Harry, old chap, excellent!" Then leaning over to the Solicitor-General, "I think, Finlay, you had better get up now and explain the clause." Sir Robert accordingly caught the Speaker's [? Chairman's] eye, and in a few sentences made everything perfectly clear, showing the absurdity of Sir William Harcourt's argument.

Chaplin, who had always been an agricultural Protectionist, was a hearty supporter of Mr. Chamberlain's fiscal policy, and took an active part in the campaign of 1903–5. He was rejected by his Lincolnshire constituency at the election of 1906, and found refuge for the remaining years of his House of Commons life in the unfamiliar atmosphere of the metropolitan borough of Wimbledon. For a short time after the formation during the War of the Coalition of 1915, he sat opposite me as the nominal "leader of the Opposition," and thoroughly enjoyed the duty of putting questions as to the order of business and the sittings of the House. But I had reason to believe that he thought that his House of Commons career was closed, and that he would welcome a transfer to another place. Accordingly in April, 1916, he was created a viscount.

He was a picturesque and in some ways an interesting figure. Though he lived in a large and lavish way, he gave much time and pains to his parliamentary work. He would have formed an admirable model for a character part in one of Disraeli's novels.

LORD MILNER

I made Alfred Milner's acquaintance when he came up to Balliol, and we sat together at the Scholars' table in Hall for three years. We then formed a close friendship, and were for many years on intimate terms and in almost constant contact with one another. I ceased to see him, except when now and again he came home on leave, during his long absence first in Egypt and afterwards in South Africa; and when he finally settled down in England, we drifted apart, though we maintained to the end of his life perfectly friendly relations.

At Oxford we both took an active part at the Union in upholding the unfashionable Liberal cause, and for many years afterwards Milner, who by nature and temperament was, like Courtney, not a party man, would have described himself as a Liberal. He even stood as a Liberal candidate for the newly-created Harrow division in 1885. In my early married days (1877–85) he used often to come to my house at Hampstead for a frugal Sunday supper, when we talked over political and literary matters, for the most part in general agreement.

He began about this time to see much of two remarkable men of wholly dissimilar personalities — Goschen, for whom he acted for a time as private secretary, and Stead, the editor of the *Pall Mall Gazette*, of whose staff he became a leading member. He had, I think, laid aside, if not definitely abandoned, parliamentary ambitions. With Goschen he had intellectual affinities —amongst others, a native faculty for dealing with economic and financial problems—which in any case would have made their co-operation easy and congenial, and the "Imperialistic" tinge with which Goschen's Liberalism had always been coloured was altogether to Milner's taste.

His association as a fellow-worker with Stead is, at first sight, more difficult to understand. It is true that Stead also was, after his fashion, an Imperialist. Moreover, Milner shared with him an interest in social reforms which had no doubt been quickened by the influence of Arnold Toynbee: they had both been in their Oxford days under the spell of this side of Ruskin's teaching. But Stead, whichever of the many "causes" he took up was, for the time being, in the forefront of his activities—the mission of Gordon to Egypt, the "Truth about the Navy," or the "Minotaur" of London—pursued it in the temper of an evangelist, and often of a fanatic; his methods were as novel and as sensational as in another field were those of General Booth. Milner, on the other hand, though a man of strong convictions tenaciously and sometimes obstinately held, and with a distinct faculty for phrase-making—as when he described the Outlanders as "helots," or advised the Lords to reject the Budget and "damn the consequence"—had a refined and fastidious mind, great literary culture, and a sense of taste which must frequently have been offended by his editor's vagaries.

In a character sketch in the *Review of Reviews* after he had been some time High Commissioner in South Africa, Stead describes how Milner used every day to go through the proofs of his leading articles, and " tone them down."

He would squirm at an adjective here, reduce a superlative there, and generally strike out anything that seemed calculated needlessly to irritate or offend. He was always putting water in my wine. He was always combing out the knots in the tangled mane of the P.M.G., and when the lion opened his mouth Milner was always at hand to be consulted as to the advisability of modulating the ferocity of its roar. . . . His task was most useful, but when he pruned he sometimes cut to the quick, and the victim smarted while his offspring bled. And now I am sadly avenged. For by some strange Nemesis Milner seems to have been doomed to use up as material for his own dispatch all the strongest overstrained adjectives and expletives which in the whole three years he was with me he had combed out of the proofs of the *Pall Mall Gazette*. They now experience a strange resurrection in the dispatch of May 4. . . . It is a leader of the kind which we used to describe as " a regular snorter," and I cannot but smile at thinking how the Milner of other days, the Milner of the " University tip," would have dealt with the telegram of May 4 had it come before him as the proof of a *Pall Mall Gazette* leader.

But, as the classical case of Delane and Courtney sufficiently shows, the profession of journalism seems to be able to establish a conventional harmony between the strangest of bedfellows; and the partnership between Stead and Milner is not more remarkable, in this aspect of it, than that of Stead himself with his predecessor in the editorship of the *Pall Mall* — John Morley.

It was at the instance of Goschen, who had become Chancellor of the Exchequer in a Conservative Government, that Milner first entered the public service, and went as Financial Adviser to Egypt. His administration there was both efficient and successful, and after his return to England he was appointed Chairman of the Board of Inland Revenue. In that capacity he was able to show the metal of which he was made, and it is no secret that in the conception and working out of Sir William Harcourt's great Budget of 1894, Milner was from first to last his principal adviser. Harcourt, who abounded in the rare virtue of gratitude, never hesitated to acknowledge his debt. When a few years later Mr. Chamberlain selected Milner to succeed Sir Hercules Robinson in South Africa, he left to take up the most difficult and responsible post in the Empire overseas amid an almost unprecedented chorus of commendation and goodwill from the leaders of all parties in the State.[1]

I do not enter here upon the much controverted theme of the merits and demerits of Milner's South African policy and of his diplomacy with Kruger. But no one can question either his ability or his disinterestedness, and the peerage and other distinctions conferred upon him were thoroughly earned. His personality was so impressive that he founded a school of able young men who during his lifetime and since have acknowledged him as their principal political teacher. He never renounced his democratic faith, but he engrafted upon it what some of his old friends regarded as incongruous excrescences. He was an Expansionist,

[1] See "Fifty Years of British Parliament."

up to a point a Protectionist, with a strain in social and industrial matters of semi-Socialist sentiment.

He was a man of great personal charm, and guided always by high ideals independently conceived and unselfishly pursued.

CHAPTER XXI

SPEAKERS AND WHIPS

THE two Speakers of whom I had parliamentary experience before the election of Mr. Lowther were Peel and Gully.

Peel was comparatively new to the Chair when I entered the House in 1886. Like his predecessor, Brand, he had been for a time Chief Whip of the Liberal party, and partly for that reason his nomination excited some surprise. Indeed he was not Mr. Gladstone's first choice, for the post was offered to and refused by Mr. Goschen and Sir Henry James. Brand's name will always be associated with his famous *coup d'état* in 1881 when, after one of the debates on the Coercion Bill had been prolonged beyond all precedent by organized and barefaced obstruction, he interposed, and put the question from the Chair: a step which made the introduction, sooner or later, into the rules of procedure of some form of closure (then generally known by its French name, *clôture*) a parliamentary necessity.

There is always a certain glamour about the figure of the first Speaker whom as a young member of Parliament one has been accustomed to see in the Chair, and who is associated in one's memories with the battles between the giants and the gods (as they seemed) who in that heroic age waged war day and night from opposite sides of the table:

> Athos and Ida, with a dashing sea
> Of eloquence between.

No one who was a member of the House of Commons between 1886 and 1892 will deny that during those years both Chairs — the Speaker's and the one which often comes near it in importance, that of the Chairman of Ways and Means — were occupied by exceptionally strong men: Arthur Peel and Leonard Courtney. Peel had great natural advantages — a tall, commanding figure, a fine voice and admirable enunciation, unfailing dignity, a sense of presence and authority, and it must be added a temper which, though habitually under control, could on occasions blaze forth into a scorching flame. He had a complete and readily available knowledge of the rules, few personal favourites or antipathies, and though a great stickler for order and propriety, he could show tact and patience in handling an obstructive and mutinous minority.

Few who were present can forget the allocution which he delivered from the Chair in April, 1892, to a batch of railway directors who were summoned to the Bar for breach of privilege. They included a member of the House, Sir John Maclure, whose burly figure, white curly locks, and almost obstreperous geniality it was difficult to associate with an offence against its authority. A still more memorable scene was the tumult which arose on the application of the guillotine to the Committee stage of the Home Rule Bill. The Chairman (Mr. Mellor) lost control of the situation, and the Speaker was sent for.

After two or three minutes he entered and took the Chair, throwing his robe about him with his most majestic air, and for a moment glared around, without saying a word, upon the House now silent and abashed.   Mr. Gladstone looked on with an expression of pained and incredulous bewilderment, and members dispersed, many of them with hang-dog and discomfited looks, to their homes.[1]

Peel resigned the Speakership in the spring of 1895.

To the amazement and consternation of the whole Cabinet, Campbell-Bannerman, who was then approaching sixty, let it be known that he desired the vacant office.   No more flattering compliment could have been paid to him—for it was certain that, if he became a candidate, he would have been elected without a contest—than the unanimous veto which his proposal encountered from his colleagues.   The choice of Mr. Gully as Peel's successor I have described on a previous page.

Mr. Gully and I had long been friends, though up to this time our points of contact in public had been more professional than political. He had become one of the leaders of the Northern Circuit, and had the reputation of a sound and accomplished lawyer, and of a suave and persuasive advocate.   There was a legend current that when Charles Russell, Herschell and Gully, who were all more or less contemporaries, had been for some time on the circuit with disappointing results, they met and seriously considered the expediency of migrating to the Colonial or Indian Bars.   In the end they resolved to face the risks of staying at home, where in time one of them became Lord Chief Justice, another Lord Chancellor, and the third Speaker of the House of Commons.

Gully at the time of his election as Speaker had not
[1] "Fifty Years of British Parliament."

been long in the House of Commons, and through the exigencies of his profession had not been constant in his attendance. The result was that he started his career in the Chair with not more than a superficial acquaintance with the technicalities, which at first sight are formidable even to a trained lawyer, of House of Commons procedure. The experts in the House, of whom Mr. Gibson Bowles was in a class by himself, enjoyed themselves for a time by harassing and trying to trip up the new Speaker on points of order. His native acuteness, fortified by his legal experience, before long made him a master of all the twists and turns of procedure: so much so, that in the later years of his term of office he was sometimes reproached with an excessive regard for technicalities.

When the general election of 1895 returned a House of Commons with a large Unionist majority, it was for some time a matter of doubt whether Gully, who was still fresh in the saddle, would not be unhorsed, and a supporter of the new Government put in his place. More generous counsels prevailed and he was re-elected Speaker, the new Chairman of Ways and Means being Mr. James William Lowther, who in 1905 succeeded him in the Speaker's chair.

Mr. Lowther occupied the Chair for sixteen years — among the most eventful and troubled in our constitutional and national history. They witnessed the continuous and bitter struggle between the two Houses which, after the rejection by the Upper Chamber of the Budget of 1909, was at last terminated by the passing of the Parliament Act.

During the whole of that campaign the temperature

of the combatants on both sides was abnormally high throughout the country, and the belligerent spirit which was engendered found constant and vehement expression in the House of Commons. The authority of the Chair had frequently to be exercised to repress disorder, and to maintain the decent and dignified traditions of parliamentary usage; and rarely in our history has the office of Speaker called for a larger endowment of courage, patience, and judgment. Domestic controversy over an Irish settlement and the disestablishment of the Welsh Church was still in full blast when the outbreak of the Great War swept all such issues for a time into the background. For four years the mind and heart of the nation were concentrated upon the gravest and most perilous task which has ever confronted a free people, and all its fluctuations, not of resolve, but of hope and anxiety, found an outlet of expression within the walls of the House of Commons. My leadership of the House came to an end in December, 1916, and one of my last official acts was to send Mr. Lowther an invitation, which he was good enough to accept, to preside over a non-party conference to consider franchise and electoral reform. The report of the conference, which went by the name of the Speaker's Conference, was the foundation of the far-reaching legislation of 1918, which, among a number of less important changes, accepted and carried into partial effect the enfranchisement of women.

In the session of 1921 Lowther resigned the Speakership which he had held during these momentous years. The leaders of all parties and groups in the House joined in a tribute of gratitude and regret. I may

quote a few words from the speech which I made on
behalf of the Liberal party:

I entered the House only two or three years later than
yourself, and I have had as full opportunities as anybody
of watching and appreciating your discharge of your duties
to it during the twenty-six years in which you have sat first
as Chairman of Ways and Means, and then as Speaker.
I use the language not of flattery, but of sincerity and of
truth, when I say that in both capacities you have not only
maintained the best traditions of the past, but, by the exercise of a peculiar and happy endowment of personal
qualities, you have been able to transcend not a few out-
worn conventions and to bring new resources to reinforce
the authority of the Chair.

It has been your fortune to be the trustee and guide of the
House during a difficult period of transition. The House of
Commons is in many ways a different place from what it was
when you and I were among its younger members. . . .

If the House, amidst all the changes, external and internal, which you have witnessed, has preserved, as I believe
it has, its continuous identity and its characteristic atmosphere, it is largely due to the good fortune which it has
enjoyed in having in the Chair during your Speakership one
who combined deep and accurate knowledge, quick judgment, dignity, urbanity, and tact with a keen insight into
human nature, and an unfailing dexterity in the employment
of the lighter as well as of the heavier weapons in the
dialectical armoury. I speak with a feeling which, I am
sure, is shared by every man on all the benches when I say
that the House will not be the same place without you. It
is with a full heart and a grateful and abiding memory of
services which will live in history, and form the model for all
those who succeed you in that Chair, that we bid you farewell.

These words I am certain gave expression to the
general estimate in which the retiring Speaker was held
by the House of Commons. Some years after his retirement Lord Ullswater (as he had become) published

a lively account[1] of some of his experiences during his long tenure of the Chair. My own relations with him — and I was leader of the House during a large part of his term — were always of the best, and I had, and have, a very high opinion of his parliamentary instinct and judgment. As was inevitable, there were one or two occasions when I found his rulings not only unpalatable but unexpected. A notable case was when he laid it down that the question of Woman Suffrage was outside the scope of a Government Electoral Bill in which it had been generally assumed on both sides of the House that in the Committee stage that issue could be raised.

The most remarkable "scene" which was witnessed in the House during Mr. Lowther's tenure of the Chair arose in a discussion on the Financial Resolution for the Home Rule Bill in November, 1912. In a thin House on a snap division Sir F. Banbury had on the Report stage carried against the Government by a very small majority (22) an amendment to the resolution. Two days later I moved the rescission of the resolution as so amended, and the Speaker, while expressing the opinion that the course proposed to be taken was without precedent, declined to rule the motion out of order. What followed cannot be more vividly or impartially described than in Lord Ullswater's own words:[2]

Two days later (November 13), Mr. Asquith moved the rescission of the resolution as amended by Sir F. Banbury's amendment. This led to a series of violent scenes: Mr. Harcourt was denied a hearing, Sir William Bull called the

---

[1] "A Speaker's Commentaries," 1925.   [2] *Ibid.*, Vol. II, pp. 131–4.

Prime Minister a traitor, and I had to request him to withdraw from the Chamber; the Attorney-General was shouted down, and, as much uproar continued which made debate impossible, I adjourned the House for an hour, in the hopes that on its resumption we might proceed in a calmer atmosphere. But my anticipations were not realized, for on resumption the uproar was as great as ever. The Opposition were determined that no further progress should be made; they shouted down one of their own number, Lord Helmsley, and kept up a constant chorus of "Adjourn! Adjourn!" It was evident after a time that no good purpose would be achieved by allowing the pandemonium to continue, and I had to adjourn the House for the night.

Just as I had declared the House to be adjourned and was leaving the Chair, Mr. Ronald McNeill, who happened to be standing on the left of my chair, seized my small bound copy of the Orders of the House and, hurling it across at Mr. Winston Churchill, cut him on the forehead. As the House was then technically adjourned and not sitting, I could take no action, but on the following day Mr. McNeill made a full and handsome apology, which was frankly accepted by Mr. Churchill.[1]

I made the suggestion that, in conference with the Prime Minister and the Leader of the Opposition, I should endeavour to discover some method of getting out of our difficulties, which would be more in accordance with precedent than the course proposed by Mr. Asquith.

On the Monday following, the deadlock was resolved by rejecting the amended resolution and introducing an entirely fresh resolution dealing on somewhat different lines with the finance of the Bill (which was carried by 318 to 207).

Just after these incidents I received several letters from old parliamentary hands and prominent people, thanking me for the course I had adopted and, to quote one of them, " saving the House alike from the repetition of the lamentable scene of Wednesday and from the high-handed action that provoked it."

[1] The unlucky copy of the "Orders" is still in his possession, Lord Ullswater says, and a bent corner of the leather binding bears evidence of the improper purpose to which it had been applied.

WHIPS

For the smooth and effective working of the party and parliamentary machines everything depends upon the Chief Whip. In the choice of candidates, in the control of the party funds, in the arrangement of the business of the House of Commons, he has, or had until lately, the dominating voice. He sees the leader of the party more frequently and on more intimate terms than do any of his colleagues. There is no post for which it is more difficult to select the right man; for there is none which requires in its holder a larger capacity both for self-assertion and for self-effacement. Its duties are, moreover, of the most laborious and exacting kind which call for exceptional physical endurance, much elasticity of temperament, and some degree of insight into the foibles of mankind. There are stories, most of them no doubt legendary, of the exploits of the "great Whips" of the past: such as "Ben" Stanley in the days of Lord Grey's and Lord Melbourne's administrations, who was credited, as Mr. Gladstone once assured me, on a critical occasion with having passed a dead or dying member through the division lobby.

Another example of *trop de zèle* of a different order was furnished by one of my own Whips. It was understood that a certain member — who was accustomed to play the odious rôle of an "independent" critic of the leaders of his party — was, by way of exception, going to make a declaration of cordial support. As a matter of fact, he took no part in the debate. But the Whip, who had been out of the House and took it for granted that the original programme had been carried out, meeting him in the lobby all but embraced him, and assured him that he was the bearer of a special message of congratulation from the Prime Minister, who had listened to his speech with the utmost satisfaction.

I was fortunate in my Chief Whips, with all of whom my relations rested upon a basis of perfect confidence. Of those who held the post in the Liberal party in my time I will single out three, as illustrating the diversities of character and qualification which may make for success in the most strenuous and delicate of offices.

The first name is that of Edward Marjoribanks, afterwards Lord Tweedmouth, who was Chief Whip in Mr. Gladstone's last administration from 1892 to 1894. No one has ever been called upon to perform the functions of a Whip under more difficult and even desperate conditions. In the critical division on the Address which replaced Lord Salisbury's Government by Mr. Gladstone's, the majority for the Opposition amendment did not exceed forty. If the Nationalists were left out of the account, there was a substantial preponderance in the House of Commons of Unionists over Liberals. The Nationalists themselves, upon whose support in the lobby the life of the Government depended, were split up into two warring sections — Parnellites and Anti-Parnellites. The working Government majority fluctuated between 25 and 7, and of such vital consequence was every vote that when I married (in May, 1894) it seemed doubtful whether I could be allowed leave of absence even for the briefest of honeymoons.

No one could have been found better fitted to deal

with such a precarious situation than Marjoribanks. A fine upstanding man, he enjoyed unfailing health and an inexhaustible flow of high spirits. He was rich and fond of pleasure, but worked at his job like a galley-slave. He was geniality incarnate to the good party man who did his duty by listening and not replying to other people's speeches, and voting consistently in the Government lobby. Withal, he had at his command all the resources of a fiery temper and a copious vocabulary of vituperation, which were drawn upon without scruple or reserve for the punishment of slackness or "independence." The member who was detected, by one of his underlings or scouts, slinking away unpaired by some devious route at the dinner hour, was infallibly marked down for one of these bouts of exemplary castigation. Marjoribanks, it must be added, harboured no malice, and would be "hail fellow well met" the next time he encountered one of his victims. He was very popular with the rank and file, and his removal by the death of his father to the House of Lords, just about the time of Mr. Gladstone's resignation in March, 1894, was an irreparable loss to the party. His successor, Tom Ellis, a charming and gifted man, and one of my greatest personal friends, was more at home among the children of light than with the children of this world, with whom a Chief Whip is in daily and even hourly converse.

A marked contrast in every way to Edward Marjoribanks was another Scotsman, Alexander Murray, the Master of Elibank. His father was a Scottish peer and a Conservative in politics. He had for some years served with Mr. Whitley, the present Speaker, as a

Junior Whip, and was intimately acquainted with the House of Commons and its ways when I appointed him to the head of the office in the critical year 1910, which witnessed two general elections, and opened the last stage in the constitutional conflict between the Houses of Parliament. Those elections were practically identical in result, and though the first of them made considerable inroads on the unexampled strength which the election of 1906 had given to the Liberal party in the House of Commons, the Government, at the beginning of 1911 in its sixth year, was still in possession of an adequate working majority. The situation, however, was one that called for careful handling, overshadowed as it was by the declared determination of Ministers to frustrate the hostility of the House of Lords to the Parliament Bill.

"The Master," as he was always called, has probably had no superior among the incumbents of his responsible office in the art of parliamentary management. I have never seen him out of temper. His method of dealing with defaulters or cranks was the very reverse of that pursued by Marjoribanks. His round, slightly rubicund face, wreathed with its habitual smile, and his soft and almost caressing voice, were brought into play more, it would seem, in mild surprise or even in subdued sympathy than in anger, and the transgressor was lured rather than driven back to the straight path. His scouting was, as a rule, admirably organized, and the daily report which he made to me as Chief of the Staff was almost always a trustworthy reflection of the passing moods and tenses of the House of Commons. He used often to remind me of the rude men of affairs

— the Maitlands and others — who manœuvred men and business across the Border in the days of Mary, Queen of Scots.

One of his preoccupations, when we were at last nearing the rocks, was the drawing up of a preliminary list of potential peers in the event of the House of Lords proving recalcitrant. The list, so far as I know, was never shown to anyone but myself, nor were any of the gentlemen hypothetically concerned sounded as to their possible intentions. I possess a copy of this *chef d'œuvre* of "The Master," but I must own that I never studied the names with any care, or even discussed them with him, being convinced all along that good sense and good reason would in the end prevail.

The last name which I will mention is that of "The Master's" successor — Percy Illingworth, who held the office of Chief Whip at the outbreak of the War in 1914, and died prematurely a few months later. He was in many ways a typical Yorkshireman: shrewd, resolute, resourceful, inclined by nature to be pugnacious, and capable of giving a good account of himself in any company either with his tongue or his fists. He was one of the straightest men I have ever known, and one of the most lovable. His counsel and support were invaluable in the trying times when what was called the "Curragh incident" made me feel it my duty to take over the War Office into my own hands. He was a stout party man, and had he lived I should have had great difficulty in persuading him to acquiesce in May, 1915, in the formation of the Coalition Government.

CHAPTER XXII

THE C.-B. GOVERNMENT

ON the day following Mr. Balfour's sudden resignation in December, 1905, Campbell-Bannerman accepted the King's commission to form a Government. During the two succeeding days I saw more than did anyone else of the new Prime Minister.[1] The personal situation was for some hours one of delicacy, and even difficulty. There have been already given to the world two pictures of it, drawn as was inevitable from somewhat different angles: the one by Lord Morley, the other by Lord Grey of Fallodon. Those who desire to know "how it struck a contemporary" onlooker should read the extracts from my wife's diary which are to be found in "Margot Asquith: An Autobiography" (Vol. III, Chap. V.).

Lord Morley's narrative is as follows:[2]

When Campbell-Bannerman acceded, and was making his Cabinet, there were colleagues who still had singular misgivings as to his capacity of holding his own against the experienced men on the bench opposite. They threw out the truly unhappy suggestion that the new Prime Minister should go to the House of Lords, and leave the lead in the Commons to one of themselves. I wrote to the most important of them that, as the majority at the coming election must inevitably be non-imperialist (not quite the same thing

[1] Even than my friend, Lord Shaw, whose "Letters to Isabel," about this matter, are entertaining and picturesque.
[2] "Recollections," Vol. II, pp. 141-3.

as anti-imperialist), it seemed rather odd that the Prime Minister should be exiled to the Lords, and I banish myself to the Brahmaputra,[1] while my correspondent took the lead of the Commons and the chief post in administration. Asquith and I inevitably, now as always, understood one another; he agreed that the plan proposed would never do; and in his own mind he devised another plan that might be a trifle more reasonable. One evening, while these unedifying transactions were still on foot, Tweedmouth and I left Campbell-Bannerman, cool, patient, half undecided as to his course; we were to return after dinner, and the true counsellor of his life was to arrive from Scotland in the meantime. After the event, I thought of Tocqueville's account of his own wife, who by the way was English. "I found in my home," said Tocqueville, "the support, so rarely precious in time of revolution, of a devoted woman, whom a firm and penetrating intelligence, and a spirit naturally high, held without effort equal to the level of any situation, and above every reverse." Returning we found the Minister indescribably exultant. "No surrender!" he called out to us in triumphant voice, with gesture to match. The decision was iron. Detachment at once fell to a low discount among the doubters, and this must be added to the many historic cases where women have played a leading part in strengthening the counsels of ministers, sovereigns, great reformers, and even popes.

That there was nothing to justify Lord Morley's epithet of "unedifying" in these "transactions" becomes apparent from Lord Grey's account:[2]

Campbell-Bannerman had no difficulty in forming a Government, but I made difficulty for some days about joining it. I was closely associated with Asquith and Haldane in House of Commons work, and our view was that, with Campbell-Bannerman as Prime Minister, the leadership in the Commons should be in Asquith's hands. There had not been differences about foreign policy, but there had

[1] A characteristic touch.
[2] "Twenty-five Years," Vol. I, p. 62.

been about Imperial affairs such as the South African War and the Sudan, and my view was that Asquith would be the more robust and stronger leader in policy and debate in the Commons. I explained this with some frankness to Campbell-Bannerman; I had no feeling but one of liking for him personally, and I wanted him to know just where I stood, and to feel that I was not suppressing in his presence things that I had said about him elsewhere. Perhaps it was some understanding of this that made him take all I said in good part. Asquith had from the first been prepared to take office. Arthur Acland, who had retired from public life, but with whom I had worked closely and intimately in past years, had a long talk with me. Haldane decided to go into office; there were no substantial reasons for standing out alone, and, as Campbell-Bannerman still offered it, I went to the Foreign Office. . . .

Probably my wife's comment had much to do with the decision. "If we had refused office," she said, "we could not have justified the decision to the constituents."

*   *   *   *   *

The other considerations that then seemed important were based upon a mistaken sense of values. I had a notion that the public interest required that every member of the Liberal party who counted for anything should contribute his help to the Liberal Government. . . . The result of the election, with its enormous and unprecedented Liberal majority, showed what a delusion it had been to suppose that it mattered anything to the cause of Free Trade whether I joined the Government or not. . . .

I had made difficulties, as I now think unnecessarily, about going into office, but when in it I made none. Campbell-Bannerman's leadership in the Commons was accepted, and there was complete loyalty to him. Experience showed that it had been quite unnecessary to raise any question of his leaving the House of Commons. Things went well enough as they were, and the differences and divisions of opinion that had existed when the party was in opposition never reappeared.

My own personal attitude can be described in a sentence: I was most anxious that Grey should come in and go to the Foreign Office, for which his qualifications were unique, and I was equally determined not to press any claim put forward on my behalf unless it met with Campbell-Bannerman's free and full assent. He and I discussed the situation together with the utmost friendliness in all its aspects — not excluding that of health. I did not then know that the question of his going to the House of Lords had some months before been debated between him and his wife and their much trusted physician, Dr. Ott, at Marienbad. As soon as his appointment as Prime Minister was announced in the papers, it now appears that Dr. Ott wrote to him: " I am very, very shocked to read in the papers that you have the intention of remaining in the House of Commons. . . . I remember very well a time when you and Lady Campbell-Bannerman were kind enough to discuss these matters with me, and that we all three agreed that for your precarious health it would be best for you to go to the House of Lords besides occupying (sic) the Government." [1]

We had our talk and, as Morley records, he reserved his decision until he could consult his wife, who was on her journey from Scotland. When he told me the next morning of the decision to which they had come, I accepted the office of Chancellor of the Exchequer without any conditions. Arthur Acland, in whose judgment both Grey and I had the utmost confidence, and

[1] See the whole letter — Spender, "Life of Campbell-Bannerman," Vol. II, p. 199.

Mr. Spender, urged upon Grey the withdrawal of his objections, and he consented to come in.

Looking back upon the whole affair, in which from first to last there was nothing in the nature of an "intrigue," I find its most interesting feature to be the weight which each of the two statesmen principally concerned attached to the counsel of his wife. In Campbell-Bannerman's case it was undoubtedly the determining factor, and in Grey's (as he says) it had "much to do with the decision." "Never," as I wrote in "Studies and Sketches," "did two Ministers occupying the highest places work more harmoniously together than did Sir Henry Campbell-Bannerman and Sir Edward Grey in the two succeeding years." "Foreign affairs," said Sir Henry, in one of the last of his public speeches—December 22, 1907—"have never been managed with more conspicuous ability and success than by Sir Edward Grey."

I will say nothing of my own relations with him from the formation of his Government to the day of his resignation, except that, on both sides, they were marked by ever growing confidence and affection.

The one great positive achievement which the Campbell-Bannerman Government was able to accomplish, amidst derisive prophecies of failure and disaster from the official Opposition, was the grant of full responsible government to the two late South African Republics which had been so recently at war against us. The following letters passed in the summer of 1909, more than a year after I had become Prime Minister, between General Botha and myself:

SANATORIUM OF GROF. DAPPER,
KISSINGEN.
23. 8. 09.

DEAR MR. ASQUITH, —

Now that the South Africa Bill has safely passed both Houses of Parliament and thereby the Union of the four self-governing Colonies in South Africa has practically become an established fact, I cannot refrain from congratulating you and the great party of which you are the leader upon the success which has followed your liberal policy in South Africa.

It is due to the far-seeing policy of your party, carried out bravely in most difficult circumstances, that all has gone so well in South Africa and that its position as an integral portion of the British Empire has become assured. There are many to-day who claim a larger or smaller share of the credit in connection with the realization of Union in South Africa, but this one thing is certain, that only the liberal policy of your Government has made that Union possible and in South Africa at all events the great majority of the people fully appreciate this. Only after a policy of trust in the whole population of Transvaal and O.R.C. had taken the place of one of coercion could we dream of the possibility of a Union of the Colonies, and above all of the two white races. My greatest regret is that one noble figure is missing — one man who should have lived to see the fruits of his work — the late Sir Henry Campbell-Bannerman. For what he has done in South Africa alone the British Empire should always keep him in grateful memory!

I have carefully followed the debates in the House of Commons and read your able speech with great admiration.

Believe me,

Yours sincerely,

LOUIS BOTHA.

The Right Honourable H. H. Asquith.

10 Downing Street,
Whitehall, S.W.
27th August, 1909.

My dear General Botha, —

It was a great pleasure to me to receive your letter, and that pleasure is shared by all my colleagues in the Cabinet, to whom I had yesterday the gratification of communicating it.

There is nothing in our conduct of affairs during the last four years on which we look back with so much satisfaction as the full and free grant of self-government to the Transvaal and the Orange River Colony, which has rendered possible that which, at our advent to power, seemed an unrealizable dream — the Union of South Africa.

I am glad that we were able to secure the passage of the Act of Union without amendment through both Houses of Parliament.

Let me add that we feel a deep sense of gratitude to yourself and your colleagues for the splendid and single-minded patriotism with which you have devoted yourselves to the great work of reconciliation and union.

Believe me to be,

Very faithfully yours,

H. H. Asquith.

The Rt. Hon. L. Botha.

No one now questions the wisdom or foresight of this act of reconciliation.

CHAPTER XXIII

CONSTITUTIONAL CONFERENCE, 1910

THE unexpected and much lamented death of King Edward led in 1910 to the setting up, in the hope that the new reign might begin with a political concordat on the constitutional issue, of a conference between the leaders of the Liberal and the Unionist parties. It consisted of eight members, the representatives of the Government being myself, Lord Crewe, Mr. Lloyd George, and Mr. Birrell, and those of the Opposition, Mr. Balfour, Lord Lansdowne, Mr. Austen Chamberlain, and Lord Cawdor. When the names were announced the only one which aroused some surprise was that of Lord Cawdor, who, though he had been First Lord of the Admiralty in the last Unionist administration, and was a popular and efficient chairman of the Great Western Railway, was not classed by the outside public in the first rank of political leaders. He was, in fact, as those members of the conference who did not know him before soon discovered, a man of great shrewdness and common sense, and endowed with an excellent temper and a good sense of humour.

The fact that the conference was composed exclusively of representatives of the two old historic parties, and that neither the Irish Nationalists nor the Labour men were invited to take part in it, may at this distance of time seem to call for remark, but admits of easy explanation. The Nationalists, who in those days numbered 86 in the House of Commons, were content to leave the negotiations in the hands of their Liberal allies. Labour, although a growing parliamentary factor, was still generally classed for electoral and parliamentary purposes as Liberal. In the summaries in the Press of the results of the subsequent election the Liberal and Labour votes were usually lumped together, and there were, I believe, in that election not more than three or four cases in which there was a straight fight between Liberal and Labour candidates.

The conference met for the first time in my room at the House of Commons on June 17. Its proceedings from first to last were secret and informal, and it is hardly necessary to say that the seal of confidence was strictly respected. On July 29, on the eve of a long parliamentary adjournment, I was able to give on its behalf a not unsatisfactory report to the House of Commons:

> The representatives of the Government and the Opposition have held twelve meetings, and have carefully surveyed a large part of the field of controversy, and the result is that our discussions have made such progress, although we have not so far reached an agreement, as to render it, in the opinion of all of us, not only desirable but necessary that they should continue. In fact I may go farther, and say that we should think it wrong at this stage to break them off. There is no question of their indefinite continuance, and if we find as a result of our further deliberations during the recess that there is no prospect of an agreement that can be announced to Parliament in the course of the present session, we shall bring the conference to a close.

Much documentary material was provided for the conference on the subject of the working of bicameral systems in other countries, and of the referendum and other plebiscitary expedients. The feasibility of a joint session of the two Chambers in cases of difference between them, and if so under what conditions, was also a topic which was fully considered. The conference heard oral evidence from two, and according to my memory from only two, witnesses. One of them was Dr. Nicolas Murray Butler, President of Columbia University in the State of New York, a conspicuous and distinguished figure both in the educational and the political life of the United States. The other was Mr. Fielding, who had had probably a longer experience than any man then living of the practical working of the constitution of the Dominion of Canada and its provinces. He told us that in the course of his public life he had been at one time continuously in office — Dominion and Provincial — for no less than twenty-five years.

We should have been glad, if it had been possible, to have had first-hand testimony from witnesses of equal authority as to the experience of the States which form the Commonwealth of Australia, and whose constitutional history presents several cases of conflict on critical matters between the Upper and Lower Houses of the Legislature.

The conference held its last sitting on November 10, by which time it had unfortunately become clear to all its members that there was no hope that it could arrive at an agreed settlement of the problems which it had so carefully examined and debated.

I still think that the experiment was in the circumstances worth trying, but the conditions were not propitious.   Party feeling was running very high, and the ardent spirits among the rank and file on both sides viewed with a certain amount of restlessness, if not of suspicion, what they feared might turn out to be a process of bargaining and compromise carried on behind the closed doors of a *camarilla*.   It was not without a sigh of relief that the good party man heard that the thing had broken down, and that the cause to which he had become devotedly attached was still left intact. An immediate dissolution was inevitable, and the general election which followed in December — the second of the year — was conducted everywhere with the utmost vigour and enthusiasm, and in some quarters with not a little bitterness.   It left the distribution of forces in the House of Commons practically unchanged.

CHAPTER XXIV

MR. BONAR LAW AS LEADER OF THE OPPOSITION

IT is difficult to say which event caused more surprise in the political world — the resignation of the leadership of the Opposition by Mr. Balfour in November, 1911, or the election as his successor of Mr. Bonar Law. I had up to that time had no personal relations with the new leader except of the most superficial kind, and while I had been struck by his readiness and resource in debate, and his singularly retentive memory, in the prolonged controversy over the fiscal question, I had come to regard him more as a specialist than an all-round combatant: an illusion which it took little time to dispel.

At moments he could be almost disarmingly ingenuous. I remember that the first time that he and I walked side by side in the annual procession of the Commons to hear the King's Speech in the House of Lords — it must have been at the opening of the session of 1912 — he said to me on the way back: "I am afraid I shall have to show myself very vicious, Mr. Asquith, this session. I hope you will understand." I had no hesitation in reassuring him on that point. A year or more later, when he had had some experience of the worries and perils of his new office, he declared in the House of Commons:

It is one of the penalties of my position that I have to speak on many occasions whether I desire to do so or not, and the curious, and for me unpleasant, consequence is that while I have to make speeches on so many subjects, I have less time than I had before, rather than more, to try to make them adequate to the subject.

A common experience with party leaders, but rarely so naïvely confessed.

Mr. Bonar Law had, as I have said, remarkable dialectical gifts, which made him a formidable gladiator both on the platform and in the House of Commons. But he was not by nature a rhetorician, and was least effective when he yielded to the temptation to become declamatory. During the last stage of the Home Rule controversy, from the time of his famous Blenheim "pledge" (July, 1912) onwards, his were the most inflammatory speeches—not excepting Sir Edward Carson's—that were made on the Unionist side. There were in many of them a certain crudeness, which was in itself a sign that the rôle of a mudslinger was not really congenial to him.

In a speech at the Albert Hall in January, 1912, after alleging that the Government had in "six short years created a swarm of new officials (some 4,000 or 5,000) — the majority of them without any competition —who like locusts are devouring the land,"[1] he proceeded as follows: "Revolutionary Governments are always corrupt Governments. They have succeeded in six years in creating a political spoil system which already rivals that of the United States."

[1] Presumably for the administration of the Old Age Pensions Act, the Labour Exchanges Act, the Finance Act of 1910, and the Insurance Act. It may be remarked that the Old Age Pensions Act, with its immense addition to the annual national expenditure, was run with a mere handful of extra officials, who were appointed from those who had passed examinations for the Excise.

Photo: Russell, London

A. BONAR LAW

In introducing a few weeks later the first reading of
the Home Rule Bill of 1912, I quoted from a speech
recently delivered by him at Belfast in much the same
vein. He denounced the Irish policy of the Government as "nothing better than the latest move in a con-
spiracy as treacherous as ever has been formed against
the life of a great nation," and added that "the present
Government turned the House of Commons into a
market-place where everything is bought and sold."
I asked whether he was prepared to repeat these
charges on the floor of the House of Commons. He replied in the affirmative. Then I rejoined: "Let us see
what it is. It is that I and my colleagues are selling
our convictions." To which Mr. Bonar Law responded: "You have not got any."

A year later at Norwich (November, 1913) he said:

For years they [the Government] have posed as the
Pharisees of politics. They have made broad their phylacteries; they were not as other men, or even as these
Tories: and now words are unnecessary. They stand before the country for what they are — Pharisees still, but
Pharisees stripped of their phylacteries, *naked* [!], and not
even ashamed.

Or, again:

Suppose the Home Rule Bill . . . had passed through
all its stages, and was waiting for the Sovereign to decide
whether or not it would become law. . . . What would
then be the position of the Sovereign of this country?
*Whatever he did, half his people would think he had failed
in his duty.* . . . That any loyal servant of the Crown
should put his Sovereign in such a position would have been,
till a year ago, incredible. To put him in such a position
would be a *crime* greater, in my opinion, than *has ever been*

committed by any Minister who had ever held power.
[Edinburgh, January 24, 1913.]

As was pointed out the next day by Herbert Samuel, a more grotesque travesty of constitutional law and practice it is impossible to conceive.

But perhaps the most conspicuous of Mr. Bonar Law's rhetorical lapses is to be found in what he said at Dublin, of all places, about the attitude of the army (November 28, 1913):

I ask him [Mr. Asquith] to turn his mind to the history of the great Revolution.   Then the country rose against a tyranny.   It was the tyranny of a King, but other people besides kings can exercise tyranny, and other people besides kings can be treated in the same way.   I remember this, that King James had behind him the letter of the law just as completely as Mr. Asquith has now.[1]   He made sure of it. He got the judges on his side by methods *not dissimilar from those* by which Mr. Asquith has a majority of the House of Commons on his side.   There is another point to which I would specially refer.   In order to carry out his despotic intention the King had the largest army which had ever been seen in England.   What happened?   There was no Civil War.   There was a Revolution, and the King disappeared.   Why?   Because his own army refused to fight for him.

The legislative veto of the House of Lords was then a lively issue; but this was, if words have any meaning, an assertion by the leader of the Tory party in the House of Commons of an ultimate legislative veto in the army.

There can be no doubt, whatever may be thought of its taste, that Mr. Law's frequent resort to what I de-

---

[1] A bold statement in view of the trial of the Seven Bishops, which cut the ground from under the Dispensation Ordinance.

scribed as the "new style" in the early days of his
leadership aroused the enthusiasm of the more blood-
thirsty of his followers, who spoke and wrote of him
admiringly as the "Fighting Leader."

I have described in a previous book[1] the attempts
which were made in the autumn of 1913, with honest
intention on both sides, but without practical result,
to arrive by negotiation and agreement at a settlement
of the Ulster difficulty.   There was, as I have said
there, not only "much platform speaking on the subject," but "some conversations under the seal of confidence between leading men."   It was in this way that
I first came to have direct personal contact with Mr.
Bonar Law. Sir Edward Carson I had known for years
at the Bar, in the daily *camaraderie* of a great profession, of which it is the fine tradition that hot and hardly
fought contentions in the forensic arena are never
allowed to interfere with the ties and even the intima-
cies of friendship.   It was essential that these pourparlers should be carried on — so far as that is possible
— outside the ken of our ubiquitous Press; and I remember well that my first "heart-to-heart" conversation with Mr. Bonar Law took place in a country house
not far from London, to which I drove on a November
afternoon, to find him playing a game of double dummy
with his host. If we did not make much progress it was
certainly from no lack on his part of courtesy or of
honest endeavour to understand and appreciate an opponent's point of view.

The change from Mr. Balfour's methods of leadership to Mr. Bonar Law's was as striking as the contrast

"Fifty Years of British Parliament."

between their methods of dialectic. Mr. Balfour, I suppose, rarely, if ever, prepared the form, as distinguished from the main theme, of a speech: he got his material from the progress of the debate, and could safely rely upon his faculty of assimilation, of improvisation, or riposte and repartee. Mr. Bonar Law combined exceptional natural fluency with a faithful and tenacious memory. He seldom used notes — not even the long envelope upon which Mr. Balfour would jot down the vulnerable points of an adversary's speech to serve him as an *aide mémoire* when he rose to reply. I remember Law even introducing a Budget with no other material aid than a single sheet of note-paper, and he had such a rapid intuition for marking, and making effective use of, debatable points that it was impossible, even for an expert observer, to guess how much or how little preparation he had given to his speech. He equipped himself in advance with a panoply of facts and figures, possibly even of phrases, which a highly-trained memory kept in storage, and always available for immediate and appropriate use in the vicissitudes and emergencies of the parliamentary arena.

CHAPTER XXV

THE MARCONI EPISODE

IN the spring and summer of 1912 the attention of the House of Commons was from time to time diverted from political matters by grave and scandalous charges, made in a certain section of the Press, against the honour of members of the Government. The Imperial Conference held in June, 1911, had passed a resolution in favour of the establishment of a chain of State-owned wireless telegraph stations within the Empire. The Marconi Company, which had already applied for licences to construct some stations, were invited to tender. Their tender was accepted by the Postmaster-General in March, 1912, subject to its embodiment in a formal contract to be laid before the House of Commons for ratification. As soon as the terms of the contract were known, motions for its rejection were put upon the paper of the House, and after the summer adjournment the matter came on for debate in October. The rumours already referred to had by then crystallized into two definite allegations:

(1) That certain Ministers had corruptly favoured the Marconi Company in obtaining the contract because the Managing Director, Mr. Godfrey Isaacs, was the brother of the Attorney-General, Sir Rufus Isaacs:

(2) That certain Ministers, making use of the knowledge which they had acquired as Min-

isters, had dealt on the Stock Exchange in the shares of the favoured company, and thereby make considerable profits for themselves.

The first charge was mainly directed against Herbert Samuel, the Postmaster-General, who had negotiated the contract with the company. In the most scurrilous of the organs in the Press which conducted the campaign of calumny it was shortly stated as follows:

Isaacs's brother is chairman of the Marconi Company. It has, therefore, been secretly arranged between Isaacs and Samuel that the British people shall give the Marconi Company a very large sum of money through the agency of the said Samuel and for the benefit of the said Isaacs.

Mr. Samuel consulted Sir Rufus Isaacs as to whether he should seek redress in a court of law. Sir Rufus, not unnaturally, referred the matter to me. My reply was: "I have read carefully this scurrilous rubbish, and I am clearly of opinion that you should take no notice of it."

The second charge was aimed, not at Mr. Samuel, but at Rufus Isaacs himself, and in association with him, at Mr. Lloyd George, the Chancellor of the Exchequer, and the Master of Elibank, who had recently resigned the office of Chief Whip. At the end of 1911 and in the early months of 1912, there had been a spectacular rise in the shares of the Marconi Company —from 40s. in August, 1911, to about £4 and 3/8ths in March, 1912, when the acceptance of their tender was made public, and by the end of April the price had been run up to over £9. The allegation was that, acting upon the inside knowledge to which they had access as colleagues of Mr. Samuel, Sir Rufus Isaacs and his two colleagues had bought blocks of shares in this company for the rise, and had pocketed the profits.

When the debate on the Marconi contract took place on October 11, 1912, these rumours having grown in the meantime in volume and in virulence, the Government proposed the appointment of a Select Committee "to investigate the circumstances connected with the negotiation and completion" of the Marconi contract, and to "report thereupon, and whether the Agreement is desirable and should be approved."

There was not the slightest foundation in fact for either of the two sets of allegation. No attempt was made to justify or even to pursue the ridiculous charge against Mr. Samuel. Sir Rufus Isaacs and his two colleagues had not had any transactions in the shares of the Marconi Company, who were the parties and the only parties to the contract with the Postmaster-General, and whose shares had been the subject of the sensational "boom." It is true that they had bought shares in an American Marconi Company, whose prospects, through an arrangement for joint working with the powerful Western Union Telegraph Company, had substantially improved. But they had first been careful to satisfy themselves:

(1) That the American company had no interest whatever in the British company;

(2) That it had no interest in any contracts which the British company made with the British Government;

(3) That its sphere of operations was confined to the working of the Marconi patents in the United States.

They therefore considered themselves perfectly justified in thinking that it was a transaction which could not possibly conflict with their duties as Ministers. They sold some of the American shares, but retained the remainder, Mr. Lloyd George, as he told the Select Committee, considering it a " thoroughly good investment," and on balance they were substantial losers by the transaction.

In the debate on the appointment of the Select Committee, Sir Rufus Isaacs and Mr. Lloyd George confined themselves to denying the suggestion that they had ever had any interest, direct or indirect, in the English Marconi Company: that being the whole gravamen of the accusations and insinuations that had up to that time been made against them. Neither of them thought it necessary or relevant to refer to the American transaction, which was unknown both to their traducers and their friends, and had no bearing upon the charges which they were challenged to meet. This was undoubtedly an error of judgment, as both subsequently acknowledged: but it is to be remembered that they were looking forward to an early appearance as witnesses before the Committee, and might well think that it would confuse the general issue if they were to divert attention by the introduction at that stage of irrelevant matter.

The Committee issued its Report on June 13, 1913. It consisted of fifteen members, and after taking evidence for months, it considered and voted upon two draft reports, one prepared by Mr. Falconer, the other by Lord Robert Cecil. The former was in the end adopted by a majority of 2 — 8 votes to 6.

Both the draft reports acquitted the Ministers concerned of all the charges which had led to the appointment of the Committee. Upon this point the Minority Report was as explicit and definite as that of the Majority. The main point of difference between them was in the view which they took of the transactions in the American shares. The Minority found the Ministers concerned guilty of "grave impropriety." The Majority was of opinion that the Ministers were all "*bona fide* convinced"—as was the fact—that the American company had no interest in the agreement between the Postmaster-General and the English company; that "on the whole matters relating to the conduct of Ministers which have come before the Committee, all the Ministers concerned have acted throughout in the sincere belief that there was nothing in their action which would in any way conflict with their duty as Ministers of the Crown"; and that there is "no ground for any charge of corruption or unfaithfulness to public duty or for any reflection on the honour of any of them."

A few days after the publication of the Report a vote of censure on the Ministers concerned was moved in the House of Commons by Mr. Cave on behalf of the Opposition. It was based on two grounds:

(1) Their transactions in the shares of the American company;

(2) Their "want of frankness" in their communications on the subject in October to the House.

This was rejected on a division by 346 to 268, and an amendment proposed by Sir Ryland Atkins adopted unanimously: that the House having heard the state-

ments of the Attorney-General and the Chancellor of
the Exchequer in reference to their purchases of shares
in the American company, "accepts their expressions
of regret that such purchases were made, and that they
were not mentioned in the debate of October 11, acquits
them of acting otherwise than in good faith, and repro-
bates the charges of corruption brought against Ministers which have been proved to be wholly false."

Both Ministers in their speeches had acknowledged
with the utmost frankness that both the purchase of the
shares and the failure to disclose the transaction in the
debate of the preceding October were errors of judgment.

The debate was not an agreeable one, and did not,
in my opinion, show the House of Commons at its best.
There was, in particular, a marked difference in tone
and temper between Mr. Balfour's speech and that of
Mr. Bonar Law. I took the opportunity to formulate
rules, which I divided into the two categories of Rules
of Obligation and Rules of Prudence.

"The first, of course, and the most obvious is that
(1) Ministers ought not to enter into any transaction
whereby their private pecuniary interests might, even
conceivably, come into conflict with their public duty.
There is no dispute about that. Again, (2) no Minister
is justified, under any circumstances, in using official
information, information that has come to him as a
Minister, for his own private profit or for that of his
friends. Further, (3) no Minister ought to allow or to
put himself in a position to be tempted to use his official
influence in support of any scheme, or in furtherance
of any contract, in regard to which he has an undisclosed

private interest. That again is beyond dispute. Again,
(4) no Minister ought to accept from persons who are
in negotiation with or seeking to enter into contractual
or proprietary or pecuniary relations with the State,
any kind of favour. That, I think, is also beyond dispute. I will add a further proposition, which I am not
sure has been completely formulated, though it has no
doubt been adumbrated in the course of these debates,
and that is that (5) Ministers should scrupulously
avoid speculative investments in securities as to which,
from their position and their special means of early
or confidential information they have, or may have, an
advantage over other people in anticipating market
changes.

"This is not an exhaustive code, but these are Rules
of Obligation, none of which were violated by the two
Ministers involved in the case."

I added:

I think that in addition to those rules, which I have described as Rules of Obligation — because it seems to me that
they have an ethical value and sanction, as well as being
based on grounds of expediency and policy — there are, or
there certainly ought to be, Rules of Prudence specially applicable to Ministers and to persons in positions of official
responsibility, rules which perhaps never have been formulated, and which it would be very difficult to formulate in
precise or universal terms. One of those rules is that in
these matters such persons should carefully avoid all transactions which can give colour or countenance to the belief
that they are doing anything which the Rules of Obligation
forbid. It was that rule, which I call a rule of Prudence,
which in my opinion, and in the opinion of my right honourable friends and colleagues, was not fully observed,
though with complete innocence of intention, in this case.
It has always been my opinion, and it is their opinion,

as they told the House quite frankly in the fullest and most manly way.

I have been as frank as my right honourable friends were frank in acknowledging what both they and I think was a mistake in judgment. But their honour, both their private and their public honour, is at this moment absolutely unstained. They have, as this Committee has shown by its unanimous verdict, abused no public trust. They retain, I can say this with full assurance, the complete confidence of their colleagues and of their political associates.

CHAPTER XXVI

WOMEN IN POLITICS

IN these days of triumphant Feminism, when women have stormed one after another the outworks, and in the end penetrated into the citadel, of Sex Domination, the question whether their real influence in politics has grown or diminished may seem to admit of but one reply. I have witnessed almost all the stages of the campaign. I have been throughout an advocate of the admission of women on the same terms as men to professional and business callings and to the discharge of administrative functions in municipal and local affairs. As far back as 1892, when I came to the Home Office, I was the first Secretary of State to open the Factory Inspectorate to women against the almost unbroken hostility of my expert advisers. On the other hand, I was, until near the close of the War, a strenuous opponent of the extension of the political franchise to women. I gave the reasons for my change of attitude in a speech in the House of Commons on March 28, 1917. It was after the Speaker's Conference, which was called at my suggestion in October, 1916, had reported in favour of "some measure of Woman Suffrage."

I had always pointed out that, if and when the change were made, it must, sooner or later, be carried to its legitimate conclusions, which the more timid of the Suffragists were loath to face: the assimilation in all material conditions of the male and female franchise, and the eligibility of women to the House of Commons. Having once ruled out the principle of sex discrimination on the vital issue, you cannot consistently or fairly reintroduce it in what are after all subordinate matters. The result of the removal of the illogical restrictions by which the grant of the franchise was clogged must inevitably be to make the women a majority of the whole parliamentary electorate. And admission to the House of Lords can hardly any longer be denied to ladies who, if they belonged to the other sex, would sit there by an hereditary title.

This apparent victory of women all along the line is not, in practice, so significant as it sometimes seems both to enthusiasts and to pessimists. Women do not in fact now, and probably never will, vote *en bloc* and as a class. And the experts in electioneering tell us that with very rare exceptions, in any average constituency, a female candidate is handicapped by her sex.

These, however, are for the most part speculations as to a conjectural and still uncertain future. We are on more solid ground when we seek to estimate the relative influence which individual women have exercised upon politicians and on the course of government in our own times as compared with other eras in English public life. It is not necessary, nor would it be in any way instructive, to go back to the days of Queen Anne. She presided at Cabinets, and her personality was a real factor in the choice both of Ministers and policies; but she was swayed, this way and that, by the capricious interplay of the cajoleries and intrigues of female favourites. Nor need one recall the power exercised by Mrs. Howard, and much more effectively by Queen

Caroline in the days of George II. The most successful masters of the House of Commons in the eighteenth
century — Walpole, the two Pitts, Lord North — were
none of them under the personal influence of women.
The frigidity of the younger Pitt was a favourite theme
with the coarser of the Whig epigrammatists and
ballad-makers, and there is only one authentic instance
in his biography of his succumbing to the commonest
fraility of mankind. He seems really to have been in
love with Eleanor Eden, the daughter of Lord Auck-
land. He was then (1796) at the height of his fame
and power: he had been twelve years Prime Minister,
and was still well under forty. But his private debts
were already so formidable that both he himself and
the lady's father seem to have thought marriage out of
the question.

Nevertheless, the influence of the Great Ladies was
in Pitts's time a factor in politics. The Whig Opposition was in this matter better equipped than the Min-
isterialists. The liveliest picture, both of the persons
concerned and their ways and methods, is to be found
in the incomparable letters of Lady Bessborough,[1] herself, with her more famous elder sister, the beautiful
Georgiana, Duchess of Devonshire,[2] not only an ob-
servant and interested onlooker, but playing from time
to time a not inactive part in the varied and often brilliant scene. A generation later, the Princess Lieven,
the Russian Ambassadress, and Mrs. Norton were
much in the confidence of leading statesmen of the day.

[1] "Lord Granville Leveson-Gower": Private Correspondence. Edited by
Castalia, Countess Granville (1916).
[2] They were daughters of the first Lord Spencer. According to Lady Hester
Stanhope, Lady Bessborough "had ten times more cleverness than her sister the
Duchess."

When the Victorian age arrived, the Queen herself became, after her apprenticeship under Lord Melbourne, a potent and sometimes, with the guidance during his lifetime of Prince Albert, a dominating figure. Her letters show with what thoroughness she kept herself informed even of the details of administration and policy, and how frequent was her intervention, whether by way of warning, of remonstrance, or of encouragement. She had strong personal partialities and antipathies. So far as one can judge after the death of Sir Robert Peel, she liked none of her Prime Ministers until after years of suspicion and mistrust she succumbed to the spell of Disraeli.

Among those Prime Ministers there were two—Palmerston and Gladstone—who may fairly be said to have made their wives their intimate political confidantes. Each of these wrapped herself up with unfailing, and for the most part uncritical, devotion in her husband's career. Lady Palmerston's social gifts and her complete command of all the arts and technique of the *Salon* made her an active and most efficient co-partner in Palmerston's fortunes. She could also on occasion hit out fiercely but shrewdly in her husband's defence. On his dismissal from the Foreign Office by Lord John Russell in January, 1852, she writes to her brother:

John has behaved shamefully ill to Palmerston. No doubt the Queen and Prince wanted to get Palmerston out and Granville in, because they thought he would be pliable and subservient, and would let Albert manage the Foreign Office, which is what he had always wanted. . . . John has behaved like a little blackguard. . . . I am still vexed and provoked at the whole thing, but I take it much more calmly.

It is so lucky for an effervescing woman to have such a calm and placid husband, which no events can irritate or make him lose his temper [*sic*].[1]

Mrs. Disraeli used to say: "Dizzy married me for my money, but if he had the chance again he would marry me for love." She was a woman of little cultivation and less tact; but she had the kindest of hearts, and is credited by Mr. Buckle with the gifts both of feminine intuition and of judgment. Curiously enough, Mr. Gladstone had a warm friendship for her. It was, in all essentials, a most successful marriage, but in no real sense a political partnership. Lord Beaconsfield survived his wife, and the letters, published in Mr. Buckle's "Life," show that in his later years there were few political secrets that he kept back from Lady Bradford.[2]

Among the propagandists of the movement for the emancipation of women, of whom John Stuart Mill was the intellectual pioneer, the example of the Queen was a great asset as disproving the familiar gibe that the inherent incapacities of the sex disabled them from taking a place side by side with men in the transaction of serious affairs. The case of George Eliot was another of their most telling *argumenta ad feminam*. She was then at the height of her fame: sober critics like Richard Hutton placed her on the same level as our greatest creative writers in the past,[3] and many quiet supporters of things as they existed were disconcerted

[1] Guedalla: "Palmerston," pp. 324-5.
[2] Mr. Somervell aptly quotes from "Lothair": "Three-score years and ten at the present day is the period of romantic passions." ("Disraeli and Gladstone," p. 292.)
[3] See Miss Haldane's "George Eliot and Her Times" (1927).

by the baffling inquiry on what ground they denied to George Eliot the vote which was given to her gardener.

The memory of Jane Austen, and the living instances of Charlotte Brontë, Mrs. Browning, George Eliot, Mrs. Gaskell, not to dwell on those prime favourites of the circulating libraries — Miss Braddon, Mrs. Henry Wood, Miss Yonge, and later Ouida and Miss Rhoda Broughton,[1] undoubtedly had a powerful effect on Victorian opinion in helping to bring to a close the era of what Mill described as the " Subjection of Women." Perhaps a more potent cause was the opening of the platform to female oratory. Long before the militant excesses of the " Suffragettes " the cause of the enfranchisement of woman had found, among the sex, advocates who could hold their own on the platform with the best male speakers. In the 'eighties and 'nineties there was an imposing and constantly recruited array of such standard-bearers and missionaries. Mrs. Fawcett, Lady Frances Balfour, Lady Henry Somerset — to name only a few — not only displayed extraordinary gifts of persuasive dielectic and moving eloquence, but they achieved what their mothers, and in those days the large majority of " their sisters and their cousins and their aunts," would have regarded as an unseemly, because an " unwomanly " triumph: they gradually trained the stolid masculine audience at political meetings to regard the spectacle of women sitting

---

[1] Miss Broughton, whose friendship I enjoyed, exclaimed when her popularity began to wane: "I began by being the Zola and I have now become the Charlotte Yonge of English fiction." She once told me that she had seen on the bookstall at Newcastle Station a pile of second-hand novels, tied up with a string, with the inscription: "Rhoda Broughton — soiled and cheap."

on the platform — sometimes in the chair — moving resolutions and even amendments, not with a silent conventional curtsy and smile, but with flights of rhetoric and flashes of humour, as part of the normal machinery of a "demonstration" or a "rally." [1]

I will only add, as I may, without lifting the veil of necessary reserve, that there can never have been a politician who owed more than I have done to the wise counsels, the unfailing courage, and the ever vitalizing companionship of a wife.

One of the most curious episodes in the history of popular agitation was the campaign organized and carried on between 1909 and 1914 by the militant wing of the supporters of woman suffrage, who went by the nickname of "Suffragettes."

Upon the question of the grant of the franchise to women both political parties were divided, and the situation was the same in the Cabinet. I myself, Lord Loreburn, Mr. Lewis Harcourt and others were opponents, and Sir Edward Grey, Mr. Haldane and Mr. Lloyd George were supporters of the change. In these circumstances it was impossible for the Government as a Government to make it part of their programme, and a succession of private members' Bills were introduced. They made no progress, and on the eve of the second general election in 1910 I promised on behalf of the Government "to give facilities for effectively proceeding with a Bill which is framed so as to admit of free amendment." In the end a Bill dealing with

---

[1] George Eliot, though she had "many friends of the so-called 'advanced' school," when feminism was starting on its new lines of progress, "was almost angry at the 'rather tactless suggestion' from one of them that she should take to the platform." (Miss Haldane, p. 307.).

various matters connected with the franchise was introduced by the Government, with the avowed intention
of allowing the enfranchisement of women to be raised
and settled by a free vote in Committee. A number of
amendments in that sense were put down, and were believed by us and by all parties concerned to be in order.
To the universal surprise the Speaker (January, 1913),
as I have mentioned in an earlier chapter, ruled that
they were outside the scope of the Bill and must be dealt
with in a separate measure. I immediately stated that
in view of the pledges we had given we should not deem
it right to proceed with the Franchise Bill, which was
therefore withdrawn. I added that we would offer facilities for a private members' Bill in the succeeding
session, as to which members of the Government would
be free to vote at every stage as they saw fit.

This was accepted by the leading supporters of the
woman's cause in the House of Commons as the best
way of dealing with the question. But it was regarded
by the militant suffragists outside as a trick, and as far
as their representatives in the House were concerned
as a betrayal of their cause. They demanded nothing
short of the introduction of a Government measure.

The "campaign" had begun by the organized disturbance of meetings, of which Mr. Lloyd George's
famous meeting at Limehouse on July 30, 1909, was an
early example. A climax was reached when in September, the same year, I went to Birmingham to address
a huge demonstration in the Bingley Hall on the Veto
of the House of Lords. The following account from a
local newspaper is a substantially accurate narrative
of what occurred:

The city gave the appearance on this occasion of being in a state of siege, for barricades were erected everywhere the Prime Minister was expected to go, and on his arrival at the station he was smuggled into the adjoining hotel in the luggage lift. The extraordinary precautions taken to exclude Suffragettes from the Bingley Hall were successful, but two of them . . . succeeded in reaching an adjoining roof, from which point of vantage they hurled slates and other missiles into the street below, and on to the roof of the hall. They were eventually dislodged with the assistance of a fire-hose.

The next stage was marked by the resort to open violence by stone-throwing and personal assaults. "These earliest manifestations of distinctive militancy," says a sympathetic writer,[1] "were largely of a symbolic character intended to typify the strength of the movement." She no doubt had in view such incidents as a visit which I paid to Liverpool, when " two suffragettes disguised themselves as coster-girls and succeeded in getting near Mr. Asquith, and one of them contemptuously tossed an empty bottle into a car from which he had just alighted." But such "symbolic manifestations " as these were soon exchanged for others of a more practical kind.

I had my full share of their attentions. In July, 1912, I went to Dublin to speak at the Theatre Royal, which two or three of the militant ladies attempted to set on fire the day before the meeting. I was driving with my wife and Mr. John Redmond in an open carriage through the crowded streets of Dublin at night, when a woman on the pavement threw a hatchet at us. It was no doubt intended for me, but it was badly

---

[1] "Woman's Effort, 1865–1914," by A. E. Metcalfe (1917): a curious book.

aimed, and struck Mr. Redmond on the cheek. A little later, while I was engaged in trying to hole a putt on the links at Lossiemouth, two young women pounced upon me, and were driven off by my daughter, niblick in hand. The same year I was driving with my hostess to unveil a statue to Campbell-Bannerman at Stirling. As we were passing Bannockburn the carriage was held up by a band of women, armed with bags of red pepper, with which they sprinkled us, while one of them tried to belabour me with a dog-whip. The author already cited, remarks that "on both occasions arrests were made, but the matter was allowed to drop." She adds that visits which I made the same autumn to Birmingham, Leeds and Manchester were the occasion for the militants to attack pillar-boxes, to spread false fire-alarms, and to set fire to a football stand and other forms of property.

The third and last stage was reached after the withdrawal of the Franchise Bill in January, 1913. "Up to this point," says the historian of the movement, "there had been isolated cases of arson." (For instance, a woman attempted in 1912 to set fire to the children's quarters at Nuneham House, Mr. Harcourt's country residence.) "Now . . . the agitation took on a far more serious phase. . . . They determined to engage in militancy of a kind that would produce the maximum effect compatible with the retention of their individual liberty for so long as possible. With this deliberate twofold intention the campaign of arson began."[1] The same authority has been at the pains to collect from the newspapers the number of reported

[1] "Woman's Effort, 1865-1914," p. 242.

cases of arson in 1913 and 1914—some of them of a most serious character—and comments with apparent complacency on the few arrests that were made. During the same time numerous attempts were made to slash or deface works of art in the public galleries and museums, with the result that by way of precaution no fewer than fifteen galleries were closed.

The women who took part in these insensate outrages did not, of course, belong to the criminal class. They were for the most part genuine fanatics, with something of the temper of the martyr. How to deal with them, and at the same time give effectual protection to person and property, was a problem which taxed the ingenuity of successive Home Secretaries, and the most experienced officers of the police and the prisons. Forcible feeding and the "Cat and Mouse Act" were expedients which were repugnant to everybody, and most of all to those who were directly concerned in their administration. Militancy ceased with the outbreak of War. On August 11, 1914, Mr. McKenna announced that he had advised His Majesty to remit the remainder of the prisoners' sentences. "His Majesty," he said, was "confident that they could be trusted not to stain the cause they had at heart by any further crime or disorder."

Thereupon they were unconditionally released and thereafter they kept the peace.

CHAPTER XXVII

PLATFORM; PULPIT; PRESS

THE organized use of the platform as an instrument of propaganda may be said to date from the initiation of the Anti-Corn Law League, founded in 1838, in the early forties of the nineteenth century. Cobbett, the greatest master of agitation in the preceding thirty years, did the bulk of his work by tracts, pamphlets and journalism: his pen was his most effective weapon, and he wielded it to better purpose than any of his contemporaries. "Mass" meetings were not unknown, such as the famous one held by "Orator" Hunt, which was dispersed by force at Peterloo in 1818; or the demonstrations in favour of Reform in 1830-2; or the vast gatherings which O'Connell organized in Ireland in the cause of Catholic Emancipation, and later of Repeal.

But the Anti-Corn Law movement was developed upon a scale, and with a systematic and continuous use of the platform, for which there was no previous precedent. The parliamentary case for Free Trade had been repeatedly and cogently presented in the House of Commons before either Cobden or Bright entered its doors, by Charles Villiers, a Whig *pur sang*, and, amongst others, by Palmerston, who had never been and never became a Whig, and at this stage of his career may best be described as a Canningite Liberal, and who as far back as 1832 had declared in a memorable speech that "what were called Protecting

duties were in fact Disturbing duties."[1]   But the driving force, without which the Free Trade victory would
at any rate have been less rapid and complete, was supplied from outside.   The leaders of the League, if they
showed good political discernment in the choice of the
platform as their main engine of propaganda, were
singularly fortunate in finding in their ranks three men,
all of middle-class origin, with such rare and diverse
gifts for platform oratory as Cobden, Bright, and
W. J. Fox.[2]   Never since, in the eighty odd years which
have witnessed agitations almost without number, carried on through the machinery of public meetings,
with speakers of every type and class, has the art been
practised with more skill and effect than it was by this
little band of accomplished pioneers.

It has happened so often, that it has now become a
commonplace to say that the gifts which make a man
an effective platform speaker are not by any means a
passport to parliamentary success.   During my early
years at Westminster, probably the two members most
in request for public meetings in the country were Sir
Ellis Ashmead Bartlett on the one side, and Samuel
Danks Waddy, Q.C., on the other: neither of whom
was listened to gladly by the House of Commons.   I
remember that in 1891 a Bill was introduced by an
eccentric Tory called Atkinson to limit the duration
of speeches in Parliament.   The Bill proposed to enact
that, with the exception of Privy Councillors, no member's speech should exceed a quarter of an hour, at the
end of which time " the Clerk shall sound such a bell as

[1] Guedalla's "Palmerston," p. 170.
[2] The Chartists had no such luck; see Trevelyan's "Bright," p. 61.

is used at Diocesan Conferences." The accompanying
sketch, which was drawn for me in the House, on the
back of the Bill, by Frank Lockwood, depicts Waddy
on the floor in the full blast of a fiery speech suddenly
cut short by the ringing of the bell. But there could
be no doubt as to Waddy's capacity for holding and

S. D. WADDY AND THE TIME-LIMIT BELL
(*A sketch by Sir Frank Lockwood*)

moving a public meeting. I have myself seen him, during the agitation against the Balfour Coercion regime,
describe, probably for the hundredth time, the eviction
of a certain Widow Malone — producing from his
breast-pocket and brandishing aloft a soiled bundle of
"receipts" for her rent — with such dramatic effect

that a large part of the audience, who hung on his lips, were reduced to tears.

Ashmead Bartlett, whose extra-parliamentary reputation was, I believe, equally great, I never heard on a platform, owing to the unfortunate convention which prevents professional politicians, unless duly disguised, from attending the meetings of the opposite party.

Bright, in my time, had ceased to be a regular speaker either inside or outside Parliament.[1] After his practical retirement, there could be no question that the one man who was equally and easily first alike on the platform and on the floor of the House was Gladstone. His first Midlothian campaign in 1879–80 may be said to have opened a new era in the development of outside agitation. It was carefully stage-managed, amongst other fresh features being the gatherings arranged at wayside stations, and the allocutions delivered from the windows or doors of railway carriages; now, unhappily, a regular incident in the itinerary of a political leader.[2] Gladstone adapted himself to the new conditions, with the miraculous versatility, physical and intellectual, which was one of his rare endowments. In 1886, after the defeat of the first Home Rule Bill, his performances at Liverpool, Manchester, and other great centres — he was then in his seventy-seventh year — could not have been equalled by any other speaker

---

[1] Lord Salisbury's judgment was that "he was the greatest master of English oratory that this generation has produced, or, I may say, several generations past. I have met men who have heard Pitt and Fox, and in whose judgment their eloquence at its best was inferior to the finest efforts of John Bright" (House of Lords, April, 1889).

[2] Curiously enough, it seems to have been Lord Palmerston who began this practice. See Guedalla, pp. 421–2.

in the country. And, six years later, he varied the daily round of his last Midlothian campaign by a series of excursions and incursions into other constituencies.

And yet prima facie one might have thought that Gladstone's oratorical methods, full as they were of subtleties and reservations, were not of the *ad captandum* kind which is supposed to attract a popular audience. John Bright's distinction between his own and Gladstone's way of speaking deserves to be remembered. "When I speak I strike across from headland to headland. Mr. Gladstone follows the coast-line: and when he comes to a navigable river he is unable to resist the temptation of tracing it to its source." Gladstone was never at any pains to "talk down" to his hearers. Nor would he spare them details, and even minutiæ, which he thought relevant to his case, and which, in any other hands, would have tried the patience of the most sympathetic gathering.

Lord Curzon, in his Rede Lecture on "Modern Parliamentary Eloquence," delivered before the University of Cambridge in 1913, after paying a glowing tribute to Gladstone's supreme gift of speaking— "there was no resource of oratory, intellectual, emotional, or external, that was not at his command"— adds, with perfect truth, that "he was an orator to be heard rather than to be read." "His triumph on the platform, which appears to have become greater as he advanced in years, was the triumph of a moral force quite as much as an eloquent tongue." "If we take up the two volumes of the Midlothian Speeches in 1879 and 1880 . . . it is difficult to believe that these interminable and involved harangues were the spell that stirred the heart of an entire nation."

A notable instance was his speech to a vast audience of over 20,000 in the Bingley Hall at Birmingham — during the Coercion controversy — when he chose as his principal topic the conduct of the Irish police at Mitchelstown. He had even equipped himself with a series of photographs, to illustrate and confirm his theory as to the flight of a particular bullet. Many years later, in the course of the Budget agitation in 1909, I myself addressed a similar gathering in the same hall, and, realizing the conditions, was filled with amazement at Gladstone's *tour de force*. The explanation is to be found not only in his great dramatic gifts, and the magic of his personality, but in his power of suddenly lighting up a prosaic narrative, or a subtly reasoned demonstration, with one of those majestic and inspiring flashes of the highest order of oratory, of which he alone still possessed the secret. One of the finest passages in the whole range of English eloquence — the simile of Castor and Pollux — is to be found embedded in his speech at Glasgow in 1892, of which the main subject was the singularly arid theme of Maltese marriages.

It is easy to exaggerate, and equally easy to disparage, both the meaning and the effect of public meetings, and the whole function of platform oratory: their meaning as an expression of opinion; their effect, as a vehicle of propaganda. There have been in our time very few *educative* platform campaigns. The Anti-Corn Law agitation was one: Cobden's speeches, which in the long run had a greater popular effect than the rhetoric of Bright and Fox, were "unadorned" appeals to the intelligence of his hearers — masterpieces of argumentative persuasion.[1]

I may be suspected of bias if I name as another instance the controversy, carried on almost entirely at public meetings, for the parliamentary organ had been artificially put out of action, between Mr. Chamberlain and myself and other Free Traders, on the fiscal question between 1903 and 1905.

Since the days of O'Connell and Bright, among the great parliamentary speakers who have graduated on the platform perhaps the most conspicuous figures are those of Joseph Chamberlain himself, Randolph Churchill, and Lloyd George.

THE PULPIT

I have referred in previous pages to the changes which have taken place in my time in the methods and character of parliamentary oratory — many for the worse, some perhaps for the better. In another branch of the art of speaking — that of preaching — the change is equally marked, and the net result has been a definite decline, so far as the principal performers are concerned, in attractiveness and efficiency. During the greater part of the nineteenth century there was both in England and in Scotland a succession of great preachers, and the most distinguished among them were to be found in the ranks of the Presbyterians and

---

[1] Cobden was equally effective, and for the same reason, in the parliamentary arena. When he died in 1865 Disraeli in the House of Commons in a most felicitous eulogium, as Lord Curzon says, of "unusual simplicity," described him as one of those members of Parliament "who, though not present in the body, are still members of this House, independent of dissolutions, of the caprice of constituencies, even of the course of time."

Nonconformists quite as often as in the Church of England. It may be doubted whether we have ever had a greater pulpit orator in the best sense — for he had none of the histrionics of Whitefield — than Robert Hall, who was a Baptist. Quite apart from the special gifts which made him pre-eminent in the pulpit, Hall was a man of wide culture. He was a victim all his life to an excruciating internal malady which never allowed him a night's peace, and which he endured with heroic patience. When in the mood, he was a brilliant talker. Of a contemporary divine he once said: "His mind seems to move on hinges, not on wheels: there is incessant motion, but no progress."

Chalmers and Edward Irving, whom Gladstone considered the finest preacher he ever heard, could command congregations in London greater in numbers and higher in intellectual quality than any Anglican preacher of the day. Newman's sermons, unsurpassed in their way, are probably at least as good to read as they were to hear. During the first half of last century the highest level of preaching in the Church of England was reached in a moderate-sized chapel in a fashionable watering-place by F. W. Robertson of Brighton. The originality of his thought, his insight into human nature, his rare felicity in the choice of words, illustrations and metaphors, the independence of his point of view, the impressiveness of his appeals, never tainted for a moment with claptrap or maudlin rhetoric — all these qualities were set off by the gifts of eye, voice, gesture, which only a speaker of the highest order has at his command. High Churchmen and Evangelicals joined forces in the petty campaign of vilification and misrepresentation which was waged against him while he lived. Their descendants are happily wiser in their day; and we have recently been witnessing in his case a repetition of the spectacle, so familiar in history, of a later generation building the tomb of a prophet whom their fathers stoned.

As I was not born until the second half of the century had begun, I can only speak at first-hand of some successors of these great figures. My own bringing up was among the Nonconformists: all my people were great chapel-goers: and my grandfather's house at Huddersfield often sheltered the big guns of the Congregational pulpit. Among those whom I can remember in my childhood was James Parsons, of York — an impressive and venerable figure, with a somewhat husky voice and no graces of gesture, who held to the old tradition that every sermon should unfold, in greater or less detail, the whole "scheme of salvation," on the chance that "some poor wandering" sinner might for the first time see the light.

Later on, in my school-days in London, I from time to time listened to the most popular Nonconformist preacher of that era — Spurgeon of the Metropolitan Tabernacle. Spurgeon had begun to preach to large congregations when he was little more than a boy: the Tabernacle in South London had been built for him and was always crowded; and for the greater part of forty years he published and circulated to the ends of the earth his Sunday morning sermon. Probably no preacher in our history ever had a wider audience. He was a man of homely appearance, and largely self-educated, but he had the finest voice I have ever heard, all the resources of an accomplished actor, and could move his hearers at will to laughter or to tears. His theology was of the straitest and most uncompromising type of Puritan orthodoxy: he never moved an inch from the point at which he had started in his youth: and in his later years, when criticism was making destructive inroads into some of the outworks of the "faith once delivered to the saints," he was much exercised by the "down grade" tendencies of not a few of his old co-religionists.

I never had the good fortune to hear the two greatest of the Scottish preachers in the post-disruption era: John Caird of Glasgow University, and Thomas Guthrie of Edinburgh. Norman Macleod, Queen Victoria's favourite, was a burly Highlander of imposing presence and considerable rhetorical gifts. The Queen herself, as her "Letters" show, preferred the Scottish to the English sermon. But the greatest ornament of the Anglican pulpit in the latter half of the century came neither from England nor Scotland.

Magee, an Irishman born and bred, grandson of an Archbishop of Dublin, was, in the height of the controversy over Irish Disestablishment in 1868, promoted by Disraeli — at the Queen's instance — from the Deanery of Cork to the English Bishopric of Peterborough. It was one of his sermons, I believe, that provoked the famous comment of a jaundiced Irish prelate, that "there was not enough Gospel in it to save the soul of a tomtit." His pulpit accomplishments were already well known in England, as he had held cures both in Bath and London, and Disraeli reckoned, with reason, that he would be a welcome and powerful re-

cruit to the anti-Disestablishment forces in the House
of Lords. He was for a generation one of the most
brilliant speakers, if not the most brilliant, in that assembly, although for some years he sat on the bench
of bishops in the company of no less formidable a
competitor than Samuel Wilberforce. He was ultimately promoted, in the last year of his life, to the
Archbishopric of York. Of all the preachers whom I
have heard, I should be inclined to put him first for
range and versatility, for an equal command of humour
and of restrained but impressive and affecting eloquence.

Another eminent Anglican who in those days had
great acceptance as a preacher was Canon Liddon. He
was a student of Christ Church, Oxford, and after a
short novitiate as Vice-Principal of Cuddesdon College, under the wary and somewhat suspicious eye of
the great bishop, he went back to the " House," became
Dr. Pusey's right-hand man, and in time the most effective and influential of the militant leaders of the High
Church party. Though not perhaps technically a great
scholar, he had an adequate equipment of learning,
and was a most accomplished dialectician. He was a
man of great personal charm, and exercised over his
own students an influence as a teacher only comparable
to that of T. H. Green. He was as unlike Spurgeon in
every other respect as two men could be, but they had
this in common: they were both severely "orthodox"
(though no two orthodoxies could have been more
widely divergent), and neither ever moved from his
original standpoint.

It was to Liddon a painful surprise when a band of
the most brilliant of his younger disciples, under the

leadership of Charles Gore, afterwards Bishop of Oxford, combined to produce a volume entitled "Lux
Mundi," in which the extremes of Anglo-Catholic
rigidity were now and again toned down in what he
regarded as a dangerous spirit of compromise with the
Rationalism of the day. His real authority and influence, which extended far beyond the boundaries of the
Anglican Church, were due to his preaching powers.
For the pulpit he had exceptional gifts. His fine
ascetic features, his silvery voice which could penetrate
without effort the farthest recesses of St. Paul's Cathe-
dral, his complete command of all the arts and graces
of elocution, were in themselves an asset of incalculable
value. He always read his sermon, and as a rule it was
of almost portentous length; but he never failed to
absorb the attention, and, when he pleased, to enthrall
the spirit of the most crowded congregation. I myself
remember as a schoolboy standing without any sense of
weariness in the gallery of St. James's Church in Pic-
cadilly while he preached for an hour and nearly three-
quarters by the clock. He was supposed to have
modelled himself on the great French preachers of the
age of Louis Quatorze, and is said to have given lasting
umbrage to Queen Victoria by addressing a personal
appeal to her in the Chapel at Windsor after the fashion
of Bossuet or Bourdaloue. At any rate, she always
looked with disfavour upon any proposal to promote
him to high rank in the Church.

Liddon's sermons had a wide circulation among religious people of many denominations, and his Bamp-
ton Lectures at Oxford have probably been more read
than any in the whole series. Gladstone made him a

Canon of St. Paul's, but though he was a great personal friend of his, and also of Lord Salisbury's, he obtained no further advancement in the Church.

It would be invidious to pick and choose among living preachers, but so long as the Church of England can attract to her pulpits men of such diverse and original gifts as the Dean of St. Paul's (Inge) and the Bishop of Durham (Hensley Henson) she can at any rate keep alive a great tradition.

THE PRESS

"The power of the Press," wrote Lord Bryce towards the close of his life to President Eliot of Harvard, "seems the greatest danger ahead of Democracy."

Mr. Spender has devoted a section of his remarkable book on "The Public Life" to the topic of "The Press and the Public Life," upon which no man living is better qualified to speak with both knowledge and authority. He points out that the modern daily newspaper performs three functions: "(1) it supplies the public with news; (2) it is a medium for advertisements; (3) it furnishes opinion and comment on affairs of public importance."[1] He adds that "the first two of these functions are purely commercial, and the more impartially commercial they are the better. But the third becomes an imposture if it is anything but free and disinterested." In these days of syndication and "mass production," when an efficient daily newspaper, or group of newspapers, can only be run with an immense capital, the "temptation to make opinion conform to the supposed prejudices of reader and adver-

[1] "The Public Life," Vol. II, p. 107.

tiser becomes all but irresistible"; the "newspaper mind . . . habitually thinks in circulations"; it "gathers up the popular voices and gives them back as opinions."

I found recently a letter to me from Lord North-cliffe—so far as my memory goes, the only one, or almost the only one, that I ever received from him—dated November, 1914, in the first stage of the War. In those days it may, I suppose, be said that he bestrode the newspaper world like a Colossus. His letter throws an interesting light upon what he regarded as the functions and the power of journalism, not in the everyday party struggles of political life, but in a supreme national emergency.

DEAR MR. ASQUITH,—

I have been asked by the head of the Recruiting Department of the War Office to use my many newspapers as a means to aid recruiting. I think it my duty, however, to tell you that, having for some time been engaged in careful inquiries throughout England and Germany, I find that whereas there is in Germany immense enthusiasm for the war, there exist in many parts of this country apathy, ignorance, or ridiculous optimism, more especially in the provinces.

You may have noticed in this morning's *Daily Chronicle* an article on recruiting, pointing out certain defects which are hindering recruiting. I entirely agree wth the *Daily Chronicle*, but the chief hindrance is the fact that whereas the German public are supplied with the work of photographers, artists, cinematograph operators and war correspondents, our people have nothing but the casualty lists and the mutilated scraps with which it is quite impossible to arouse interest or follow the war intelligently. Members of the Government have private sources of information as regards the war, and so have we in Printing House Square and in Fleet Street, and thus we understand and are interested and anxious.

The public *cannot* be aroused by present methods, and I believe that unless the matter is taken in hand speedily you will be rapidly forced to a measure of conscription that might possibly bring about a split in the national ranks.

If you care to see me on the subject I could say very much more about the astounding ignorance of the fact among our people that we are fighting a battle for our existence as a nation.

Yours v. truly,
NORTHCLIFFE.

I doubt whether the writer's diagnosis of the situation, and especially his comparison of the relative temper of the Germans and our own people, was altogether just; but such a communication at such a time from such a quarter was, as it was intended to be, a real service to the national cause.

Dr. Johnson in the most famous of his Prologues, speaking through the mouth of Garrick of the theatrical profession, describes by anticipation the normal function of the popular journalist in our own days:

> For we who live to please must please to live.

The newspaper magnates who have annihilated, or absorbed, their smaller competitors are caterers on a gigantic scale to the public taste. This is true even of the comparatively small number of papers which are still in the old sense of the term party organs. They have gradually abdicated what, apart from the actual collection of news, used to be their primary function — political propaganda. Nothing can be more significant than a comparison between the amount of space and the scale of prominence given to politics and to other topics respectively in the newspapers of to-day and those of fifty or even thirty years ago. As Mr. Spender says:

" politics are only a small part of the activities of successful popular newspapers," and political writing
more and more " tends to be the by-product of a lively
journalism which imposes its standards and its methods
upon the political as upon other items in the daily bill
of fare."

The question is often asked: How many people take
their political opinions from their daily paper? The
average party politician finds it difficult to realize the
extent of the vague, floating, and dim formless elements
which go a long way to make up our vast electorate.
There can, I think, after our experience of some four
general elections and almost innumerable by-elections,
since the last extension of the suffrage which took effect
in 1918, be little doubt that this neutral, or rather un-
mapped, area has been substantially expanded by the
women's vote. I remember the adventures of a charming young friend of mine of the other sex who was can-
vassing for the Liberals in the election of 1918 in the
mean streets of one of the poorer London suburbs. In
one of the houses she visited the man was out, but his
newly enfranchised wife was at home. She declared
at once that they had both promised their votes to the
Tory candidate. Undaunted, the attractive canvasser
plied all her persuasive arts, until at last the good
woman said: "Well, dearie, if it would really please
you so much, I don't see why we shouldn't vote for
your man."

Probably this ingenuous member of the new electorate had never read, and will never read, a leading
article in her life.

The Scots are, and always have been, great newspaper readers, and being a political race, take their leading articles seriously. I was for over thirty years member for a typical Scottish county, and during almost the whole of that time the Home Rule question was, directly or indirectly, the chief issue in the arena of party controversy. The two great Scottish newspapers, each of them with a long Liberal tradition— the *Scotsman* and the *Glasgow Herald*—were throughout ardent supporters of the Unionist cause, and I myself was one of their principal targets. Yet, at election after election, my own polling figures rose, and, what is more important, a substantial majority of the electorate remained immovable and impenitent Home Rulers.

An equally and indeed a more striking case, because it affected the whole of Great Britain, was the Liberal majority at the general election of 1906—of which there were of course many premonitions, but nothing to presage its unexampled dimensions. As Mr. Spender truly says, "the Liberals had nearly all the largest circulations against them."

Notwithstanding, therefore, some disquieting and even menacing symptoms, I am unable to associate myself with Lord Bryce's foreboding that the Press is likely to be "the greatest danger ahead of Democracy." A far greater is the apathy and waywardness of large strata of the electorate. None the less, we have had abundant evidence both during and after the War that, when public opinion is nervous and unbalanced, and when the diverse ephemeral interests which in quiet times are the stock-in-trade of contemporary journalism are overshadowed for the moment by national and international emergencies, a Press which distrusts or suppresses facts, allows itself to become the instrument of personal and political intrigue and uses its power over uninstructed minds to manufacture or manipulate opinion, may become a potent and even a poisonous engine of mischief.

We have never had in England a "reptile Press" such as was habitually employed by Bismarck in Germany. Nothing can surpass in equivocal candour his own avowals as to the working of their infamous institutions. "My official proceedings against Arnim had been provoked by his refusal to obey official instructions. I said nothing in the legal proceedings about the fact of his having used the money which had been given him to represent our policy in the French Press (6,000 to 7,000 thalers) in attacking our policy and my position in the German Press."[1] What magnanimity! and what righteous indignation! He found tools ready to his hand, and fit for the vile work with which they were entrusted, in such creatures as Busch, who seem to have felt no degradation in their daily task of falsifying dates, forging gossip and slander, and inventing and floating every kind of kite balloon, under the instructions of a master who never hesitated, when the immediate purpose had been served, to disown the handiwork of his mercenaries.

Though the relations of English Ministers with the Press have been at times pregnant and intimate, the Government has never had an official organ,[2] still less a subsidized Press Bureau. There have been indis-

---

[1] Quoted by Spender, "The Public Life," Vol. II, p. 135.

[2] An exceptional case was the *British Gazette*, conducted by Mr. Churchill during the General Strike of 1926. The circumstances were abnormal, and the experiment was happily of brief duration.

cretions on the part of individual Ministers, like Lord Brougham's "The Queen has done it all" at the time of the dismissal of the Whig Ministry by William IV in the autumn of 1834, or revelations like Lord Aberdeen's, when he disclosed to Delane the Cabinet secret of the proposed Repeal of the Corn Laws in 1845. As Mr. Spender points out,[1] *The Times,* which was the recipient of both these communications, was habitually favoured with news and forecasts of official policy from the Foreign Office, either exclusively or in advance of the rest of the Press, during the editorship of Delane. But no one ever ventured to suggest that Delane allowed himself to become the automatic mouthpiece of the Government of the day.

The "interview," which may be said to have been introduced as a regular feature into respectable English journalism by W. T. Stead, has become a settled institution. Public men have got completely into the habit of blowing off their steam through this sometimes convenient but often dangerous medium. I have myself for a long time past made it a rule not to give interviews to the Press. I have been a good deal criticized both by friends and opponents for such old-fashioned austerity, but on the rare occasions when I have deviated from my practice I have generally regretted the result.

As is the case with most professions, the great journalist may either be born or made. I have had personal relations with many, if not most, of the distinguished men among them, and I will speak only of those who have passed away. Further, I confine myself to those,

[1] "The Public Life," Vol. II, p. 136.

for the most part connected with the daily Press, to whom journalism was the main, if not the sole, business of life, and exclude men like — for instance — John Morley and Fitzjames Stephen, with whom it may be said to have been a casual, though strenuous, interlude in a literary or political career.

"The number of new daily newspapers," says Mr. Spender, "established in the last thirty years, is very nearly zero: the number that have been extinguished or amalgamated into syndicates is lamentably large. Not so many years ago there were eight evening newspapers in London; at the time when I am writing there are only three, though the population has enormously increased in the interval. . . . To write a short leading article well is a fine art which I would by no means disparage, but it is inevitably the art of assertion or declamation rather than of argument, and if for convenience two writers are employed, the aggregate work in the week is certainly not more than would occupy about half the time of one able-bodied writer. . . . So far as quantity goes, W. T. Stead could easily have produced all the leading articles of a political kind that now appear on an ordinary day in three or four of the most successful London papers."

Stead was, no doubt, an exceptional man — a born journalist if ever there was one. With John Morley as editor, Stead as sub-editor, and Alfred Milner as Chief of the Staff, the *Pall Mall Gazette* was personally as well equipped as any daily journal of our time. Three men with such varied and seemingly incongruous tastes and faculties have rarely been harnessed in a single team. Morley contributed a literary reputation somewhat in excess of his deserts, which has not successfully defied the ravages of time. Milner had the precision of thought and of style of the best type of Balliol man. It was Stead who left the stamp of his individuality on the paper, and made it a live and influential organ. He had the *flair* of the new journalism. Morley was sucked into the current of official life, Milner was carried off to a distant and historic proconsulate; but Stead, after all his adventures and escapades, continued (even after he had taken to Spiritualism) to interest the public, who saw a certain dramatic fitness in his tragic end.

He was, as I have said, a unique figure in the life of Victorian journalism. In his own class there was nothing, as Horace says, *simile aut secundum*. He had, however, two contemporaries without whom the new journalism would not have put on its characteristic features: they were both primarily not writers but organizers of news. George Newnes conceived the idea of a weekly paper of snippets, to which he gave the title of *Tit-Bits*. It was in the original form nothing more than a collection of readable stuff, with prize competitions for the solution of acrostics and similar puzzles, of which the crossword is the latest development. Alfred Harmsworth, the eldest of an enterprising family of brothers, launched a rival venture which he christened *Answers*.

From these small beginnings there sprang two forests which have overshadowed and indeed revolutionized the English newspaper world. Harmsworth invented the *Daily Mail*, and in time acquired *The Times,* which he remodelled into an organ of the most modern

fashion.   Newnes became the pioneer in a new type
of monthly—the *Strand Magazine*—which has had
many imitators.   The Harmsworth group, though it no
longer includes *The Times,* and its founder, Lord
Northcliffe, is dead, is still the most formidable aggregate in the syndicated domain of our modern Press.
In no other department of activity has free and independent initiative been so successfully invaded by rings
of rival monopolists.

As a people we are jealous of the freedom of our
Press, but this once sacred catchword of democracy has
not only been trampled under foot by the new dictators
in Italy and Spain, it is steadily disappearing in the
United States, and it is not using the language of exaggeration to say that there is growing apprehension
lest it may fail to survive in Great Britain.

CHAPTER XXVIII

POLITICIANS AND AUTHORSHIP

I RECENTLY came across in an old newspaper a report of a speech delivered by Mr. Winston Churchill when he was Under-Secretary for the Colonies — some time between 1906 and 1908 — at a house dinner of the Authors' Club. Mr. Churchill was by that time already the father of a small family of books, and his " Life " of his own father, Lord Randolph, then only recently published, had given abundant proof of exceptional literary gifts. My readers will be grateful to me for citing some passages from his reply to the toast of his health, proposed by an old pupil and friend of mine, Mr. Anthony Hope Hawkins.

Mr. Churchill said that:

Authors were the happy people in the world, whose work was a pleasure. They had all heard about the dignity of labour; but it had not impressed him as it should. He did not wonder for a moment that the great mass of human beings envied the fortunate few who were able to earn their living by the visions of their fancy.

No one could set himself to the writing of a page of English composition without feeling a real pleasure in the medium in which he worked, the flexibility and the profoundness of his noble mother tongue. The man who could not say what he had to say in good English could not have very much to say that was worth listening to at all. It was a privilege to sit at a table on a sunny morning and feel that there were four hours of uninterrupted security, with plenty of white paper and a pen, away from the vexations of daily life.

What did it matter to a man in that position what went on outside his study door?

The House of Commons might do what it liked, and so might the House of Lords; the American market might have its bottom knocked out; the heathen might rage in every part of the globe; Consols might fall, and the suffragists might rise; but the author was secure as almost no other man was secure — not even *The Times* Book Club could have a depressing effect upon his sales.

He had sometimes fortified himself amid the vexations, vicissitudes, and uncertainties of political life by the reflection that he might find a secure line of retreat in the pleasant, peaceful and fertile country of the pen, where one need never be idle nor dull.

Mr. Churchill, when he conjured up this breezy and exhilarating vision of the war-worn politician finding a haven of refuge from the "vexations and vicissitudes" of his profession in the quietude of his study, with "plenty of white paper and a pen," was still a young man. If my dates are right, he had quite recently added to the vocabulary of politics a terse circumlocution for an unparliamentary term. Happily he still finds time, in the interludes allowed him by the "uncertainties of political life," to ply his pen and cover his "white paper" for the benefit and enjoyment of all who can relish the art of English composition.

In no country has the man of letters played such a part in politics, or the politician been such a conspicuous literary figure as in France. Yet Napoleon, the greatest of men of action, has left on record his estimate of the men of letters: "*Ce sont des coquettes avec lesquelles il faut entretenir un commerce de galanterie, et dont il ne faut jamais songer à faire ni sa femme ni son ministre.*"

Authorship is a tradition of old standing among English statesmen. Walpole, the Pitts—both father and son—Peel and Palmerston are exceptions; though Palmerston's dispatches and letters, of which some admirable specimens are to be found in Mr. Buckle's "Letters of Queen Victoria," show that he could write as good English prose, manly, lucid, pointed, as the best professionals of his time. It is no disparagement to Halifax and Bolingbroke—the Trimmer and the Tory—to say that of the two great parties which for more than two centuries divided the government of the country, the Whigs were perhaps more at home in literary composition. Burke and Sheridan, both of them great orators, immersed in all the everyday business, open or tortuous, of the parliamentary life of the eighteenth century and too ready to "give up to party what was meant for mankind," may nevertheless be truly said to have been more illustrious as writers than as combatants in the political arena. Burke, who was the dinner-bell of the House, poured out in pamphlets dealing with current events a wealth of reasoned and majestic compositions which took, and will always keep, their place among the classics of English literature. Sheridan, whose famous, but now forgotten, speech on the Begums of Oude was regarded by his contemporaries as the finest performance in that age of great orators, was the author of what is still recognized as the best of English comedies. But among the "pedestrian" politicians whose primary interest was always in the debates in the House of Commons, Charles Fox in one generation and Lord John Russell in another devoted not a little time and pains to other forms of composition, though it

must be admitted that the Tory, Canning, far outshone
them both.

To come down to our own time, we find in the annals
of Queen Victoria and her successors no lack of literary
statesmen.   Here again, Lord Morley's is an exceptional case.   He was by temperament, as well as by
training, primarily a man of letters, though he liked to
think otherwise.   He told me once, with a humorous
twinkle, that Mill, in a letter of introduction which he
gave him to Emerson, on his visit to America, had
described him as "a young man who, if I mistake not,
will some day make his mark in periodical literature."

There are some admirable remarks which are appropriate here in the chapter on "Some Eminent Mod-
erns" in Mr. Spender's book on "The Public Life."[1]

Balfour and John Morley had more in common in their
mental make-up than any other two men in public life during these years.   Had Balfour been required to earn his
living as a young man, he too would surely have started
as a writer. . . . Throughout his life he has spoken
as the writer speaks, delicately picking his words, amending
and erasing as he goes along, never hesitating to keep his
audience waiting while visibly in their presence he searches
for the perfect mode of expression.   Morley had actually
more of the rhetorical in his composition than Balfour, and
on the full-dress occasions, of which he had received adequate notice, he could deliver stately and highly-polished
orations which are beyond Balfour's compass.   But he
was always oppressed by the difficulty of satisfying his literary conscience in impromptu speech, and having entered the
House of Commons comparatively late in life, he never
acquired the unembarrassed ease and familiarity with its
ways which made Balfour a great House of Commons man.

There was nothing Morley disliked more than the sug-

[1] Vol. I, pp. 102-4.

gestion that he was the literary man who had strayed into politics. He had high political ambitions, and protested that his writing was part of his politics. The claim was well founded,[1] *but the pen and the tongue have essentially different techniques.* . . . To take his career as the test of the literary man in politics would be a serious mistake. He was Morley — a fascinating, gifted, exceptional man, as unlike other literary men as he was unlike most politicians. He was in fact less a literary man than a moralist with the pen.

To every word of this, after years of close observation of these two distinguished men, I entirely subscribe, with the addition that what Mr. Spender says of Morley — that he was " as unlike other literary men as he was unlike most politicians " — is equally true of Balfour. I have been honoured with the friendship of both, and it is difficult to say which was the more charming companion. I have been a student of their writings, and watched them day by day and year after year in the controversies, ephemeral or momentous, of the House of Commons. They were both, when they sat down in the study, with Mr. Churchill's " pen and white paper " before them on the table, consummate masters in their different styles of English prose. But neither was by nature a speaker, though each of them acquired by practice the faculty of impressing and delighting great popular audiences, and the more difficult art of holding the House of Commons. Morley was at his best when he was carefully prepared; Balfour, when he spoke impromptu, and could revel in the absurdities and inconsistencies of previous speakers in the debate. The platform and the House of Commons can ill spare such "men of letters" as these.

[1] As it would have been in the case of a greater writer — Burke.

Take the Prime Ministers of my lifetime. I have already mentioned Lord John Russell. Lord Derby, who divided his leisure between racing and the classics, produced a translation of the "Iliad." Lord Salisbury graduated in the art of writing as a professional journalist, and anyone who reads his "Collected Essays" will recognize the unmistakable signs of an accomplished and experienced man of letters. Lord Rosebery and Mr. Balfour, if they had done nothing in politics, could, in their different fields of composition, have always counted on a select band of admiring readers.

There remain the two greatest names — Disraeli and Gladstone. Mr. Gladstone's writings are spread over many volumes, and upon some of them, such as his earliest work on "Church and State," which Macaulay honoured with his famous review, and his Homeric studies, he bestowed much time and infinite care. But without subscribing to Disraeli's disparaging and contemptuous estimate of his rival's literary faculty, one may say that on the whole he is difficult to read, and still more difficult to remember. Disraeli's warmest admirers must concede that his books at their worst abound in flimsy and glittering rubbish. But so accomplished and impartial a critic as Sir Leslie Stephen is a warm though most discriminating admirer, and speaking with particular reference to his earlier work, such as "Contarini Fleming" and "Henrietta Temple," asks the question: "May one not lament the degradation of a promising novelist into a Prime Minister?" Of all our literary Prime Ministers, he is probably the one who will be the longest read.

Bryce, in his "Biographical Studies," records that Disraeli "early in his political life said one night to Mr. Bright (from whom I heard the anecdote), as they took their umbrellas in the cloak-room of the House of Commons: 'After all, what is it that brings you and me here? Fame! This is the true arena. I might have occupied a literary throne; but I have renounced it for this career.'"

Will the union of literary with political activities and interests, illustrated in the past and in our own day by so many notable examples in our public life, be continued in the future? It is difficult to prophesy, and the pessimist is generally wrong, but I confess that I do not augur favourably from such omens as I can discern. As Mr. Spender truly says, "the literary habit makes autocrats of writers";[1] and to the more fastidious and sensitive among them it is torture to see, under the stern exigencies of politics, their work "flattened to the average of common opinion." Nor do the conditions which now govern parliamentary life in the House of Commons seem likely to make it as attractive a place as it used to be to the Cornewall Lewises and Mills, the Bryces and Leckys, the Jebbs[2] and Butchers, the Thackerays and Trollopes of the ages. I trust I may be wrong.

This chapter may fitly conclude with a characteristic outburst from one of the greatest of Victorian writers

---

[1] *Loc. cit.*, p. 104.

[2] Sir R. Jebb, perhaps our most eminent Greek scholar, sat for years as member for the University of Cambridge. I can only remember his making a single speech. It was on an amendment in Committee on the Welsh Church Bill proposing to retain the Welsh cathedrals for the disestablished Church. It was such a fine performance, both in sentiment and expression, that it profoundly moved the House, and induced me to consent to the amendment.

who was also in his time a favourite orator in the House
of Commons.   Macaulay writes from his exile in Calcutta to his friend Ellis:

That a man before whom the two paths of literature and
politics lie open, and who might hope for eminence in either,
should choose politics, and quit literature, seems to me
madness. . . .

For what is it that a man who might, if he chose, rise
and lie down at his own hour, engage in any study, enjoy
any amusement, and visit any place, consents to make himself as much a prisoner as if he were within the rules of the
Fleet; to be tethered during eleven months of the year
within the circle of half-a-mile round Charing Cross; to sit,
or stand, night after night for ten or twelve hours, inhaling
a noisome atmosphere, and listening to harangues of which
nine-tenths are far below the level of a leading article in a
newspaper? For what is it that he submits, day after day,
to see the morning break over the Thames, and then totters
home, with bursting temples, to his bed? Is it for fame?
Who would compare the fame of Charles Townshend to
that of Hume, that of Lord North to that of Gibbon, that
of Lord Chatham to that of Johnson? Who can look back
on the life of Burke and not regret that the years which he
passed in ruining his health and temper by political exer-
tions were not passed in the composition of some great and
durable work?

Who can read the letters to Atticus, and not feel that
Cicero would have been an infinitely happier and better
man, and a not less celebrated man, if he had left us fewer
speeches and more Academic Questions and Tusculan Dis-
putations; if he had passed the time which he spent in brawl-
ing with Vatinius and Clodius in producing a history of
Rome superior even to that of Livy?

But these, as I said, are meditations in a quiet garden,
situated far beyond the contagious influence of English faction. What I might feel if I again saw Downing Street and
Palace Yard is another question.[1]

---

[1] Trevelyan's "Life of Macaulay."

Macaulay's concluding premonition was well founded. When he got back home he seized the first opportunity to re-enter the House of Commons, and in time became a Cabinet Minister. He was never more than a secondary figure in politics. But what he says of Gibbon — who was a silent member — can be applied, *mutatis mutandis,* to himself:

We have not the smallest doubt that his campaign . . . and his parliamentary attendance were of far more use to him than years of retirement and study would have been. If the time that he spent on parade and at mess in Hampshire, or on the Treasury Bench and at Brooks's during the storms which overthrew Lord North and Lord Shelburne, had been passed in the Bodleian Library, he might have avoided some inaccuracies; he might have enriched his notes with a greater number of references; but he would never have produced so lively a picture of the Court, the Camp, and the Senate House.[1]

[1] Essay on Sir J. Mackintosh.

CHAPTER XXIX

THE CIVIL SERVICE

THERE was published in the year 1831, when the agitation over the Reform Bill was at its height, a volume entitled "The Extraordinary Black Book," which purported to be "a complete view of the Expenditure, Patronage, Influence and Abuses of the Government," and which contains amongst other curious information "Lists of Pluralists, Placemen, Pensioners and Sinecurists." The book is avowedly a propagandist work, written and compiled from the point of view of those who at that time were labelled extreme "Radicals," and its authors, as the editor avows in his dedication, were "not of the number of those who inculcate patient submission to undeserved oppression." But there seems to be no reason to doubt the accuracy of the bulk of the figures and other materials made use of in the body of the work, which purports to be drawn for the most part from official reports and returns laid before Parliament.

No just comparison is possible between the aggregate or the net cost of Civil administration as it was a hundred years ago and as it is to-day. But a few salient illustrations of the general change that has been brought about may form a useful preface to what I have to say, after much direct and personal experience, of the Civil Service of our own time.

Roughly speaking, in 1830 the total annual cost of the salaries of persons employed in the public depart-

ments was about 2¾ millions.   That was the aggregate
payment for the work actually done for the State by its
Civil servants.

Side by side with this figure must be set the amount
annually paid for sinecures and pensions.   The sinecures fell into two classes — offices to which no duties
were any longer attached, and offices of which the
duties, such as they were, were performed not by the
holder but by his deputy.   The most lucrative of these
were in the gift of the judges, who thus had the opportunity, of which they took full advantage, to provide
for their families and dependents.   For example, Lord
Ellenborough, son of a Chief Justice, received as
"Clerk of the King's Bench" a salary of £9,600; one of
the Kenyons, brother of a Chief Justice, as "Filazer
and Clerk of Outlawries," between £7,000 and
£8,000; while the "Rev. Thomas Thurlow," relation
of the famous Lord Chancellor, was paid as "Clerk of
the Hanifer Emoluments" sums averaging between
£2,000 and £3,000.   The value of the colonial sinecures,
i.e. the payment made by the local officer, who did all
the duties, to the non-resident holder in England, was
estimated at over £75,000 a year.   The total cost of sinecures of all kinds was over £350,000. Charles Greville,
the diarist, was not only Clerk of the Privy Council
here, but Secretary and Clerk of Enrolments in Jamaica,
at a salary of £3,000. A Select Committee of the House
of Commons investigated this and other kindred matters in 1835, the Chancellor of the Exchequer (Sir F.
Baring) strongly pressing for the abolition of
Greville's sinecure. His account of his struggles to
escape "from the determination of this morose and

rigid millionaire," of his wire-pulling with members of the Committee and other men of influence, and of his final victory by a majority of one (10 to 9) is ludicrous and at times almost pathetic reading. Mr. Gladstone, who was a member of the Committee, voted with the pro-Greville majority.[1]

The pensions (exclusive of all grants, allowances, half-pay and superannuations for actual service) reach a figure of over £750,000. Lord Sidmouth, who had been Prime Minister, received under this head £3,000 a year, together with the valuable sinecure of Clerk of the Polls for his son. Lord Bexley, better known as Vansittart, a most incapable Chancellor of the Exchequer, also drew a pension of £3,000. The list as printed in the Black Book is full of curiosities: among them, a pension of £600 to the "Countess Dowager of Mornington, mother of the Duke of Wellington, and of Lord Wellesley and Lord Cowley."

These good old days were, even in 1831, drawing to a close. The whole system of sinecures and ornamental pensions was gradually brought to an end: not without many protests on the part of the victims—Lord Ellenborough, for instance, who complained to a Committee of the House of Lords that, according to the rules of natural justice, abatement of emolument ought to be accompanied by reduction of duties, and in his case there could be no such reduction, for he had no duties to discharge.

My personal acquaintance with our modern Civil Service lasted off and on from 1892 to 1916. The curtailment of the area of patronage, and the introduction

[1] "Greville Memoirs," 1st Series, Vol. III, pp. 266 sq.

of competitive examination, opened a new era in its history, and in the departments which I myself administered, as well as in those with which as Prime Minister I was constantly brought into contact, the standard of efficiency was, with rare exceptions, of the highest. The position of a permanent Civil servant, especially when he has reached the upper ranks of the hierarchy, is one which calls for a certain amount of flexibility in addition to administrative ability. He has to accept and serve the head whom for the moment the caprice of fortune and the hazards of politics have placed over him. The new head may turn out to be a mere figurehead; he may be a good, honest mediocrity, anxious to learn the technique of the office and to give full weight to the judgment of his expert staff; he may be by nature a meddler and muddler, or what is even more troublesome to his subordinates, a man of the best intentions with limited vision and an obstinate will: he may be, as Campbell-Bannerman once said to me of a colleague of ours: "Maximus in minimis, minimus in maximis." Or, on the other hand — for there are infinite varieties of possibility — he may be, if not a heaven-born administrator, at any rate one who will never let his office down either in the Cabinet or the House of Commons. Who can tell in advance? And the task of prophecy becomes more difficult when the new Minister comes with a reputation already made in other fields: such for instance, to take wholly dissimilar cases, as Cornewall Lewis, or Morley, or Randolph Churchill, or John Burns.

The English Civil Service is unique in the world. Performing as it does, in a country where party divisions often cut deep, and where the House of Commons is jealously on the watch to guard against the encroachments of "bureaucracy," the most confidential and responsible functions, essential to the efficiency and continuity of successive Governments, it has never incurred even the suspicion of corruption or of bias, and is carried on with rare disinterestedness by men who are debarred from publicity or self-advertisement, and many of whom have deliberately forgone the rewards of successful ambition which would have been almost certainly theirs in other walks of life.

On the whole, our Civil servants, without losing their independence of judgment, or cloaking or dissembling their opinions in the advice which they give, show a tactful adaptation to the varying idiosyncrasies of their successive chiefs.

My first direct experience of them was at the Home Office, where under my regime Sir Godfrey Lushington was succeeded as Under-Secretary by Sir Kenelm Digby, and Sir Edmund Du Cane as head of the Prison Commission by Sir Evelyn Ruggles-Brise. Though I made a good many administrative changes, some of which cannot have been altogether palatable to the veterans of the staff, I never lacked their cordial co-operation in carrying out a definite decision. Of all the innovations, the institution of female inspectors for factories and workshops was perhaps regarded in the office with the most misgiving; the physical risk—greater then than it is now—of the entanglement of petticoats in machinery, and the moral hazards of being out late at night, being dwelt upon in some of the minutes of the junior clerks. But we were a happy and hard-working family, and I believe I can safely say that we parted with mutual regret.

As I was for eleven years in daily contact with Treasury administration, it may be of interest that I should say something in detail of its personnel and working in pre-war days.

The department, when I first came to it, was steeped in the Gladstonian tradition. The older members of the staff had in their earlier days worked either under Gladstone's personal guidance, or while the memory of his methods and example was still fresh and dominant. The Great Man himself had sat in his political youth at the feet of Peel, and his finance was coloured to the end by the two primary precepts of the Peelite gospel: rigid economy in expenditure, and the simplification of the revenue by the abolition, not only of protective duties, but of the host of minor imposts which had been allowed to creep into the tariff, relatively unproductive in yield, expensive to collect, hampering to trade, and a burden on the consumer. His fame as a financier rests far more on the zeal and the success with which he carried through this double task than on his skill in exploring new sources of revenue, and in what was called in the political slang of a later day "broadening the basis of taxation."

His most memorable achievement in that field was the invention of the Succession Duties in his first Budget of 1853. They were destined to develop into the fully-fledged Death Duties of Sir William Harcourt's "predatory" Budget of 1894, which were looked upon somewhat askance in his old age by Gladstone himself, but of which every subsequent Chancellor of the Exchequer, of whatever political party, has taken the fullest advantage. The most original of Gladstone's later experiments in new taxation—his proposal in 1863 to impose income tax on charities—upon the elaboration of which he expended an enormous amount of time and pains, and which he expounded in one of the most brilliant of his Budget speeches, he was compelled to withdraw, in face of the clamorous and well-organized opposition of "vested interests."

But, as I have said, his main preoccupation from first to last was so to regulate both expenditure and revenue as to enable the earnings and savings of the people, so far as possible, to "fructify in their pockets." For that purpose, not a penny was to be exacted in taxation which could not be demonstrated to be indispensable for the essential services of the State. And, equally for that purpose, trade was to be set free from any artificial fiscal hindrances, and the exuberant forest of old duties, which still confronted the Chancellor of the Exchequer, lopped off and levelled to the ground, to clear the way for the natural growth and expansion of our national resources. The imposition of pettifogging duties in the supposed interest of limping or lagging industries, is a violation of the first canons of Gladstonian finance.

Gladstone's proposal, in 1874, to abolish the income tax, which had then sunk to 3d. in the pound, was denounced at the time, and is still often represented, as an electioneering bribe. A Budget without an income tax would be in these days an unthinkable freak. But it is to be remembered that the income tax was in its origin a war tax, and that it was revived in time of peace by

Sir Robert Peel, as a temporary expedient to make good the loss of revenue caused by his simplifications of the tariff. It was renewed from time to time, after it had served its original purpose, but was never regarded by Gladstone as an integral and permanent part of our fiscal system. In 1873, when, as Robert Lowe said, a prosperous country had just " drunk itself out of the *Alabama* award," it produced a little more than five and a half million pounds and might legitimately be regarded as being, for the time at any rate, an unnecessary tax.[1]

I remember that, when preparing my first Budget, I proposed to my experts to establish a differentiation for purposes of income tax between earned and unearned incomes. I was at once met with the objection, which was considered fatal, that Gladstone had always declared that any such scheme was impracticable. I therefore thought it wise to fortify myself with an inquiry by a strong Select Committee of the House of Commons, appointed *ad hoc* and presided over by Sir Charles Dilke, which presented a formidable report before I submitted the project to the House. It received general approval, and has become an essential part of our income tax machinery.

The most important post in the Civil Service, the office of Permanent Secretary to the Treasury, had been filled for years by a succession of past masters in all the arcana of Gladstonian finance — Lord Lingen, Lord Welby, Sir Francis Mowatt. Mowatt, who found

[1] Sir Stafford Northcote the following year proposed to reduce the income tax to 2*d*. He estimated the cost at £1,800,000. The yield of every penny, which when Peel proposed the tax was £728,000, had risen by £1,000,000.

himself completely out of sympathy, not only with Mr. Chamberlain's full-blooded protectionism, but with the relatively anæmic policy or policies of the then Prime Minister, resigned his post during the fiscal controversy of 1903 before the advent of Campbell-Bannerman's Government.

A new experiment was then resorted to in Treasury administration: the appointment of two joint permanent secretaries. The men selected for the partnership were Sir Edward Hamilton and Sir George Murray, who were in the saddle when I took over in December, 1905, the Chancellorship of the Exchequer. Sir E. Hamilton, the son of a well-known and much revered Bishop of Salisbury, one of Gladstone's closest friends, had spent his official life in the Treasury, and had been for a considerable time the Great Man's private secretary. In the division of labour which followed the dual headship, he took over, as his special province, what may be called the sphere of pure finance.

Sir George Murray had begun his Civil Service career in the Foreign Office, and was transferred to the Treasury in 1880. He had been private secretary to Gladstone and to Lord Rosebery when they were Prime Ministers, and afterwards had been at the head both of the Board of Inland Revenue and the Post Office. On his return to the Treasury he took especial charge of its administrative side. The important Division II, whose business it was to act as watchdog on the two departments, the Navy and the Army, which were justly regarded as the standing and most formidable enemies of public economy, was fortunate in having as its chief a man with the vigilant eyes and the suave but persistent faculty of scrutiny and criticism of Mr. Chalmers (now Lord Chalmers), who ultimately succeeded to the post of Permanent Secretary. The Treasury had always been the favourite department with the candidates who came out at the top of the Civil Service examinations, and who had the first choice among the various offices. In my time the members of the staff, almost without exception, had taken First Classes at one or other of the Universities, and it would have been impossible to find a set of men more highly qualified for what are perhaps the most arduous and responsible functions in the regular service of the State.

"Treasury control" was certainly in those days by no means an obsolete or an empty formula. The permanent officials are, of course, in the long run powerless, unless they can rely on the firm backing of the Chancellor of the Exchequer. Sir William Harcourt and Sir Michael Hicks-Beach — both men with a formidable facility in strong and explosive language — were as stern and rigid economists as Mr. Gladstone himself. Harcourt would even sometimes — in the intervals of browbeating his spendthrift colleagues — take to lecturing his subordinates for their laxity and softheartedness: offences from which, to do them justice, they were as a rule conspicuously free. I remember once, in the days when I was Home Secretary and he was Chancellor of the Exchequer, happening to come into his room at the back of the Speaker's chair. There I found some half-dozen of the highest officials of the Treasury, standing in a row with Sir R. Welby at their head, while Harcourt was pouring out a stream of vitriolic objurgations, ending up with the words:

" All I can say is that if any firm in the City were run in the way the Treasury is, it would be in the Bankruptcy Court in a week!" This, however, as his experienced hearers well knew, was only "pretty Fanny's way": for he was in reality the most appreciative of chiefs, and in another half-hour he would be cracking jokes with them as though they were the best fellows in the world.

To illustrate both the meticulous care and the occasional gusto with which new demands, especially from the "fighting departments," were handled, I may instance a case which I think I once mentioned to the House of Commons. Soon after the War Office was removed from Pall Mall to Whitehall, there came a request from the Army Council to the Treasury to sanction the expenditure of a small sum (some £600 or £700) for the construction of a subway under Whitehall, in order that, in the event of invasion, the archives of the War Office might be secretly conveyed to a place of safety. This precious document, after going through the usual official routine, came up to me, the final minute upon it, initialled by Sir George Murray, being in the following terms: "This application must be refused. The last objective of any intelligent invader of this country would be the War Office."

In the protracted and continuous struggle between the spending departments and the Treasury, the former had always from a popular point of view the best cards in their hands. Economy is an uninspiring catchword: it cannot easily be transferred into what is now called a "slogan." On the other hand there is nothing easier than to get up a crusade for "National Safety." Stead's

"Truth about the Navy" in 1884–5, the agitation whose war-cry was "We must have Eight" in 1908–9, and Lord Roberts's campaign for compulsory military service, are instances within the memory of most of us. And apart from large questions of policy, which it is for the Cabinet to decide, the Treasury is always at a disadvantage when attacking extravagance in detail in the fighting services. It is absurd of course to speak of such men as Sir George Murray and Lord Chalmers as in any sense amateurs, but when it came to particulars they fought both the experts of the Navy and Army on uneven terms. A notable illustration is the case of Lord Spencer's Naval Estimates in 1894, which led to Gladstone's resignation. Harcourt in the character of Chancellor of the Exchequer was in the first instance their severest and most formidable critic. I may quote from some notes which Lord Shuttleworth, who was then Secretary to the Admiralty, has been kind enough to send me:

"More than once," he writes, "when I was sitting with Lord Spencer in his room at the Admiralty discussing business, he looked at his watch and said: 'I must be off to face the blizzard.' This meant an interview with the Chancellor of the Exchequer. In the end Harcourt, who used to go over personally to the Admiralty to beard the experts, found himself compelled to capitulate."

CHAPTER XXX

RECREATIONS

I HAVE never been a gambler, not because I think gambling wrong, but simply from lack of the gambling temperament, which in greater or less degree is inbred in the average Englishman. The law will not in these modern days enforce purely gaming contracts, but except where on special grounds of policy it has been thought expedient to intervene, it does not prohibit them. From the ethical point of view, it is impossible to distinguish even the cruder forms of betting from the speculative transactions of the Stock Exchange or of the metal and cotton markets.

It is difficult to understand the seemingly haphazard fashion in which the practice of gambling invades some forms of sport, and leaves others almost severely alone. It may not be true that the abolition of betting—if such a thing were possible—would put an end to horse-racing; there would still be sufficient enthusiasts for the breeding and training of blood-stock to keep it alive; but it would almost certainly cease to be a national institution. Football, again, one of the oldest of our games, would probably not attract the enormous crowds which now follow the fortunes of the Association teams if gambling on the result were effectively prohibited. On the other hand, such popular sports as cricket, golf, and boat-racing have for all practical purposes remained outside the range of money speculation.

The only one of our national games (for I suppose I cannot include croquet among them) which I have habitually played is golf, but I learnt it too late in life to become anything more than a very indifferent, though a very keen, performer. But I have always taken a strong interest in cricket and horse-racing, though my actual participation in them, even as a spectator, has been of necessity confined to occasional days at the big matches at Lords and the Oval, and to two visits to the Derby and one to the Ascot meeting. In the years when my wife rode regularly to hounds, I used often to spend Sundays in Leicestershire, and though I made no attempt to earn such a compliment as the Master of Hounds in Sussex paid to Dr. Johnson,[1] yet I gained a certain consideration in the hunting world when it was bruited about that I knew the names of the last twenty winners of the Derby.

Later on, when I saw my first Derby in 1920, I was fortunate enough to predict the success of the winner, Spion Kop, who was by no means the favourite: he started at 100 to 6. The news of my prophetic insight leaked out, and I was for some months assailed by letters and telegrams (reply paid) from all parts of the country, asking for my "tip" for such races as the Royal Hunt Cup and the St. Leger. I had an interesting correspondence on the subject with Mr. Gilpin, the eminent trainer of Spion Kop. And though I do not go racing, I enjoy now and again on Sunday afternoons a visit to the Berkshire stables of my friend and neighbour, Mr. R. C. Dawson, where I made the acquaintance of the fascinating Mumtaz Mahal.

[1] See Piozzi, "Anecdotes," p. 206. "Why Johnson rides as well as the most illiterate fellow in England." Mrs. Piozzi says that "though he would follow the hounds fifty miles on end sometimes, he would never own himself either tired or amused." He complained that the "dogs" were lacking in sagacity.

In shooting I can only claim credit for a single achievement. Soon after my second marriage, while I was still Home Secretary, I shared for a season with my brothers-in-law a small forest in the north of Scotland. I had no previous experience of stalking, but I went out twice, with the result that I fired two shots and killed two stags. Content with this proof of my prowess, I put by my rifle, and have never used it since. I believe I still hold the record among deer-stalkers, of never having fired a shot without killing my quarry. A similar feat was credited to my friend, the late Lord Rayleigh, who became President of the Royal Society.

In indoor games, the principal innovation in my day has been the introduction and development of bridge, which seems likely to hold its own for some time to come. I wish we could see a revival on a larger scale of chess. As anyone who reads the correspondence between Lord Granville Leveson-Gower and Lady Bessborough must have noticed in the early years of the nineteenth century chess was a favourite after-dinner pastime in country houses. One rarely sees it in such surroundings now, though within my experience it has made great progress in popularity in the smoking-rooms of the House of Commons, from which cards and billiards have always been excluded. There is no gambling over chess, which is one of the few games where the element of chance does not come in. In its highest forms, as played by the so-called "masters," it seems to demand a specialized gift, which has little relation to the other intellectual faculties. Napoleon is said to have been a very indifferent player.

I have sometimes amused myself by going to see the

prodigies of simultaneous or blind-fold play. I once asked Pillsbury—one of the most brilliant of the American masters—who was playing against twenty boards without seeing one, whether he visualized each board as its turn came round. He told me that he did not: that his grasp of each successive situation was a pure act of memory which came to him without any sense of effort. But without soaring to the heights where only the specialist can breathe freely, there is a pleasant sense of concentration and absorption in chess which makes it one of the best distractions for the leisure time of busy men.

The favourite recreations of the Prime Ministers of our time have been of all sorts and kinds. Lord Palmerston, Lord Derby and Lord Rosebery were fond of racing. Lord Rosebery has won the Derby three times, twice in the two years when he was at the head of affairs. It was a bitter disappointment to Lord Derby when in the second of his brief Prime Ministerships his horse Toxophilite was beaten. Disraeli in one of his early novels—"The Young Duke"—makes the hero say: "I have hunted: it was not very disagreeable. I sometimes shoot: it is not very stupid." Mr. Buckle conjectures that these may well have been the writer's own sentiments when he was a young man.[1] Gladstone's two chosen pastimes were tree-felling and backgammon. Lord Balfour, who was, I believe, a tennis-player in his younger days, has in his maturity condescended to lawn tennis: and will always be remembered in the annals of sports as the man who anglicized golf.

[1] Buckle, "Life of Disraeli," Vol. III, p. 160.

CHAPTER XXXI

CLUBS

I HAVE belonged for a good many years to two dining clubs — "The Club" and "Grillion's" — each of which is of peculiar composition, and has a long and distinguished history. Neither of them has any local habitation, beyond the private room in an hotel or restaurant in which for the time being its dining quarters are fixed. In both, the dinners only take place during the session of Parliament: weekly in case of Grillion's, fortnightly in case of The Club. Members come to the dinners casually without any previous notice of their intention, with the result that it is a mere hazard whether the company present on any given evening is, relatively to the total membership, large or small. There are instances in the annals of each of the two clubs of a dinner attended by only one member. Oddly enough, in two of the cases the solitary diner was a Prime Minister: Lord Liverpool, at The Club, in December, 1825, of whom it is recorded that he drank only "one bottle of Madeira": and Mr. Gladstone at Grillion's in April, 1885, who records himself as having had "one bottle of champagne." He added to the record two quotations:

"Among the faithless, faithful only he"

and

"The mind is its own place, and in itself
Can make a heaven of hell, a hell of heaven."

Lord Houghton was invited to celebrate this occasion in verse, and produced a poem beginning:

Trace we the workings of that wondrous brain,
Warmed by one bottle of our dry champagne;
Guess down what streams those active fancies wander,
Nile or Ilissus? Oxus or Scamander?

Other members who are recorded to have dined alone at Grillion's are Sir Edward Grey (twice, in 1909 and 1912) : and Mr. Balfour (in 1909). I have myself dined there with only one companion, but I suppose the average attendance in these days may approach a dozen, and sometimes at the last moment an unusual influx requires the provision of an additional table.

"THE CLUB"

"The Club" was founded in 1764, by Sir Joshua Reynolds, with whom were associated Samuel Johnson, Edmund Burke, Christopher Nugent, Bennet Langton, Topham Beauclerk, Oliver Goldsmith, and Anthony Chamier.

The total number of its members was 20 in 1775; enlarged to 30 in 1778; and to 35 in 1780, with 40 as its future maximum, which has since been observed.

All of the members, with only eight exceptions, who died before the "Dictionary of National Biography" was completed, have found a place in its pages.

None of the meetings are recorded before 1775, when among those present were Boswell (elected in 1773) and Gibbon, and the absentees, who incurred the penalty of a fine, included Charles Fox and Garrick.

Among others who became members in the eighteenth century were Adam Smith, elected the year before "The Wealth of Nations" was published; R. B. Sheridan, elected in the year "The School for Scandal" was put on the stage; and George Canning. Early in the nineteenth century came Sir Humphry Davy, Sir Walter Scott, Lord Liverpool, Henry Hallam, and Brougham. Then in Queen Victoria's reign: Sydney Smith, Macaulay, Clarendon, Gladstone and Lord John Russell (both in 1857), George Grote, Dean Stanley, Robert Lowe, J. A. Froude, Tennyson, Lord Salisbury, Sir A. Cockburn, Lecky, Lord Kelvin, Sir H. Maine, Matthew Arnold, Huxley, Bishops Wilberforce, Stubbs and Creighton, A. J. Balfour, John Morley, Sir R. Jebb, Goschen, Lord Bowen.

It may be interesting to give the list of members at the time I write, arranged in order of priority of election. It will be noticed that each of the three senior members has held the office of Prime Minister.

1. Earl of Rosebery.
2. Earl of Balfour.
3. Earl of Oxford and Asquith.
4. Viscount Grey.
5. Archbishop of Canterbury.
6. Viscount Haldane.
7. Archbishop of York.
8. Lord Hugh Cecil.
9. Lord Tennyson.
10. Sir George H. Murray.
11. Honourable John Fortescue.
12. Sir Frederic Kenyon, *Treasurer*.
13. Sir John Simon.
14. Lord Stamfordham.

15. Sir Charles Oman.
16. Lord Sumner.
17. Mr. Rudyard Kipling.
18. Viscount Dunedin.
19. Mr. M. R. James.
20. Mr. H. A. L. Fisher.
21. Sir Henry Newbolt, *Treasurer.*
22. Mr. John Bailey.
23. Mr. John Buchan.
24. Marquess of Salisbury.
25. Mr. F. W. Pember.
26. Sir Maurice Hankey.
27. Bishop Gore.
28. Mr. George M. Trevelyan.
29. Bishop of Durham.
30. Mr. D. G. Hogarth.
31. Earl of Crawford and Balcarres.
32. Viscount Irwin.
33. Mr. Stanley Baldwin.
34. Lord Hewart.
35. Sir Austen Chamberlain.
36. Mr. H. P. Macmillan.
37. Prof. A. S. Eddington.
38. Sir D. Hogg.
39. Bishop of Oxford.

Honorary Members.

Sir E. Maunde Thompson.
Marquess of Lansdowne.
Sir George O. Trevelyan.
Lord George Hamilton.
Lord Carnock.

The chairman is changed at each meeting. The only official is the treasurer. This post has been held amongst others by Edmund Malone, Dr. Charles Burney, Dean Milman, Henry Reeve, Sir M. E. Grant Duff, and the present Librarian of the British Museum, Sir F. G. Kenyon.

The formula which announces to a new member his election remains as it has always been: "I have to inform you that you have had the honour of being elected to The Club."

The meetings were at first held at the "Turk's Head," in Gerrard Street, and the members assembled for supper; but ere long they agreed to dine together once in every fortnight during the sitting of Parliament, and Tuesday was fixed for the meeting. It continued to meet at the "Turk's Head" till 1783. After several migrations it transferred itself in 1890 to the Grand Hotel, and subsequently to the Café Royal, where it still dines about ten times during the session.

Dr. Johnson seems rarely to have attended after the first few years. It was at a meeting in 1775 that he uttered, in a "strong, determined tone" his famous dictum: "Patriotism is the last refuge of a scoundrel."

In the Journal of Madame D'Arblay (Fanny Burney) there is a letter from Dr. Burney to his daughter which describes a meeting of The Club immediately after the execution of Louis XVI:

At The Club, on Tuesday, the fullest I ever knew, consisting of fifteen members, fourteen seemed all of one mind, and full of reflections on the late transaction in France; but when about half the company was assembled, who should come in but Charles Fox! There were already three or four Bishops arrived, hardly one of whom could look at him,

I believe, without horror. After the first bow and cold salutation, the conversation stood still for several minutes.

The mixture of politicians, artists, men of literature and science, churchmen and lawyers, with an occasional soldier and sailor, which is the tradition of The Club, has been on the whole well maintained. Politics are as a rule eschewed. Grant Duff, in a privately printed history of "The Club" (1905), extracts from his diary the report of a dinner which took place in June, 1895, immediately after the resignation of the Rosebery Government—the Duc d'Aumale being in the chair. After the others had gone, Lord Acton remarked that it was a curious testimony to the interest and variety of the topics which had come up that "in the middle of a great political crisis, we being what and who we are, have not said one single word about it." The French Revolution was among the topics which had "come up," and the diarist records a number of stories told by the chairman of the experiences of his father, Louis Philippe—amongst them, an anecdote of a conversation he had in Paris immediately after the September massacres with Danton, who had obtained permission for him to serve at the front against the Duke of Brunswick. This I transcribe as I do not remember to have read it elsewhere:

DANTON: "I have a word to say to you. You came here yesterday morning. I know every one you have seen and everything you have said. You have talked a great deal of nonsense (*vous avez déblatéré beaucoup*) about things of which you know nothing, amongst others about what you describe as the massacres."

LOUIS PHILIPPE: "But surely everybody must speak with abhorrence of them."

DANTON: "You don't know anything about the matter. I made them. It was necessary that a stream of blood should flow between the aristocracy and the people. Do not spoil such a future as you have before you."

Grant Duff, who was himself an exceptionally well-furnished *raconteur*, and a constant habitué of The Club, expresses the opinion that the "conversation is best when about seven are present, because then more general, with a great deal of anecdote and pleasant interchange of ideas." There is at any rate no limit to the variety of the topics which come up for discussion. I can remember, shortly after I became a member in the 'nineties, an animated controversy between Bishop Creighton and Lord Kelvin, in which the greatest of living physicists stoutly maintained that the twentieth century would begin on January 1, 1900.

GRILLION'S[1]

Lord Houghton, in a preface to "Annals of Grillion's Club," compiled in 1880 by Sir Philip de Malpas Grey-Egerton, one of the secretaries, says there remained in the far-stretching memory of Lord Stratford de Redcliffe, in his ninety-second year, a clear recollection of the visit of an Etonian school-fellow, Mr. Fazakerly, to him at Constantinople, in 1811, and of a conversation that occurred between them on the serious damage that London society suffered from the violence of political controversy. The possibility of founding a club, open to members of both contending parties, was then and there discussed, and it was agreed that

---

[1] All the material facts in the history of Grillion's are to be found in "Grillion's Club: A Chronicle, 1812–1913. Compiled by the Secretaries," of which a limited number of copies were printed at the Oxford University Press, 1914.

whoever first returned home should do his best to carry out this intention. . . .

When Startford Canning returned to England the following year (1812) he found Grillion's Club established, and himself one of its members.

From that time to the present (Lord Houghton writes) the main characteristic of the Club has been its generous and courteous comprehension of diversities of political views. It has thus not been uncommon for the most uncompromising opponents, in the most important crises of our political history, to meet round its table in perfect freedom of conversation, and even of banter, secure alike from affront and misapprehension.

The occasional admission to the club of other than political members, besides eminent ecclesiastics, is an innovation of late years.

The membership has always, in my time, been variegated, on the whole with a high intellectual average — politicians, judges, bishops, literary and scientific men of all parties and schools, who would probably not meet together anywhere else. The attendance varies from one to twenty or thirty: rarely, I suppose, exceeding from eight to ten.

The club took its name from an hotel kept by Mr. Charles Grillion at 7 Albemarle Street. After various migrations it now dines in its private room at the Hotel Cecil.

Mr. Gladstone's last recorded attendance was on March 25, 1895; he had then been a member of Grillion's for fifty-five years and was in his 85th year.

The members present were fourteen, and included Mr. Lecky, Mr. Bryce, and Sir E. Grey; the Archbishop of Canterbury (Dr. Benson) being in the chair.

"The conversation" (we are told) "during the earlier part of the evening was mainly on the subject of forest trees. Mr. Lecky started some historic topics, and Mr. Gladstone at the close of the evening recounted several parliamentary and official anecdotes."

For some years after I was elected in 1893, the two veteran members of the club, who rarely missed a dinner, were Earl Fortescue and Lord Norton, both octogenarians. The records show that on May 7, 1900, "this being the 60th anniversary of Earl Fortescue's election to the club, he was present at dinner and his health was drunk with cordial good wishes for his continued presence. The toast was drunk in 70-year-old whisky, of which he brought some bottles as a present."

It is a curious contribution to the history of social habits that it was not till 1888 that smoking was permitted. The old Victorians were not smokers: I doubt whether either Gladstone or Lord Salisbury (except perhaps as a casual experiment) ever had any converse with tobacco. It is recorded that on June 25, 1888, the Earl of Carnarvon moved the suspension of the standing orders, with the object, it was understood, of obtaining permission to smoke. . . . Nobody voted either way, thereupon the chairman declared the motion carried, and the Earl of Carnarvon smoked a cigarette. The consumption of *two* cigarettes is noted in the dinner book.

The most interesting possession of Grillion's is the series of engraved portraits of more than 200 members which hangs on the walls of the dining-room, and which was begun in 1826. The best of these as works of art are from drawings by George Richmond, who was for many years artist to the club, in which office he was succeeded by H. T. Wells, R.A. Since his death in 1903, it has been left to members to select any capable artist, whose work could be reproduced in accordance with the scale and style of the existing portraits.

A few desultory notes which I have kept of the table talk at Grillion's or The Club may be of interest.

December, 1920. I hadn't been at Grillion's for the best part of a year. The interesting people there were Hugh Cecil, Haldane, and Sir. W. Raleigh, of Oxford. I said that doctors of the best repute had told me that they had been under the strongest temptation to kill — which they can do easily and without any real danger of detection — either babies just being born, whom the doctor could see were incurably afflicted — often from the sins of their parents: or mature people, stricken with cancer or some other hideously painful and quite irremediable disease. The conventions of the profession forbid them in such cases to do what is the really humane thing.

Hugh Cecil, who is an *acharné* High Churchman, maintained that, apart from the convention, it is a mortal sin to take life. I asked him whether — from his point of view — it was not equally sinful to drench the disease-ridden patient with stupefying drugs, which deprive him of will, intelligence and emotion, and only postpone death. He replied: " No. You can never tell what may happen, and you ought to leave it to God: pain is a discipline, and may bring out latent and unsuspected qualities of character, etc."

My rejoinder was that that was *pro tanto* an argument against all kinds of anæsthetics. When chloroform was first introduced into practice it was denounced by such an intelligent and unclerically minded man as F. W. Robertson of Brighton, who used to declare that the Saviour had refused an anæsthetic on the Cross. H. C. would, I think, have been on stronger ground if he had insisted on the uncertainty and fallibility of the doctors' diagnosis and judgment.

The Professor (Raleigh) was paradoxical and on the whole I thought rather foolish. With all his knowledge and cultivation he is yet a great master of attractive nonsense and irresponsible whimsicality.

April, 1921. They were talking yesterday of what martinets some dramatic authors are at rehearsals — Gilbert, Shaw, and others: including even Barrie, who in a moment of irritation went up to Dennis Eadie and said solemnly: "Eadie, I want you to indicate by your expression that you have a younger brother who was born in Shropshire."

At Grillion's I found myself again next to W. Raleigh, who did not shine in conversation with Arthur Balfour, Bob Cecil, and one or two others. His paradoxes were too thin and laboured. We got into a general discussion (there were twelve or fourteen men there, almost all of them of distinction in some walk of life) about the physical progress of the race. It emerged that the average height of those present — none of them under 50 — was from 6 ft. to 6 ft. 1 in. Raleigh with his 6 ft. 6, and Lord Balfour of Burleigh (6 ft. 4) and Bob Cecil (6 ft. 2) helped to swell the total, but I think that Gosse and I were almost the only men under 5 ft. 10 in.

(*Undated*). I dined last night at Grillion's, where there was a fairly good company — the Archbishop, Lulu Harcourt, Haldane, and some other great lawyers. I was near Gosse and had what I thought were two quite good scores off him. He did n't know the lines about the four Georges (Landor's), or Moore's about Lord Castlereagh. Someone asked why is Lord Castlereagh like a pump, to which Moore at once replied:

> Because it is a slender thing of wood
> Which up and down its awkward arm does sway
> And spout and spout and spout away
> In one weak, washy, everlasting flood.

May, 1922. I went last night, not to Grillion's, but to "The Club," where Sir Joshua's portrait of Dr. Johnson hangs on the walls, and the book of attendance, which every one signs, begins with his signature and those of Burke, Garrick, and Boswell. It was a curious little company of six or seven — all Oxford men: the Archbishop of Canterbury in the chair, and the others Bishop Gore, Fisher (the Education Minister), Kenyon (of the British Museum), and Dr. Hogarth. The conversation was rather "shoppy" — all about collections and the latest archæological finds. Hogarth, who talked much the best, told us of a fraudulent factory recently discovered in Crete, where two infernally clever Greeks had turned out for years a series of Minoan and pre-Minoan "masterpieces," which had been eagerly bought by American experts for their University museums and galleries. Kenyon agreed that they were almost indistinguishable from originals, and huge sums had passed to the forgers.

(*Undated*). I dined last night at Grillion's, and found with pleasure that my brother-in-law, Ribblesdale, was in the chair. We were only five, of whom two — the old Field-Marshal Lord Grenfell and Lord Sanderson — were over 80, and the third, Edmund Gosse, over 70. None of them, however, showed any of the infirmities of age, and we had a good talk about Gordon, Wolseley, and other military heroes.

June 14, 1922. I found an unexpectedly good gathering at dinner at "The Club" last night: A. J. Balfour, Haldane, Bishop Gore, Kenyon (of the British Museum), and a strange figure whom I have not encountered for years — Lord Tennyson, eldest son of the poet. He has a curious, slightly abbreviated reproduction of his father's magnificent head — on the whole the finest I have ever seen, not excluding Mr. Gladstone's. We had some very good talk — largely about Ireland, and books.

July, 1922. Dined at Grillion's and sat by Lord Fitzalan, the Lord-Lieutenant of Ireland, who is very wisely on the point of going to take a cure at some watering-place in Normandy. He told me of a good saying about Ireland, which I don't remember to have heard before: "a country in which the impossible always happens and the inevitable never." There is a French *netteté* about that which I like.

There was a discussion in which Fisher, Gosse and others took part, as to whether there was any good American lyric poet since Poe. The general opinion appeared to be in the negative.

April, 1923. I dined at Grillion's and had a good talk with the Archbishop of Canterbury, Haldane and Stanley Baldwin — a curious trio — on the latest developments of the Einstein theory.

July, 1923. I was delighted to find myself last night in the company at Grillion's of two bishops. I took the opportunity of talking faithfully about the Ten Commandments and the Psalms, and the various foolish innovations and Bowdlerisms which they and their kind are said to be contemplating and engineering in the Bible and the Prayer Book. They didn't show much fight.

February 14, 1924. I dined at Grillion's last night — where there are often only half a dozen present. It was, as it turned out, a record in the history of the club — both in number and quality of attendance. I sat next George Curzon, who is very good company, and I took the opportunity of opening up the subject of the Ruskin School, and at his request sent him when I got home one or two copies of the appeal. He was quite well disposed.

March, 1925. We had an unusually good company at Grillion's where I went to dinner last night — Baldwin, Archbishop of York, Austen Chamberlain, Fisher, Gosse, etc. — and had quite an excellent talk about books. I challenged them to produce a better twenty years of literary output in England than 1740 to 1760 in the despised eighteenth century.

February, 1926. I had quite a pleasant womanless evening at Grillion's last night. I sat between the Archbishop and Stamfordham, and we had a large company — Baldwin, Buckmaster, etc.

The last dinner which I was able to attend was on March 30, 1927, and I asked Sir E. Gosse, who is one of our secretaries, to be good enough to preserve for me a list of those who dined. Here it is (the order being that in which the diners sat on each side of the table) :

Sir A. Chamberlain.	Archbishop of Canterbury.
Lord Fitzalan.	Sir John Simon.
Lord Finlay.	Mr. Geoffrey Dawson.
Genl. Sir N. Lyttelton.	Mr. Hugh Macmillan.
Lord Oxford (in the Chair).	Archbishop of York.
Bishop of Durham.	Sir G. H. Murray.
Lord Stamfordham.	Sir E. Gosse.
Lord Byng of Vimy.	Lord Londonderry.
Sir Owen Seaman.	Lord Haldane.
Lord Eustace Percy.	Lord Dawson of Penn.

CHAPTER XXXII

THE NATIONAL BALANCE SHEET ON THE
EVE OF THE WAR

WHEN the War broke out in August, 1914, a Liberal Government had been in power for the better part of nine years. The direct responsibility for the national finance during that time had fallen upon the shoulders of two Chancellors of the Exchequer—myself and Mr. Lloyd George. After I became Prime Minister in 1908 in the large area of administrative work which I had constantly to survey there was no field in which I took a more continuous and lively interest. The colossal figures of debt, and of both income and expenditure to which we have become accustomed since the War, make it difficult to realize in their true proportions the problems of pre-War finance. The three governing aims of our policy in this department were: (1) the reduction of debt; (2) the concentration of new expenditure, as far as possible, upon naval defence and social reform; (3) the re-adjustment of the burden of taxation both in regard to old and new imposts. A few figures will show the main lines upon which we proceeded.

(1) *Reduction of Debt*. The actual reduction of deadweight debt and other capital liabilities between 1906 and 1914 was £97,846,964. Under the Budget of 1914 (the last peace Budget) it was estimated that there would be in the coming year a further reduction of £16,500,000. The total capital sum, therefore, which

by the end of the financial year 1914–15 the Government would have paid off, or provided for paying, would have exceeded £114,000,000, and the annual expenditure on the service of the debt would have been proportionately lessened by the interest on that amount.

(2) *New Expenditure.* In the last year (1905–6) of the administration which preceded ours, the amount *raised by taxation* was £129,776,290. The corresponding sum in the Budget estimate of 1914–15 was £173,675,000: an increase during the nine years of £43,898,710.

The three heads which accounted for the whole, and more than the whole, of this increase were:

(a) The Navy: an *additional* £18,250,000. The expenditure on the Army had remained stationary. During the same period the naval and military expenditure of the great Continental Powers had risen by at least 115 millions.

(b) Social Reform (Old Age Pensions, Health Insurance, Unemployment Insurance, Labour Exchange, etc.)—all *new* services—£22,022,000.

(c) Public Education—*additional* and *new* services—£3,785,000.

(3) *Readjustment of Burden of Taxation.* As the net result of the alterations in the relative scale of direct and indirect taxation, which in 1905–6 was, as it had been for a considerable number of years, roughly 50 per cent. to 50 per cent. it had become, after the Budget of 1909–10–11, 43 per cent. indirect and 56 per cent. direct. Under the further modifications proposed in the Budget of 1914–15 it would be, omitting decimals, 30 per cent. indirect and 60 per cent. direct.

The indirect taxes reduced or abolished between 1906 and 1914 were as follows:

	Annual Relief. £
Coal (Export duty of 1*s.* per ton abolished)	2,600,000
Tea (reduced from 6*d.* to 5*d.* per lb.)	1,120,000
Sugar (reduced from 4*s.* 2*d.* to 1*s.* 10*d.* per cwt.) . . .	3,650,000
Minor duties	340,000
	£7,710,000

The actual yield of the taxes increased or imposed by the famous Budget of 1909 in its final form was, in the last completed financial year before the War (1913–14), a little over £27,000,000: of which over £8,000,000 came mainly from spirits, tobacco and liquor licences, £7,000,000 from death duties, and nearly £9,000,000 from income and super tax. Of this the super tax contributed £3,320,000, which it was estimated would under the new scale, set up by the Budget, of 1914–15, be increased in a normal year to £4,500,000. The land value duties had so far only added to the revenue £700,000. It is to be remembered that the Income Tax for the financial year 1914–15 was at the rate of 1*s.* 3*d.* in the pound.

It is clear from this review that notwithstanding the heavy new demands that had to be met for naval defence and social reform, the financial position of the country at the outbreak of war was one of exceptional strength. It was indeed unique in Europe: as was actually proved

"AN ASQUITH TO THE RESCUE"

War Minister (to Premier). "Hold Tight! I'll see you through."

Reproduced from "Punch," April 8, 1914, by permission

(Mr. Asquith assumed the War Secretaryship after the Curragh Incident. See page 192.)

when, while the struggle was still in its early stages, it became apparent that our resources and our credit would have to be drawn upon, not only to make good our own necessities, but also those of our Allies.[1]

[1] Notwithstanding contemporary Jeremiads, a well-known and much respected sporting journal in an article on December 27, 1913, paints the situation in the darkest colours: "The one word which sums up all these discords is as regrettable as it is inevitable. Insecurity. . . . But there are even worse symptoms [than the Parliament Act] of the dangers to land, to property, to finance, to national existence, with which we have been menaced since August, 1911. This is the true reason for an insecurity which has been, strangely enough, reflected even in the thoroughbred form of the past racing season."

CHAPTER XXXIII

ANGLO–AMERICAN RELATIONS BEFORE
THE WAR: HENRY JAMES

FOR twenty years and more before the War we had been very fortunate in the succession of eminent Americans whom the United States had sent as their representatives at the Court of St. James's, whether the Republicans or the Democrats were for the time being in power at Washington. It was difficult to follow men like Motley and Lowell; but it would be impossible to find a more distinguished list of contemporary names than those of Phelps, Robert Lincoln, Bayard, John Hay, Joseph H. Choate, Whitelaw Reid, and Walter Hines Page. Literature, Journalism, the Bar, all contributed their quota; such men as Phelps and Choate were among the most felicitous and effective orators in the English-speaking world; Bayard had a dignity of presence and a weight of wisdom which impressed all who were brought into contact with him; and John Hay, who had been private secretary to President Lincoln, and was an author of humour and originality, had singular personal charm.[1]

Mr. Whitelaw Reid, who came here direct on a special mission for the Jubilee of 1897, held the post of American Ambassador for the exceptionally long term of nearly eight years (1905 to the end of 1912). He

---

[1] He wrote me a kindly farewell letter (September 13, 1898), in which, alluding to some public reference which I had made to his approaching departure, he says: "Dear Asquith, Good Bye! and a thousand thanks for embalming my insignificant name in the ambit of your eloquence."

was, with his wife, proprietor of a great New York journal, with large means and of unbounded hospitality, and during his tenure of office he and Mrs. Reid made Dorchester House one of the central meeting-places of all that was best in London Society. He was, like his immediate predecessor, Mr. Choate — the leader in his day of the United States Bar — an ardent supporter of Anglo-American friendship.

I remember an amusing incident which happened to me on the railway. I had been invited to spend Sunday at Sudbury in Derbyshire with an old friend and colleague at the Home Office, Lord Vernon, who while still a young man was physically disabled by paralysis. I got into the railway carriage at St. Pancras with a single fellow-passenger, whom to the best of my recollection I had never seen before. After a time he opened conversation with the words: "Your face, sir, seems to be familiar to me. May I ask whether you were not the first walking gentleman in Tree's company at Washington last fall?" I disclaimed the flattering unction; for to be mistaken for a *jeune premier* was a gratifying tribute to my looks and get up. As we drew near the wayside station at Sudbury, where the train had been ordered to stop, I noticed that my fellow-traveller began to gather up his belongings, and I followed suit. We found a carriage waiting for us at the station and drove together to our common destination. I found my wife waiting for me and we made merry over the conjectures of our American fellow guest, who it turned out belonged to one of the best families in New York.

The American Ambassador, whoever might be for

the time being the incumbent of the office, had come —
as I said in my speech in the House of Commons after
the death of Mr. Whitelaw Reid on December 16,
1912 —

to hold a position of his own, which is independent of his
status and his functions as diplomatic representative of an
external Power. We regard him as a kinsman, who is also
an honoured and a welcome guest, having sprung from our
own race, speaking our own language, sharing with us, by
birth and by inheritance, not a few of our most cherished
traditions, and participating, when he comes here, by what
I may describe as a natural right, in our domestic interests
and celebrations. The office has been held and adorned by
a long succession of distinguished men, and I am not using
the language of exaggeration when I say that none of them
has more fully entered into its spirit and more maintained
its special authority than Mr. Whitelaw Reid. He brought
to the discharge of its manifold and exacting duties the
gathered experience of a veteran in public affairs, the endowment of a man of the highest culture, social gifts of the
most genial and generous kind, a keen sympathy with all
the many sides of our British life, a mind always open and
receptive, and the warmest of hearts.

We propose to suggest to the American Government that
one of His Majesty's battleships or battle cruisers should
convey the remains of the late Ambassador to his native
land. I am certain that I interpret the sentiments of the
whole House when I venture in their name to offer to his
family, and to the President and the people of the United
States, our deep and heartfelt sympathy at the loss of one
who was a great American, but who none the less had his
home amongst us and in a true and real sense was felt by
all of us to be one of ourselves.

Mr. Balfour, on behalf of the Opposition, spoke in
the same sense:

We in Great Britain have always been anxious to extend,
and have always extended, to the representatives of the

United States not merely the consideration due to those who represent a great and friendly Power, but something much more, something much deeper, and something much more intimate. We have welcomed them, as Mr. Asquith has truly said, to the very arcana of our social life. The functions which fall upon the representative of the United States, being thus in their nature peculiar, have been most admirably fulfilled by the departed statesman.

The more you knew of him, the more any man knew Mr. Whitelaw Reid, the more competent he was to appreciate, not only the ardent and enlightened patriotism which distinguished him, but those broad bonds of generous sympathy which made us feel, when he was talking to us, that he was not less sympathetic to England because he never allowed one to forget that he was the representative of another, though kindred nation.

During the term of Mr. Whitelaw Reid's ambassadorship here, and while Mr. Taft was still President, our representative at Washington, Mr. Bryce, who enjoyed in a unique degree the respect and confidence of the whole American people, was engaged, under the instructions of Sir Edward Grey, in negotiating a general Treaty of Arbitration between Great Britain and the United States. The story of what happened is vividly told in Mr. Fisher's admirable life of Lord Bryce.[1]

The business proceeded pleasantly with goodwill, and indeed with enthusiasm on either side. On May 1, 1911, the draft agreed upon at Washington was sent over to London, and on August 3 the Treaty was signed by Mr. Bryce and Mr. Knox, the Secretary of State. The preamble recited that the two nations, being equally desirous of perpetuating the peace which had

[1] "James Bryce," Vol. II, pp. 67–74.

happily existed between them since the Treaty of Ghent
in 1814, had appointed plenipotentiaries to conclude a
treaty "which should provide means for the peaceful
solution of all the questions of difference which it shall
in future be found impossible to settle by diplomacy."
The articles of the Treaty declared that all such questions should be referred either to the Court of Arbitration at The Hague, or to such other arbitral tribunal as
may be decided in each case by special agreement.

Sir Edward Grey expressed the hope that the example would spread and that one or more great Euro-
pean Powers would eventually make similar agreements with us and the United States. "The effect of
such agreements upon disarmament and the morale of
international politics should be considerable."

These high hopes were almost immediately dashed
to the ground. The Treaty was in 1912 wrecked and
rendered worthless by the Senate of the United States:
an event which, Bryce's biographer tells us, was "the
keenest disappointment of his diplomatic career."

In the following year (1913) a movement was initiated, spontaneously and not at the instance of either of
the two Governments, to celebrate in 1914 the centenary of the Treaty of Ghent and the hundred years of
peace among British-speaking peoples. I spoke in its
support at the Mansion House on February 4, 1914,
little foreseeing the calamities which that fateful year
had in store for the civilized world. I pointed out that
since the Treaty of Ghent, despite diplomatists and
soldiers, and despite popular passions and misunder-
standings, the peace then concluded had been unbrok-
enly maintained.

It was not (I said) because there had not been during those hundred years occasions, and frequent occasions, upon which matters of controversy have arisen between the two peoples — controversies about territorial adjustments, controversies upon matters which as history shows are as much or even more apt to lead to actual warfare — controversies upon points of honour. . . . If controversies of that kind had taken place between any other two peoples in the world they must, in all human probability, have led to effusion of blood. It is not so between us and the United States of America — and why? Not because there is any special sacrosanctity in the Treaty of Ghent or any other piece of parchment which is covered with diplomatic ink, but because the deep-rooted feelings of which the Treaty of Ghent was, perhaps, the earliest formal embodiment have year by year and generation after generation grown and solidified, until we two great kindred races have come to feel that the shedding of one another's blood in any cause, for any difference, would be a matter diverse not only in degree but in character to the outburst of war between any other two nations.

The celebration of the Treaty of Ghent and of the hundred years of Anglo-American peace never took place. Within a few months Europe was being devastated by the most murderous war in history, and Flanders was its first victim. The smoke of the battlefield has long since rolled away, and, thanks largely to the League of Nations, post-war diplomacy is gradually recovering its sanity. Amidst all the changes that have altered the face of the world, the possibility of a conflict between the English-speaking nations is happily as unthinkable as it was thirteen years ago.

One of our oldest and best friends was the distinguished American writer, Henry James. After the War broke out in 1914, he never concealed for a moment his ardent sympathy with the Allies and their

cause.   In the early summer of 1915 he paid us a visit
at Walmer Castle, and on his return to London I received from him the following letter.   Needless to say,
I gladly consented to his request.

21 CARLYLE MANSIONS,
CHEYNE WALK, S.W.
June 28th, 1915.

MY DEAR PRIME MINISTER AND ILLUSTRIOUS FRIEND, —

I am venturing to trouble you with the mention of a fact
of my personal situation, but I shall do so as briefly and
considerately as possible.   I desire to offer myself for
Naturalization in this country, that is, to change my status
from that of American citizen to that of British subject.
I have assiduously and happily spent here all but 40 years,
the best years of my life, and I find my wish to testify at this
crisis to the force of my attachment and devotion to England, and to the cause for which she is fighting, finally and
completely irresistible.   It brooks at least no inward denial
whatever.   I can only testify by laying at her feet my explicit, my material and spiritual allegiance, and throwing
into the scale of her fortune my all but imponderable moral
weight — "a poor thing but mine own."   Hence this re-
spectful appeal.   It is necessary (as you may know!) that
for the purpose I speak of four honourable householders
should bear witness to their kind acquaintance with me, to
my apparent respectability, and to my speaking and writing
English with an approach of propriety.   What I presume
to ask of you is whether you will do me the honour to be
the pre-eminent one of that gently guaranteeing group?
Edmund Gosse has benevolently consented to join it.   The
matter will entail on your part, as I understand, no expenditure of attention at all beyond your letting my solicitor
wait upon you with a paper for your signature — the affair
of a single moment; and the "going through" of my application will doubtless be proportionately expedited.   You
will thereby consecrate my choice and deeply touch and
gratify yours all faithfully

HENRY JAMES.